The Australi

# The Australian Economy

## 3rd edition

*Edited by Peter Kriesler*

ALLEN & UNWIN

First published in 1999
Allen & Unwin
9 Atchison Street, St Leonards NSW 1590 Australia
Phone:    (61 2) 8425 0100
Fax:       (61 2) 9906 2218
E-mail:   frontdesk@allen-unwin.com.au
Web:      http://www.allen-unwin.com.au

National Library of Australia
Cataloguing-in-Publication entry:

The Australian economy.

  3rd ed.
  Bibliography.
  Includes index.
  ISBN 1 86448 783 6.

  1. Monetary policy—Australia. 2. Australia—Economic
  conditions—1945– . 3. Australia—Economic policy.
  I. Kriesler, Peter.

330.994

Set in 10/11 pt Sabon by DOCUPRO, Sydney
Printed and bound by Brown Prior Anderson, Victoria

# Contents

| | | |
|---|---|---|
| Tables | | vii |
| Figures | | x |
| List of contributors | | xii |
| Glossary | | xiv |

1 The Australian economy after the 'Asian crisis'  1
PETER KRIESLER

2 Economic growth  6
STEVE DOWRICK

3 Inflation in Australia  26
BILL JUNOR

4 The Australian unemployment experience  52
T. STEGMAN

5 The Asian financial crisis and Australia's balance of payments  75
ELAINE HUTSON AND COLM KEARNEY

6 Fiscal policy 60 years after Keynes  93
J.W. NEVILE

7 Money and monetary policy  113
MARK CROSBY AND ROSS MILBOURNE

v

8   Public expenditure: Taming Leviathan for the next
    millennium?                                                      129
    PETER GROENEWEGEN

9   Taxation and tax policy in Australia                            146
    NEIL WARREN

10  The labour market since Howard                                  181
    JOHN BURGESS, WILLIAM F. MITCHELL AND
    MARTIN J. WATTS

11  Industry policy in Australia                                    201
    ROBERT CONLON

12  Australia and the Kyoto Protocol                                224
    ANTHONY D. OWEN

Notes                                                               236
Bibliography                                                        244
Index                                                               256

# Tables

| | | |
|---|---|---|
| 2.1 | 1997 Australian real consumption compared with 1975 and 1960 | 7 |
| 2.2 | GDP growth by decade | 10 |
| 2.3 | Growth of population and employment | 11 |
| 2.4 | Weekly hours worked per person aged 15–64 | 13 |
| 2.5 | Sources of growth of labour productivity in the market sector (% p.a.) | 18 |
| 2.6 | Economic development 1950–92 in East Asia and OECD | 21 |
| 2.7 | Contributions to annual growth of real GDP in Australia relative to average OECD growth | 23 |
| 3.1 | The CPI (All Groups) and alternative measures of the 'underlying' inflation rate | 32 |
| 3.2 | CPI-weighted average of eight capital cities | 33 |
| 3.3 | Indicators of labour market performance before and after the Accord | 42 |
| 3.4 | Sacrifice ratios for Australia | 47 |
| 4.1 | The Australian unemployment record | 56 |
| 4.2 | Unemployment rates by age and sex | 58 |
| 4.3 | The composition of changes in unemployment | 61 |
| 5.1 | The current account: 1996/97 | 77 |
| 5.2 | The financial account 1996/97 | 78 |
| 5.3 | Australia's historical balance of payments | 79 |
| 5.4 | Australia's foreign indebtedness | 80 |
| 5.5 | Australia's debt service ratios | 81 |
| 5.6 | Asian exchange rate regimes | 89 |

6.1     The structural deficit and its components, Australia
        1973/74 to 1997/98                                          107
7.1     The transmission mechanism of monetary policy              119
8.1     Outlay by purpose, relative importance (% of total)
        by level of government, 1990/91, 1995/96                    142
9.1     Commonwealth, state and local tax revenue: 1996/97         151
9.2     Outlays and tax revenue by level of government:
        1995/96                                                     154
9.3     Growth of taxes in OECD countries                          155
9.4     Real effective tax rates by country for domestic
        investments                                                 157
9.5     Tax revenue to level of government: 1994                   159
9.6     State taxes as a percentage of GDP: 1994                   159
9.7     Local taxes as a percentage of GDP: 1994                   160
9.8     Tax expenditures classified by taxpayer affected           161
9.9     Estimated taxes paid and other characteristics of
        households, 1996/97                                         162
9.10    Estimated taxes paid and other characteristics of
        households, by family type, 1996/97                        162
9.11    Efficiency gains from consumption tax reforms:
        1990/91                                                     163
9.12    Compliance cost of Federal taxes, 1994/95                  164
9.13    The hidden costs of taxation                               164
9.14    Personal income tax schedule 1996/97                       165
9.15    Growth in companies, trusts, partnerships and
        employment: 1991/92 to 1995/96                             171
9.16    Distribution of taxes by tax type: Australia 1969/70
        to 1995/96                                                 173
9.17    All Federal, State and local taxes on assets and asset
        transfers as a percentage of total taxes                  175
9.18    Estimated distribution of household assets by asset
        type                                                       177
10.1    Unemployed people by age and whether looking for
        full- or part-time work, November 1997                    182
10.2    Part-time employment as a percentage of total
        employment                                                 184
10.3    Changes in employment and labour force, March
        1996 to January 1998                                       184
10.4    Percentage changes in industry employment, May
        1996 to November 1997                                      186
10.5    Wage and salary earners—employment, full-time,
        part-time by sector and level of government               187
10.6    Average weekly earnings, November 1983 to August
        1997                                                       188

| 10.7 | Growth in award indexes, November 1983 to June 1997 | 189 |
|------|---|---|
| 10.8 | Key features of the Workplace Relations Act | 190 |
| 10.9 | Average wages growth per different wage measures (%) | 193 |
| 11.1 | Average effective rates of protection: manufacturing industries and agricultural sector | 207 |
| 11.2 | Employment in manufacturing | 208 |
| 11.3 | Existing and proposed funding of business programs | 209 |
| 11.4a | Summary: Commonwealth (State and Territory) budgetary outlays on industry | 210 |
| 11.4b | Major components of Commonwealth budgetary outlays on manufacturing | 211 |
| 11.5 | Major Commonwealth export measures—industries in all sectors | 219 |
| 12.1 | Estimated increases in $CO_2$ emissions | 233 |

# Figures

| | | |
|---|---|---|
| 2.1a | Real GDP—total and per capita | 9 |
| 2.1b | Annual growth rate of real GDP | 9 |
| 2.2 | Demographic ratios 1960–98 | 12 |
| 2.3 | Participation rates of males and females | 13 |
| 2.4 | Public and private investment 1960–97 | 15 |
| 2.5 | Take-off and slowdown in OECD and East Asia | 22 |
| 3.1 | The path of Australia's inflation since 1960 | 30 |
| 3.2 | Annual rate of inflation | 34 |
| 3.3 | Actual and expected inflation in Australia | 49 |
| 4.1 | Unemployment: % of labour force | 57 |
| 4.2 | Real GDP: % change on previous year | 63 |
| 4.3 | The Australian Beveridge Curve: 1979:3–1997:3 | 66 |
| 4.4 | Labour market flows | 69 |
| 6.1 | Budget deficits as a percentage of GDP and short-term interest rates | 99 |
| 6.2 | General government current revenue as a percentage of GDP | 102 |
| 6.3 | Structural deficits as a percentage of GDP and unemployment | 109 |
| 6.4 | Savings by sector as a percentage of GDP | 111 |
| 7.1a | The relationship between selected interest rates | 117 |
| 7.1b | The yield curve for three different periods | 118 |
| 7.2 | The growth rate of M3 versus the rate of growth of real GDP | 122 |
| 7.3a | The growth rate of real income versus the nominal cash rate | 123 |

7.3b     The growth rate of real income versus the real cash
         rate                                                            123
7.4      The growth rate of real income versus the nominal
         cash rate lagged 6 quarters                                    124
7.5      The growth rate of M3 versus the rate of inflation
         (change in the GDP deflator)                                   124
9.1      Nominal company tax rates                                      158
10.1     Unemployment rate and average duration of
         unemployment in Australia                                      183
10.2     Average annual percentage changes in industry
         employment, 1984–89, 1990–95 and 1996–97,
         Australia                                                      185
11.1     Manufacturing: effective rates of protection                  206

# Contributors

JOHN BURGESS is in the Economics Department at the University of Newcastle.

ROBERT CONLON is in the School of Economics at the University of New South Wales.

MARK CROSBY is in the Economics Department at the University of Melbourne.

STEVE DOWRICK is in the Faculty of Economics and Commerce at the Australian National University.

PETER GROENEWEGEN is in the Economics Department at the University of Sydney.

ELAINE HUTSON is in the School of Finance and Economics at the University of Technology, Sydney.

BILL JUNOR is in the Economics Department at Macquarie University.

COLM KEARNEY is in the Economic and Social Research Institute, Dublin.

PETER KRIESLER is in the School of Economics at the University of New South Wales and is Deputy Director of both the Centre for Applied Economic Research and the Australian Human Rights Centre.

ROSS MILBOURNE is Deputy Vice-Chancellor (Research) at the University of Adelaide.

WILLIAM MITCHELL is in the Economics Department at the University of Newcastle, and is Director of the Centre of Full Employment and Equity.

JOHN NEVILLE is in the School of Economics at the University of New South Wales.

TONY OWEN is in the School of Economics at the University of New South Wales.

TREVOR STEGMAN is in the School of Economics at the University of New South Wales.

NEIL WARREN is in ATAX, Faculty of Law at the University of New South Wales.

MARTIN WATTS is in the Economics Department at the University of Newcastle.

# Glossary

This glossary in no way attempts to be all encompassing. Rather the index should be used as well, with the location of the definition of all major terms being noted.

ABS: Australian Bureau of Statistics. A federal bureau charged with gathering and processing all major economic, social and other statistics on Australia.

ACCORD: A prices and incomes policy resulting from agreement between the former Labor government, the trade union movement and employer representatives.

APPRECIATION/REVALUATION: An increase in the value of the $A against other currencies. Appreciation refers to a floating exchange rate regime, where the currency market sets the value of the $A. Revaluation refers to the fixed exchange rate regime where the value of the currency was set by the Reserve Bank.

BALANCE OF PAYMENTS: A record of all financial transactions between the residence of one country (Australia) and the rest of the world.

CAPITAL ACCOUNT: That part of the balance of payments which records international purchases and sales of assets, such as stocks, bonds and land.

CPI: Consumer price index. The most cited measure of inflation, this index is based on the price of a basket of consumer goods.

CROWDING OUT: The idea that an increase in government expenditure will reduce (crowd out) private expenditure so that the increase in total expenditure is less than the increase in government expenditure.

CURRENT ACCOUNT: That part of the balance of payments which records trade in goods and services, as well as net income flows and transfer payments.

DEPRECIATION/DEVALUATION: A reduction in the value of the $A against other currencies. Depreciation refers to a floating exchange rate regime, while devaluation refers to the fixed exchange rate regime.

DEREGULATION: The removal of controls and government regulation over an industry. During the 1980s both the financial markets and the setting of the exchange rate were both deregulated in Australia.

ELASTICITY: The responsiveness of the changes in one variable as a result of changes in another. For example, price elasticity measures the responsiveness of changes in demand to changes in price.

FISCAL POLICY: Concerned with changes in government expenditures and revenues.

FOREIGN DEBT: The debt/liabilities owed by Australian residents to the rest of the world.

GDP: Gross domestic product. The main measure, from the National Income Accounts, of the value of all goods and services produced within a country.

INDIRECT TAXES: These are paid by the producer or the seller, rather than 'directly' by the income earner.

INDUSTRY COMMISSION: A body established by the Federal Parliament to inquire into the operation of industries in the private and/or public sector. It reports to Parliament.

INFLATION: Upward movement in the general price level.

INTERMEDIATE GOOD: A good which is not itself consumed, but is used in the production of other goods. Examples include raw materials and machinery.

J-CURVE: The idea that things have to get worse before they get better; applied to the balance of trade (exports minus imports) as the result of a depreciation.

LABOUR FORCE: Those of working age who are willing and able to work.

MONETARY POLICY: Concerned with government intervention in the financial system.

NAIRU: Non-accelerating inflation rate of unemployment. The level of unemployment which is believed to have a neutral impact on inflation; also called the natural rate. It has been argued that unemployment below this rate will tend to accelerate inflation, while unemployment above it will lead to inflation decelerating.

NEW CLASSICAL MACROECONOMICS: A theory which believes in perfectly functioning markets and rational expectations, so that the effects of changes in policy variables occur extremely rapidly (in theory, instantaneously).

NOMINAL VALUES: Money values of economic variables, influenced by both actual changes in those variables and changes in their price. Nominal values are not corrected for the effects of inflation.

NRH: Natural rate hypothesis. See non-accelerating inflation rate of unemployment (NAIRU).

OECD: Organisation for Economic Co-operation and Development. A forum for discussion of policy, a think-tank for new ideas and an agency for collecting international economic statistics.

OPEC: Organisation of Petroleum Exporting Countries.

PARTICIPATION RATE: The proportion of the working age population in the labour force.

PHILLIPS CURVE: The idea that there is an inverse relationship between inflation and unemployment; that is, as one goes up, the other comes down.

PRODUCTIVITY: Output per hours worked.

PUBLIC TRADING ENTERPRISES: Government-owned enterprises which finance their operations from sales to the private sector.

RATIONAL EXPECTATIONS: The idea that people do not make persistently biased (incorrect) errors in their expectations in the long run, or, more strictly, the idea that expectations are formed on the basis of the best economic theory extant.

REAL VALUES: Actual changes in the money values of variables corrected for price changes. Real values are calculated by correcting nominal values (or current prices) for inflation.

SAVINGS: All income that is not consumed.

SEASONALLY ADJUSTED DATA: Some events affecting economic quantities occur each year, such as Christmas or school leavers entering the work force. These events have an independent effect on economic quantities, such as retail sales figures and the unemployment rate. Seasonally adjusted data remove the effects of these seasonal events from the statistics.

STAGFLATION: The coexistence of high inflation with high unemployment.

TERMS OF TRADE: The ratio of export prices to import prices.

UNEMPLOYMENT: That part of the labour force actively looking for work, but unable to find it.

'UNDERLYING' OR 'CORE' INFLATION: The inflation rate corrected for the effect of government policy and certain one-off factors.

# 1 The Australian economy after the 'Asian crisis'
## *Peter Kriesler*

Over the last few years, a number of important economic issues have emerged. While some of these have moved to the forefront of debate for the first time, others have continued in importance. Among the issues which have remained unresolved despite being on the agenda for some time are those associated with industrial relations and with industry policy. On the other hand, the tax debate is like a phoenix, rising from its own ashes at various intervals. All of these issues have had, and will continue to have a significant impact on the economy, and are discussed below. However, since the last edition of *The Australian Economy*, the major influence on the Australian economy has been the Asian crisis. This was expected to have a profound impact on the Australian economy due to the increased openness of the economy and in particular, by lowering the growth rate. However, the economy has remained surprisingly buoyant in the face of the crisis. To understand why, as well as to comprehend the implications of the events in Asia, it is important to examine the channels by which we would expect the events in Asia to influence Australian economic activity.

As we would expect, the major impacts on the Australian economy are through international trade, particularly through exports and imports. In addition, we would expect events in Asia to cause changes to capital flows into and out of Australia. All of these would lead to changes in the value of the Australian dollar, which, in turn influences domestic inflation as well as international competitiveness.

To understand this, we need to briefly consider events in Asia. A 'dramatic and sudden withdrawal of international capital from a

1

number of Asian countries' led to collapses in their exchange rates and serious problems with international debt. These, in turn, led to the countries applying contractionary fiscal and monetary policy which seriously reduced their growth rates, to the extent that some of the countries experienced contractions in the size of their national outputs (documented in detail in Chapter 5).

Although the Asian economies affected are not our major trading partners (Japan and the USA are) nevertheless, they account for most of the growth in trade over the last decade. So the fall in their national incomes should have had a substantial contractionary impact on Australia's exports. At the same time, the fall in the value of their currency relative to the Australian dollar, coupled with the increased efforts to sell exports would be expected to lead to increased domestic imports.

The value of the Australian dollar has increased with respect to these Asian countries, making exports less attractive and imports more so. At the same time, it has depreciated with respect to USA and Europe, having the opposite effect. One of the startling effects of the crisis has been the successful diversion of exports to new markets, so that the fall in exports has not proved to be anywhere near as severe as was originally predicted. The significant fall in exports to the Asian economies has been, until the end of 1998, offset to a large degree by increased exports elsewhere, especially to Europe.

On the other hand, the lower Asian exchange rates plus their attempts to address their external account problems have led to major export effort from those countries. These have had some impact on increased Australian imports from the region.

The net effect has been a substantial deterioration of the balance of trade (exports minus imports). As is demonstrated in chapter 5, Australia's net foreign debt has risen as a result. Associated with this increased debt has been an increase in the net income component of the current account. However, since the mid-1990s, the impact of the increase in foreign debt has been largely offset by lower world interest rates. In other words, despite the fact that Australia's net foreign debt has risen, because the interest rate on that debt has fallen, interest payments and, therefore net income, have not risen as substantially as may be expected. Of course, if there is any increase in world interest rates, this would immediately increase repayments of debt and so would lead to a further deterioration in the current account through increased net income outflows. This is discussed in greater detail in Chapter 5.

The overall current account position, in recent years, has not been particularly favourable, with many of the 1999 outcomes representing new records for the size of the deficit.

In previous years, current account deficits near these levels have led to government responses through contractionary policy in order to attempt to alleviate the problems by reducing imports into Australia. The rationale was that, since imports were strongly related to domestic income, by reducing the growth in income, imports would fall, leading to improvements in the current account position. This was usually achieved via tight fiscal policy, via reductions in government expenditure or increased taxation (see Chapter 6) or by tight monetary policy through increased interest rates (see Chapter 7), the effects of which are to reduce the level of economic activity, reducing both GDP and employment. This, for example, was the sequence which led to the 'recession we had to have' at the beginning of the 1990s.

However, there are extremely important drawbacks to such a strategy. As well as causing increased unemployment, contractionary policy, while treating the symptoms makes the underlying cause worse. Given the size of Australia's foreign debt, the long-term solution requires increased exports, and/or a reduced reliance on imports as a result of domestic import substitution. Both of these require investment in value added. The problem is that the solution to the short-term crises in the forms of high interest rates and contractionary fiscal policy, do not provide a conducive environment for investment, either private or public (Chapter 6). In other words, the more today's problems are solved by such policies, the lower will be investment, and so the lower will be future levels of domestic capacity, which, in turn will increase reliance on imports and reduce export competitiveness. The upshot of all of this is that the policies will, themselves, lead to further deterioration in the current account in the longer term.

However, contemporary current account deficits, unlike previous episodes, have not led to government action. It appears that the government has succeeded in its rhetoric to the extent that such current account figures are not regarded as being problematic by either the media or by financial markets. In fact, many top public servants have explained exactly why it is that we do not need to worry.

The effects of the Asian crisis on the capital account are more ambiguous. Clearly, the effect on Asia as a whole has been to change the general perception of investors away from the view which dominated international markets until 1997, that Asia was a safe place for investment, with high returns. In fact, it is the change in this perception which led to the capital flight that accentuated the crisis. To the extent that Australia is associated with Asia, it is clear that we would expect foreign investment to fall. Counterbalancing this is the fact that investment in Australia would represent the safest haven in the area. Foreign investment also is extremely sensitive to expected exchange rate changes. Here too we would expect

investment in Australia to be relatively favourable, as the exchange
rate would depreciate less against the US dollar, the Japanese yen
and European currencies than would the exchange rates of the other
Asian economies. In fact, there has been a significant increase in net
capital inflows following the Asian crisis.

Chapter 5 shows that in the short run, capital inflows are
important in maintaining balance in balance of payments. However,
in the longer run, those capital inflows are associated with a deterioration in the current account due to income payments moving
in the opposite direction. However, as has been noted, the effects
of this on the net income component of the current account has
been mitigated due to low world interest rates which have reduced
the burden of foreign debt.

The overall impact of all of this has been that the growth rate
of the Australian economy does not seem to have been affected by
the Asian crisis. The record strong growth during recent years has
not been interrupted by international factors. This is despite
increased current account deficits, which, due to benign interpreta-
tions by the government and financial commentaries, has not had
the usual impact on economic policy. However, as chapter 4 indicates, this strong growth in output has not made significant inroads
into the unemployment rate.

The impact of the Asian crisis on the inflation rate is likely to
come through its impact on the exchange rate. The immediate effect
would be to reduce the inflation rate, as a result of cheaper imports
feeding through to the domestic price level. This has been accentuated by the relative appreciation of the Australian dollar against the
exchange rates of the Asian economies. The important counter-
vailing influence came from the depreciation of the domestic
currency against the USA and Europe. Despite the increasing importance of Asian imports, imports from Europe account for over
25 per cent of imports in January 1999, imports from the USA were
over 20 per cent, while those from the ASEAN countries were
12.5 per cent of total imports for the same period.[1] So, as is
discussed in chapter 3, the positive impetus for inflation resulting
from the depreciation of the currency against the European and
American economies should dominate the opposite tendency arising
from the appreciation with the ASEAN economies. However, given
the extremely low level of inflation on which these are acting, the
overall impact is unlikely to raise the inflation rate to one which
will be of concern for policy makers. As a result we are unlikely to
see any contraction in monetary policy which, as chapter 7 notes,
is currently targeted at maintaining an underlying inflation rate of
less than 2 per cent.

Associated with growth, employment, inflation and the balance of payments, are the major policy instruments used by the various levels of government to attempt to influence these. The emphasis on the traditional tools of monetary and fiscal policy has been decreasing. Rather, governments have come to rely increasingly on other policies. This is particularly true of both the current Coalition government and of its predecessor. For both of these, the emphasis of policy shifted away from macroeconomic policy to microeconomic policy. Of great importance to both was industry policy, which was seen as a key plank to the microeconomic reform agenda. The underlying goal of industry policy, as chapter 11 makes clear, is to attempt to make Australian industry 'keen and mean' to boost international competitiveness. Similarly, labour market deregulation was seen as a panacea towards solving the unemployment problem. Debate about labour markets reform has been seen, especially by business and by the government, as a key aspect of policy debate. The government is attempting to further the goals of microeconomic reform by deregulating the labour market. However, this has clearly met with mixed success. Chapter 10 argues that recent changes to the labour market have accentuated inequalities, while not addressing the key issues influencing employment.

As well as the macro impact of fiscal policy, its composition is likely to also have a significant impact on the economy. As a result, separate analysis of public expenditure and of taxation can contribute to our understanding of the economy. The latter, in particular, has dominated policy debate, and been a major issue in elections. There is almost universal agreement about the inadequacies of the current tax system, but no agreement as to how to rectify this. The government has had great rhetorical success in equating the need for taxation reform with a need for a general goods and services tax (GST). One of the main contributors to the current policy debate, Neil Warren, examines Australia's current taxation system, clearly identifying the need for reform. At the same time, he examines the merits of the various alternatives, including GST, commenting on the controversial question of the treatment of food.

Finally, international environmental goals agreed to in Kyoto, Japan in December 1997, led to the release of the Kyoto Protocols. These imposed legally binding obligations on countries, including Australia, to reduce emissions of greenhouse gases. The agreements will have a significant impact on the structure of many economies, as they regulate the nature of emissions, and hence impose constraints on industry. As a result, it is important to understand the implications of the Kyoto Protocols for the Australian economy. This is examined in chapter 12.

# 2 Economic growth
## *Steve Dowrick*

There are several reasons why we might be interested in the rate of growth of the Australian economy. Most important is the fact that faster economic growth will reduce the rate of unemployment. Indeed, much of the policy debate over the short-run performance and management of the economy is concerned with trade-offs between growth and inflation over the business cycle. These important short-run aspects of economic growth are analysed in detail in later chapters. In this chapter the emphasis is on longer-run trends in growth. Is the average rate of growth over one business cycle higher or lower than the average over another? If so, why? What do we expect to be the average rate of growth over the next five to ten years, and what can be done to influence that rate?

Our concern with the growth of economic output is not because more production is necessarily better, but because it is closely linked to the growth of consumption. The link is not perfect because a part of what we produce is owed to overseas investors (and some of what we consume is likewise derived from overseas assets owned by Australian investors). We also trade about one-quarter of what we produce in order to buy foreign goods and services, which sometimes become relatively cheaper or dearer. Furthermore, our net national production does not all get consumed immediately; some of it is invested in buildings and equipment. Nevertheless, national consumption does rise pretty much in line with national output.

The Australian Bureau of Statistics reports how Australian consumption has grown since 1975. Over this period the output of the Australian economy, as measured by real Gross Domestic Product

**Table 2.1  1997 Australian real consumption (1989/90 prices) compared with 1975 and 1960**

|  | Ratio 1997/1975 | Ratio 1997/1960 |
|---|---|---|
| Food | 1.7 | |
| Cigarettes & tobacco | 0.6 | |
| Alcoholic drinks | 1.2 | |
| Clothing, fabrics & footwear | 1.3 | |
| Household appliances | 4.1 | |
| Other household durables | 1.4 | |
| Health | 2.2 | |
| Dwelling rent | 2.2 | |
| Gas, electricity, fuel | 1.6 | |
| Fares | 2.2 | |
| Purchase of motor vehicles | 1.8 | |
| Operation of motor vehicles | 1.8 | |
| Postal & telephone services | 5.9 | |
| Entertainment & recreation | 2.5 | |
| Financial services | 3.9 | |
| Other goods | 2.5 | |
| Other services | 2.7 | |
| Net expenditure overseas | –5.2 | |
| Private final consumption: Total | 1.96 | 3.84 |
| Real GDP: Total | 1.95 | 3.88 |
| Population | 1.34 | 1.8 |
| Private final consumption: *per person* | 1.46 | 2.18 |
| Real GDP: *per person* | 1.46 | 2.20 |

*Source:*  Australian Bureau of Statistics Cat. No. 5206.0

(GDP) has nearly doubled. What has happened to consumption? Consumption of cigarettes has fallen, but every other consumption category has increased. Some items, such as purchases of alcohol, clothing and furniture, have risen only 30 or 40 per cent—in line with the growth of the population—but consumption of items like health services, cars and entertainment has doubled, while we have seen a quadrupling in annual purchases of household appliances, telephone services and financial services. Details are given in Table 2.1.

Overall, the Bureau estimates that total consumption has risen 96 per cent over 22 years, arriving at this estimate by valuing all consumer purchases in 1975 at 1979/80 prices, and doing the same to consumer purchases in 1997. Applying the same constant price valuation to the total output of the economy (real GDP) produces an almost identical figure—actually 95 per cent. (If we compare 1997 consumption and output in 1997 with their 1960 counterparts, we find ratios of 3.84 and 3.88 respectively.)

So Australian consumption has risen at almost exactly the same rate as output. This is the principal reason why we are interested in the growth of the economy—it translates into more goods and services for consumers. But does that mean that the 'average Australian' is actually better off? Critics of economic growth point to the failure of measured consumption to take account of important side effects such as environmental degradation and the depletion of natural resources. Moreover, consumption as measured in the national accounts ignores the value of non-market activities such as raising children and enjoying leisure. Thus measured economic growth is not necessarily the same thing as economic welfare.

An ideal social accounting would measure economic growth with full weight given to non-tangible benefits and costs. The Australian Bureau of Statistics is working towards such a system of social accounting. As it stands now, however, we are reliant for most purposes on measures of consumption and output which are driven largely by the quantities and values of market transactions. As long as we realise that these market-based accounts relate to only a part, albeit an important part, of our economic activities, then we can argue that measured economic growth is an important indicator of social welfare.

Other things being equal, economic growth yields greater access to goods and services and should allow more choice. Those who prefer to grow their own vegetables and weave their own clothes can still do so, while economic growth gives access, for those who want them, to modern medicine, home computers and international travel. Of course the 'other things' are not necessarily kept equal. For example, a full social accounting of economic progress should take account of the noise pollution of aircraft and the increasing inequality of incomes which may result from the revolutions in transport and information technologies.

Accepting these limitations to the measurement of economic growth, this chapter examines Australia's growth record from two perspectives. First, we examine how our growth has changed over time, and the major factors which account for our growth performance. Then we look at international comparisons of economic development in order to assess our comparative success and failure. These two approaches enable us to then make some predictions for the future path of Australian economic growth.

## Growth performance over four decades

The truly remarkable feature of post-war economic development has been the huge increase in the output of goods and services. The output of the Australian economy has increased nearly fourfold since 1960 and consumption of goods and services has risen accordingly.

**Figure 2.1a  Real GDP—total and per capita**

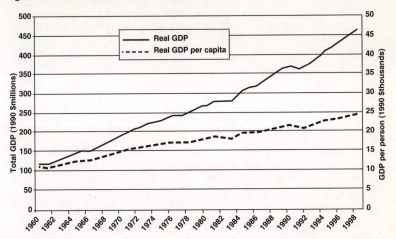

**Figure 2.1b  Annual growth rate of real GDP**

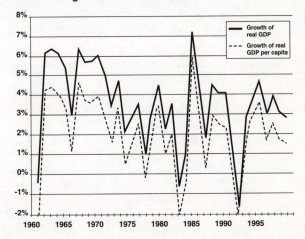

This does not mean that average consumption has risen as fast, however, since the population has been growing at the same time. The population has grown by 80 per cent since 1960, but economic growth has been sufficient to more than double the quantity of goods and services available to the 'average' Australian.

The graph of real output in the Australian economy is shown in Figure 2.1a, measured against the left axis. The annual rate of growth of the economy is displayed in Figure 2.1b. The upper line shows the growth rate of real output while the lower line refers to

**Table 2.2 GDP growth by decade**

| | Average annual rates of growth | | | | |
|---|---|---|---|---|---|
| | 1960–69 | 1970–79 | 1980–89 | 1990–98 | 1992–98 |
| Growth of real GDP | 5.1% | 3.3% | 3.2% | 3.1% | **4.0%** |
| less growth of population | 1.9% | 1.4% | 1.5% | 1.2% | **1.2%** |
| equals growth of real GDP per capita | 3.1% | 1.9% | 1.7% | 1.9% | **2.7%** |

output per person. The gap between the two lines represents the growth rate of population.

The growth path over the last 40 years is subject to sharp downturns of the business cycle occurring every five years or so. It is also evident that the 'golden years of growth' occurred in the 1960s, with an annual average over 5 per cent (3 per cent in per capita terms), before the sharp slowdown of 1973 saw the growth rate halved over the following 20 years. This pattern of growth was common to almost all of the world's industrialised economies.

Most recently, after a sharp recession at the beginning of the decade, the 1990s have seen the growth rate of real GDP in Australia average 4 per cent per year, and GDP per capita growing at 2.7 per cent—rates not sustained since the 1960s. This remarkable turnaround has not been observed in most other industrialised economies. The causes of this apparent sea-change in Australian economic growth has been based substantially on growth in productivity rather than growth in employment, so although living standards are rising the rate of unemployment has been falling only slowly.

One of the ironies of popular economic commentary is that, despite the post-war bonanza in Australia's economic production and consumption, it is commonly accepted that Australia's economic performance has been poor. In particular, it is common to hear calls that Australia should emulate the 'miracle' rates of growth—in the range 5 to 8 per cent—achieved by some of the successful economies of East Asia prior to the financial crisis of 1997. Such criticisms are commonplace in the media from commentators who wish to argue that particular policies or institutions need to be reformed. In fact, however, Australia's economic growth has been unprecedented. Moreover, a proper measurement of living standards—taking account of the different prices faced by consumers in Australia and East Asia and taking account of the greater opportunities for leisure enjoyed by Australians—shows that Australians enjoy the higher standard of living.

If we want to explain the growth path of the economy, an important initial consideration is to distinguish the short-term fluc-

**Table 2.3 Growth of population and employment**

| | average annual growth rates | | | | |
|---|---|---|---|---|---|
| | 1960–98 | 1960–69 | 1970–79 | 1980–89 | 1990–98 |
| Population (total) | **1.5%** | 1.9% | 1.4% | 1.5% | 1.2% |
| Population (15–64) | **1.8%** | 2.2% | 1.8% | 1.8% | 1.2% |
| Labour force | **2.0%** | 2.5% | 1.9% | 2.3% | 1.3% |
| Employment | **1.9%** | 2.4% | 1.5% | 2.2% | 1.2% |
| Hours worked | | | | 2.2% | 0.9% |

*Source:* ABS Labour Force Statistics

tuations of the business cycle, typically consisting of booms and recessions over a five- or six-year period, from the longer-term trends. Trend growth can then be explained in part by the contribution of labour, in part by the contribution of capital, and then in terms of underlying technical progress.

## The labour force's contribution

The biggest single explanator for economic growth in Australia is the rapid rise in population. Australia has had the fastest growing population of all the advanced industrial economies in the post-war period, fuelled by a combination of immigration and a sustained baby boom. Population has grown by an average of 1.5 per cent per year since 1960, although the rate has slowed considerably in recent years as the natural rate of increase has dropped and, particularly, as immigration was cut in the wake of the recession of the early 1990s. The data are summarised in Table 2.3.

A fast growing population will, other things being equal, lead to a rapidly growing labour force which will generate economic growth by expanding employment and its associated output. Indeed, if the capital stock is induced to grow at the same rate as the labour force, and if there are constant returns to capital and labour in production, then we can say (loosely) that since 1960 population growth accounts for 1.5 per cent per year growth in GDP—nearly half of the total growth rate of 3.6 per cent. On the other hand, if we ignore the impact of population growth on the development of the nation's capital stock and assume that a 1 per cent increase in labour input will raise output by 0.7 per cent (a fairly typical estimate of the output–employment elasticity) then the contribution of population growth is 1.1 per cent per annum, which is still a very substantial contribution of one-third.

The raw population figures actually understate the demographic contribution to the labour force. In the 1950s Australia had, as a result of the post-war baby boom, a high proportion of its population under the age of 15. As the baby boomers have moved into

**Figure 2.2  Demographic ratios 1960–98**

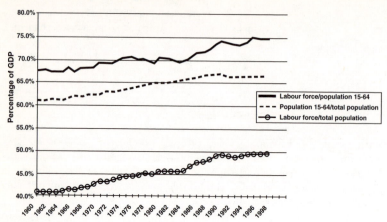

the adult age group, so the potential labour force has expanded faster than the total population—compare the second row with the first in Table 2.3. This baby boom effect has added 0.3 percentage points to the growth of the potential labour force.

The demographic story does not end there. The proportion of the working age group who choose to participate in the paid labour force has also been steadily increasing—as indicated by the figures in row three of Table 2.3, which show that the labour force has grown faster than the 15–64-year-old population. In 1960, 67 per cent of the population aged between 15 and 64 years was in the labour force. By 1998, that proportion had risen to 75 per cent and would probably have been one or two points higher still if high unemployment had not discouraged several hundred thousand potential workers from actively seeking employment. This rise in participation comes despite the facts that young people are increasingly choosing to continue their education well beyond the minimum school leaving age and that many older people are taking the option of early retirement in their early 60s or late 50s.

These trends are illustrated in Figure 2.2. The uppermost line shows how participation has increased. Three-quarters of the working age population are now in the labour force. The middle line shows how the demographic structure has changed, with 15–64 year olds now accounting for over two-thirds of the total population. The bottom line shows the product of these two trends. Over half of all Australians are now in the labour force, compared with only four out of every ten a generation ago.

This rise in participation reflects a revolution in Australian

**Figure 2.3  Participation rates of males and females**

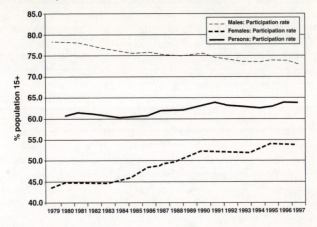

social and economic life—the net movement of over a million women into the labour force. The proportion of the adult female population in the labour force increased from 43 per cent in 1978 to 54 per cent by 1998 and is still increasing. The trends are displayed in Figure 2.3.

Although the largest increase has occurred amongst women working part-time, it still remains the case that the majority of women are working full-time. In considering the relative participation rates of men and women, it is important to take account not only of numbers of people employed but also of hours of work. Selected data on men's and women's working hours are displayed in row 1 of Table 2.4 below. Men in full-time work were working longer hours (44 hours per week in 1995 compared with 41 hours per week in 1978), but less of them were in full-time work, so the average hours of all men had fallen.

Despite the large increase in the numbers of women participating in the labour force, their contribution to total hours worked is only just over half that of men. In other words, the supply of labour by

**Table 2.4  Weekly hours worked per person aged 15–64**

|                                              | 1978 | 1990 | 1995 |
|----------------------------------------------|------|------|------|
| 1. Full-time men (hours per worker)          | 41.4 | 42.6 | 44.0 |
| 2. Men 15–64 years (hours per man)           | 33.6 | 32.3 | 31.4 |
| 3. Women 15–64 years (hours per woman)       | 14.2 | 17.0 | 17.6 |
| 4. Female share (% of total hours worked)    | 29.0 | 34.0 | 35.4 |

*Source:* ABS 6203.0, 6204.0, 6101.0. Hours of work are for all employees, in August of each year

women outside the home is increasing strongly but the potential supply is still substantially unused.

Probably the biggest single driving factor in the continuing choice of women to join the workforce is the improvement of access to schooling. The increase in female educational attainment across recent generations is remarkable. Only one-quarter of women born before 1938 have post-school qualifications, and two-thirds of that cohort left secondary education early. Of the cohort born in the 1960s, however, one-half have post-school qualifications and only one-third left secondary education early. In other words, between successive generations the proportion of women leaving school early has halved and the proportion with tertiary education has doubled. For the current generation of labour market entrants, young women are on average at least as well educated as their male counterparts. Although young men are more likely to have a trade qualification, young women are more likely to have a tertiary degree.

The economic link between education and labour force participation is straightforward. Education increases potential earnings and therefore makes joining the labour force relatively more attractive compared to leisure, child-bearing and home production activities. As successive cohorts of highly educated women move through the life-cycle, we can expect birth rates to decline and labour force participation to rise even higher.

The effect of more women working has substantially outweighed the withdrawal of younger and older people from the labour force. This participation effect, allied to the demographic effect of the baby boom generation, has produced a substantial increase in the proportion of the total population active in the labour force. If we take account of the fact that much of this increase in participation over recent years has been in the part-time sector, the supply of hours per head of total population has been somewhat slower, but the trend increase in participation has been substantial.

The contribution to measured economic growth of women moving from traditional domestic roles into the labour force probably overstates the true increase in economic activity. This is because national accounts fail to measure the contributions of both men and women to home child care, home maintenance and catering, etc. Nevertheless, it is indubitably the case that the rapidly rising trend in labour supply has been the biggest single factor in driving up the measured output of the Australian economy over the past few decades. Measured output has grown at an annual average rate of 3.7 per cent, and labour supply probably accounts for nearly half of that growth—with a contribution of around 1.2 per cent from pure population growth and around 0.4 per cent from the increasing

**Figure 2.4  Public and private investment 1960–97**

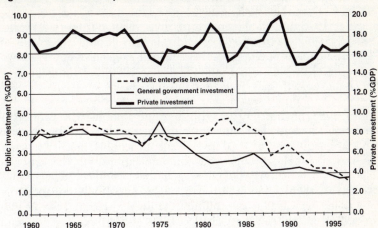

supply of hours of work coming in particular from the baby boom generation of well-educated women.

## The contribution of physical investment

While labour force growth can stimulate economic activity, it is not likely to be very productive unless the new workers are equipped with the tools, machinery, buildings and communications equipment which are necessary for modern production. Indeed, the rapidity of the growth of the Australian labour force makes new investment in capital equipment particularly important if productivity levels are not to fall behind.

Figure 2.4 shows levels of public and private investment over the last four decades, each expressed as a percentage of GDP measured at current prices. Private investment (the uppermost line, calibrated against the right axis) has been consistently in the range of 16 to 18 per cent, with fluctuations outside that range partly caused by and partly contributing to the economic cycle. The sluggish recovery in private investment since the low of 1991 has undoubtedly contributed to the slow recovery of the economy from the recession. Nevertheless, the longer-term trends show that the relatively high rate of private investment in Australia (compared with other industrialised countries) has undoubtedly contributed substantially to long-run growth.

The progress of public investment (both government investment and the investment of government enterprises) has been rather different. Levels of public investment are shown by the two lower lines, measured against the left axis. Each starting at around 4 per cent of GDP in the 1960s, general government investment began to fall after 1975 and public enterprise investment started to fall after 1985. By 1997, both categories had fallen to around 2 per cent of GDP. The cuts in public investment helped to achieve governments' aim of fiscal surplus in the late 1980s and 1990, but the impact on longer-run growth may well be damaging.

Of course public investment (as with private investment) covers a multitude of both productive and non-productive projects— bureaucratic white elephants and political pork-barrels, on the one hand, are included with vital investments in schools, hospitals, water and power supplies, roads and communications, on the other. If only the former non-productive categories were cut from public investment, then economic growth might actually be enhanced by reductions in wasteful expenditure. However, recent econometric evidence from the USA (Aschauer 1989 and Munnell 1992) and from Australia (Otto and Voss 1994) suggests that, on average, public investment tends to be very productive. Quite apart from the direct benefits to consumers of better roads, schools and hospitals, these studies find that increasing the stock of public capital actually increases the productivity of the private sector. Better public provision of transport and communications, or of healthier and more educated workers, reduces substantially the costs of private production. Moreover, several studies suggest that although there is some crowding out of private investment in the short run, the enhanced productivity of the private sector causes private sector investment to increase in the longer run. It follows then that the decline in Australian public sector investment since 1985 may well have reduced incentives for private investment. The combined impact of sluggish private and public investment may well have reduced the potential for future growth.

There is also some concern that private investment may over-emphasise housing and office blocks at the expense of investment in machinery and equipment. International evidence from De Long and Summers (1992) suggests that investment in equipment is likely to bring substantial spillover benefits. Workers learn to use and adapt the new technologies embedded in new equipment and this acquired knowledge becomes a public good which stimulates productivity in other firms and sectors. To the extent that these spillover benefits are not captured fully by the firm making the investment, there is a tendency for private investment in equipment to be sub-optimal. If so, Australian tax and financial incentives, which tend to favour investment in housing and other tangible assets like offices, are perhaps misdirected.

## The contribution of technical progress

The previous sections have suggested the extent to which economic growth has been driven by: (i) cyclical fluctuations in economic activity; (ii) the growth of the labour force; and (iii) the growth of private and public capital stocks. After taking account of these contributions, it is usual to find that there is some residual component to growth which is not explained by a simple factor input model of production. This residual or unexplained growth is sometimes labelled technical progress. A more accurate description is, however, to label it 'multi-factor productivity growth' or 'MFP growth'.

Pure technical progress—new ideas or 'blueprints' for ways of satisfying human wants—is impossible to measure. Nevertheless, looking back over the history of human technology and civilisation leads to a very strong presumption that such technical progress is at the heart of economic development. Indeed, without technical progress we might expect physical investment to run into diminishing returns which would cause the economy to reach a steady state where growth ceases. Rather naively, economists often identify technical progress with multi-factor productivity growth, although if pushed they will typically admit that this identification is really an expression of their ignorance about the other contributions to growth, that is, contributions other than the growth of capital and labour inputs.

In principle we know that investments in education and training contribute to growth, improving the skill levels of the workforce, and that the discovery (or depletion) of natural resources can also contribute. These contributions are, however, notoriously difficult to measure. So this section will concentrate on the rather easier task of identifying trends in multi-factor productivity—trends which represent some combination of true technical progress and the contribution of these other unidentified factors.

Before we can seriously measure productivity, the amount of output provided by one unit of input, we need to understand how we measure output itself. Up until this point we have used the national accounts aggregate of GDP. Unfortunately, some outputs which are important components of GDP are not amenable to measurement—particularly the non-marketed services of government and some of the services of the financial sector. Lacking adequate measures of real output in these sectors, the Australian Bureau of Statistics (1989) report that they value these services at the cost of their inputs. This procedure is tantamount to assuming zero productivity growth for these sectors. If we want to examine productivity, it is then important to use the statistics for those sectors

**Table 2.5   Sources of growth of labour productivity in the market sector (% p.a.)**

|  | 1 | 2 | 3 | 4 | 5 | 6 |
|---|---|---|---|---|---|---|
| Financial year ending June | Growth of output | Growth of hours | Growth of capital services | Growth of labour productivity | Due to growth in capital intensity | Due to trend MFP growth |
| 1965–98 | 3.3 | 1.0 | 4.3 | 2.3 | 1.1 | 1.5 |
| 1965–73 | 4.5 | 2.1 | 6.5 | 2.7 | 1.4 | 2.2 |
| 1973–83 | 1.7 | –0.5 | 4.1 | 2.2 | 1.4 | 0.8 |
| 1983–90 | 4.5 | 2.7 | 3.9 | 1.3 | 0.3 | 0.8 |
| 1990–98 | 2.9 | 0.1 | 2.8 | 2.8 | 0.9 | 2.0 |

*Source:*  ABS Catalogue 5204.0, April 1999, 'Australian System of National Accounts', Table 1.17 for output and input measures. The contribution of capital intensity is calculated as the growth in the capital labour ratio × 0.32; the trend is estimated by Dowrick (1998); the unreported contributions are cyclical adjustment and random factors.

of the economy where real output is measured directly. Accordingly, the following analysis of productivity is restricted to the output of the market sector of the economy.

Labour productivity is defined as the ratio of real output to the number of hours worked. A strong cyclical pattern is evident. When the economy moves into recession, labour productivity tends to fall as firms hold onto overhead labour and hoard skilled workers who might be difficult to replace. Then, when the economy begins to recover, labour productivity can rise very fast as under-utilised labour is put back to work.

In the late 1960s and early 1970s, annual growth in labour productivity averaged 2.7 per cent. This rate of growth declined to 2.2 per cent in the ten years after the watershed of the 1973 oil crisis, and declined even further to just 1.3 per cent over the remainder of the 1980s before climbing back to 2.8 per cent in the 1990s. The productivity slowdown and subsequent pick-up have been the subject of intense analysis at both academic and political levels.

It is now widely accepted that the slowdown following 1973 was part of a world-wide phenomenon whereby the exceptionally rapid growth of industrialised economies in the aftermath of the Second World War was brought to an end by the oil price rises of 1973 and the associated period of economic stagnation and in-flation. The subsequent slowdown in the growth of labour productivity in the 1980s has, however, been seen as an event particular to Australia. At the time it triggered widespread criticism of labour market institutions, particularly the centralisation of wage setting which was set in place under the 1983 Accord between the incoming Labor government and the Australian Confederation of Trade Unions. Partly as a result of this productivity, there were moves in the 1990s to deregulate the labour market and, in particular, to replace centralised wage bargaining with bargaining at enterprise level.

Much of the evidence of the productivity slow-down in the 1980s was misinterpreted. Part of the aim of the 1983 Accord was to encourage employment growth through wage restraint. To a substantial extent that aim was successful, as evidenced by the strong growth in hours worked in the ten years from July 1983 (1.7 per cent per year) compared with the fall in hours worked over the previous ten years (–0.7 per cent p.a.).

One result of strong employment growth induced by wage restraint is that firms favour more labour intensive methods of production. This in turn implies that output *per unit of labour* will not be as high as it would have been under higher wages and more capital intensive production. This is not to say that wage restraint has been harmful for productivity, rather that labour productivity is a misleading measure. We should, instead, estimate the combined productivity of both labour and capital, i.e. multi-factor productivity.

The way we do this is summarised in Table 2.5. Subtracting labour growth from the growth of output gives the growth rate of labour productivity (column 4). Subtracting labour growth from the growth of the capital stock gives a measure of the growth of capital intensity. We then subtract from labour productivity growth the contribution of increased capital intensity and the contribution of cyclical fluctuations. These contributions are estimated from production function relationship estimated by Dowrick (1998). The resulting measure of trend multi-factor productivity growth is given in the last row of the table. We can regard this as an estimate of the rate of technical progress.

This preferred measure of underlying productivity growth tells a substantially different story from the crude measure of labour productivity. Almost all of the labour productivity slowdown after 1983 can be attributed to the much faster growth of employment and the slower growth of capital intensity. The sharp fall in productivity growth actually occurred from 1973, in line with the productivity slowdown in the USA and Europe. There is no evidence that MFP growth slowed after the introduction of the 1983 Accord.

More recently, the decade of the 1990s has seen a very strong recovery in underlying productivity growth. A possible explanation, canvassed by the Industry Commission (1997), is the series of microeconomic reforms, including some deregulation of the labour market, discussed elsewhere in this volume. A problem with this explanation is that we would expect greater efficiency in the allocation of resources to be accompanied by faster growth in both output and inputs. But the 1990s has seen a jobless recovery, with hours of work hardly increasing at all. The growth of capital has been lower than in any previous period since 1965 and output growth has been below average. So the source of recent productivity growth is yet to be satisfactorily explained.

**International technology transfer and comparisons of economic growth**

It has become a habit amongst economic commentators to bemoan Australia's economic performance, frequently citing faster growth rates of other OECD and Asian countries as evidence of their superior economic policies and institutions. What these comparisons ignore is that Australia is at a very different stage of development from most of the countries with which it is being compared. In particular, many southern European and East Asian economies have been able to capitalise in the post-war period on the 'advantage of backwardness'—the opportunity to catch up on the world's most advanced economies by importing or copying their products and technologies. As these countries catch up on the productivity levels and living standards of the advanced economies, so there is a strong tendency for their growth rates to slow down.

Table 2.6 presents data on levels and growth rates of per capita GDP for a selection of industrialised and industrialising countries. Note that the data here go only as far as 1997 and therefore do not capture any of the growth slowdown occasioned by the East Asian financial crisis of 1997. Amongst this sample, Australia began in 1950 as one of the richest economies, second only to the USA. Australian growth rates have in fact roughly equalled those of the USA over the five decades. By 1990, a number of countries had caught up with Australian levels of per capita GDP.[1] Japan and Hong Kong had experienced particularly fast growth of 7 per cent per year or more in the 1960s, but Japanese growth rates have been falling since 1970 and economic growth in Hong Kong has slowed since 1980. The southern European economies of Italy and Greece, which had been catching up on Australia in the post-war reconstruction period of the 1950s and 1960s, have slowed down in more recent decades. In the late 1980s and early 1990s, some of the new East Asian 'tigers' such as Korea, Indonesia and China were experiencing the rapid growth spurts which characterised Japan and Hong Kong several decades ago.

These observations suggest the existence of a consistent pattern whereby rapid growth is possible for countries which are entering into the process of industrialisation. Once through the phase of

**Table 2.6  Economic development 1950–92 in East Asia and OECD**

| | A: Level of real GDP per capita (thousands of 1997 US dollars) | | | | | |
| | 1950 | 1960 | 1970 | 1980 | 1992 | 1997 |
|---|---|---|---|---|---|---|
| Australia | 10.1 | 11.8 | 16.3 | 19.0 | 21.9 | 25.2 |
| New Zealand | 10.1 | 12.1 | 14.2 | 15.7 | 17.2 | 19.2 |
| W. Germany | 5.2 | 10.0 | 14.3 | 18.1 | 22.3 | 23.4 |
| USA | 13.3 | 15.0 | 19.6 | 23.2 | 27.2 | 30.2 |
| Japan | 2.2 | 4.5 | 11.1 | 15.3 | 22.9 | 24.3 |
| China | | 0.9 | 1.1 | 1.5 | 2.3 | 3.6 |
| Hong Kong | | 3.4 | 6.8 | 13.2 | 25.0 | 28.5 |
| Indonesia | | 1.0 | 1.1 | 1.9 | 3.2 | 4.1 |
| Korea, Rep. | | 1.4 | 2.5 | 4.7 | 11.0 | 14.8 |
| Malaysia | | 2.2 | 3.3 | 5.8 | 8.7 | 11.4 |
| Singapore | | 2.5 | 4.6 | 10.7 | 19.2 | 25.5 |
| Thailand | 1.3 | 1.4 | 2.3 | 3.3 | 6.0 | 7.6 |

| | B: Growth rate (annual average) (%) | | | | |
| | 1950–60 | 1960–70 | 1970–80 | 1980–92 | 1992–1997 |
|---|---|---|---|---|---|
| Australia | 1.5 | 3.2 | 1.5 | 1.2 | 2.8 |
| New Zealand | 1.8 | 1.7 | 1.0 | 0.8 | 2.2 |
| W. Germany | 6.5 | 3.6 | 2.3 | 1.8 | 1.0 |
| USA | 1.2 | 2.7 | 1.7 | 1.3 | 2.1 |
| Japan | 7.3 | 9.1 | 3.2 | 3.4 | 1.2 |
| China | | 2.0 | 3.3 | 3.6 | 9.4 |
| Hong Kong | | 6.9 | 6.6 | 5.3 | 2.7 |
| Indonesia | | 1.1 | 5.8 | 4.1 | 5.1 |
| Korea, Rep. | | 6.2 | 6.1 | 6.5 | 5.9 |
| Malaysia | | 4.2 | 5.7 | 3.4 | 5.4 |
| Singapore | | 6.0 | 8.5 | 4.9 | 5.7 |
| Thailand | 1.0 | 4.8 | 3.6 | 4.9 | 4.9 |

*Source:*  Penn World Tables 5.6 and IMF Financial Statistics

economic acceleration, growth performance comes to resemble the growth of the other advanced economies.

We can examine more closely this relationship between economic growth rates and level of development by plotting the decade average growth rates against the level of per capita GDP for each country at the beginning of that decade. Figure 2.5 displays the resulting scatter plot. There appear to be two strong relationships. Below $US4000 per capita, economic backwardness appears to be a handicap. The very poorest of these economies tend to grow much more slowly than the richest—a phenomenon which is analysed in greater detail by Abramovitz (1986) and Dowrick (1992). Economic growth rates of around 7 per cent are quite common for economies at the US$4–6000 level, but as these economies grow richer there is a pronounced tendency for their growth to slow down.

These tendencies are illustrated in the figure by an inverted V

**Figure 2.5  Take-off and slowdown in OECD and East Asia**

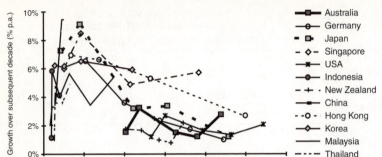

Source: Penn World Table 5.6 and IMF Financial Statistics

shape which peaks at around $US5000. One of the most interesting features of this picture is that this pattern of growth appears to have held as much for the advanced OECD economies, such as West Germany, as for the East Asian economies such as Japan and Singapore.

The Australia–Japan comparison is particularly interesting. The Japanese 'miracle' growth rates occurred in the 1950s and 1960s when the Japanese economy was embarking on rapid industrialisation. In the 1970s and 1980s, the Japanese growth performance was not dramatically better than the Australian performance of the 1950s and 1960s when Australia was at a similar level of economic development. Indeed, the Australian economy outgrew the Japanese economy over the recent period 1992–97. Moreover, much of Japanese economic success in the 1980s was due to their very high savings and investment rates rather than to any continued 'miracle' of technical progress.

This analysis tends to suggest that the Australian growth performance, since 1960 at least, has been pretty much what would be expected for an economy at the high end of the economic development scale. It cautions against the doomsayers who compare Australian growth with that of the Asian economies which are at a very different stage of economic development.

Indeed, we can make use of these international comparisons to compare Australia's productivity performance with that of its peers. In a recent paper (Dowrick 1998), the growth rates of OECD economies are explained in a growth-accounting framework by the contributions of technological catch-up, investment, employment growth, common shifts in technical progress, and residual multi-

**Table 2.7  Contributions to annual growth of real GDP in Australia relative to average OECD growth**

|          | Growth of Australian output | Average OECD growth | Contribution of investment | Contribution of employment growth | MFP growth |
|----------|------|------|------|------|------|
| 1960–73  | 4.9% | 4.7% | 0.7% | 0.9% | –1.4% |
| 1973–79  | 2.9% | 2.6% | 0.3% | 0.1% | –0.1% |
| 1979–90  | 3.1% | 2.5% | 0.3% | 0.8% | –0.5% |
| 1991–96  | 2.9% | 2.2% | –0.2% | 0.1% | –0.8% |
| 1960–96  | 3.4% | 3.0% | 0.3% | 0.5% | –0.3% |

factor productivity (MFP) growth. The results for Australia are summarised in Table 2.7.

The contributions are all measured relative to the OECD average. We see that Australian investment was above the OECD average up until 1990, but has since slipped below average and therefore makes a negative contribution to relative growth.

Most interesting is the finding that whereas up until 1990 Australian MFP growth was below the average of the OECD, over the period since 1990 it has been well above average. This lends additional weight to the evidence from time series analysis, that there has indeed been a sea-change in Australia's productivity performance. The cause of this substantial improvement has yet to be established. It may be related to changes in industrial relations, to the privatisation and deregulation of various sectors of the economy, to increased skill and education levels, or to better performance of research and development activities by Australian companies and public institutions.

## Concluding comments

Most of the preceding analysis has been concerned with the proximate determinants of growth—particularly the inputs of labour and capital into production and technical change—but has not delved into the deeper determinants, the factors influencing people's decisions of whether to enter the labour market, whether to save, where to invest in physical capital, when to invest in education or research. These more fundamental determinants of growth are presumably linked to both social and market institutions and also to culture.

There is a fast expanding economics literature which is trying to develop adequate theoretical models of the growth process. Drawing on some of the insights of earlier economists such as Schumpeter and Kaldor (see Hanusch 1988), the 'new growth theories' of Romer (1986, 1990) and others emphasise the importance of spillover benefits which can occur when a firm or individual makes investment decisions. Investment in research, or learning to use new equipment and techniques, can create new knowledge which is readily available to others and generates benefits which are not necessarily captured by the individual making the investments. There may be an important role for government to use taxes and subsidies to encourage or provide socially beneficial investment in education and research as well as in public infrastructure.[2]

Culture and institutions also matter. A harmonious society characterised by trusting personal relationships may not only be more pleasant than an aggressive cut-throat environment but also more conducive to economic progress. At the same time, a culture which values new ideas, and institutions which encourage training and innovation, are likely to promote growth.

The measurement and contribution to economic growth of these less tangible factors is, however, particularly difficult if not impossible to identify. Nevertheless, we can draw some tentative conclusions from the evidence which has been presented here and from the wider economic debate which is summarised in recent publications such as Temple (1999).

First, we can expect an expanding labour force to continue to generate substantial economic growth over the next decade, although the baby-boom effect will diminish as those born in the 1940s start to contemplate early retirement (voluntary or compulsory). Most of the labour force expansion will come from immigration and from a new generation of women seeking careers commensurate with their educational attainment. The feminisation of work and the workforce is a substantial source of growth in the Australian economy.

Second, comparative analysis of economic growth over the last 30 or 40 years suggests that Australian institutions and policies are performing well by international standards. Strong and sustained growth since the recession at the beginning of the 1990s constitutes particularly good performance in terms of productivity growth, substantially stronger than that of comparable economies over the same period. There is a *prima facie* case that the productivity recovery is the result of those policy and institutional reforms to labour, finance and industrial markets since the early 1980s that have been labelled 'micro-economic reform'. To the extent that this is so, we may expect rapid productivity growth to continue. On the other hand, lowered levels of public investment in physical and social infrastructure and a sluggish recovery in private investment do not augur well for longer term growth.

Australian economic growth is likely to continue in the range between 3 and 4 per cent per year. One point will be attributable to the rate of increase of population and the continuing increase in women's participation in the labour market; another point to underlying technical progress; the third point to a moderate level of investment by both the public and private sectors. A more buoyant scenario might see the trend rate of growth continue as high as 4 per cent, but this will occur only if there is a resurgence of investment activity, in both the private and public sectors, in the physical and social infrastructure which drives economic growth.

# 3    Inflation in Australia
## *Bill Junor*

In May 1998, Ian Macfarlane, the Governor of the Reserve Bank of Australia, in testimony before the House of Representatives Standing Committee on Financial Institutions and Public Administration noted that:

> Underlying inflation has been $1\frac{1}{2}$ per cent over the last 12 months. We are still expecting that it will rise over the next 12 months, largely because falling import prices, which were pushing inflation down, have given way to increasing import prices . . . these changes are not alarming, but they do tend to suggest that we have passed the low point in the inflation cycle. (Macfarlane 1998, p.1)

In its 'Semi-Annual Statement on Monetary Policy' in May 1998, the Reserve Bank indicated that it expected the inflation rate to be 2 per cent per year by the end of 1998, increasing to 'around $2\frac{1}{2}$ per cent by the middle of 1999' (Reserve Bank of Australia 1998, p.52). This upward pressure on the inflation rate is attributed largely to rising import prices in the wake of the depreciation of the Australian dollar. Expectations of inflation, derived from surveys of both consumers and producers, also seem to be undergoing upward revision, albeit tentatively.

The expected increase in the inflation rate is a modest one, from what is, in the post-World War II period, very low inflation. What then accounts for this concern about inflation and the expectation on the part of some sectors of the economy that inflation rates will not remain at their current low level? Macfarlane (1995, pp.10–11)

26

suggests that the double digit inflation in many countries in the 1970s and the consequent emergence of an 'inflationary mentality' generated adverse economic consequences. These adverse consequences mean that inflation imposes costs on the economy.

What are these costs of inflation? Economists have identified several effects of inflation that give rise to economic costs. These effects include increased uncertainty regarding the profitability and appropriate financing of investment, redistribution of income and wealth, increased nominal interest rates, balance of payments problems, and unemployment. Although the costs of inflation can readily be identified conceptually, it is, as Nguyen (1991) points out, very difficult to estimate these costs directly. For this reason most empirical studies attempt to estimate the costs indirectly, by considering the effects of inflation on either the level of real output or its rate of growth.

A convenient starting point to a discussion of these various aspects of inflation is with a definition of inflation.

## A definition of inflation

Attempts to define inflation tend to fall into two broad categories. First, those which define inflation by reference to what are claimed to be its *causes*. Two examples of this 'causal' approach to a definition of inflation are 'too much money chasing too few goods' and 'money wages rising faster than labour productivity'. The problem with this approach is that it offers various (and often competing) *explanations* of the causes of the inflationary process, rather than a *definition* of inflation.

Falling into the second category are those definitions which focus on the *effects* of inflation. An example of this 'symptoms' approach is the particular definition that will be employed here: *inflation is upward movement in the general level of prices*.

## Measurement of inflation

The notion of *the general level of prices* can be captured by a price index which weights the prices of the various goods and services covered by the index by their relative importance in a selected base year. This weighting process ensures that the resulting index provides an adequate representation of the various price changes, positive and negative, that occur in a particular period of time. Inflation can then be measured as the percentage change in the price index:

$$P_t = \frac{(PI_t - PI_{t-1})}{PI_{t-1}} \times 100$$

where $P_t$ is the rate of inflation in period t, $PI_t$ is the value of the price index in period t, and $PI_{t-1}$ is the value of the price index in the previous period $t - 1$. Inflation is therefore expressed as a percentage change per unit of time; most commonly per quarter or per year.

The Australian Bureau of Statistics publishes many different price indexes—they differ on the basis of their method of construction and on their coverage. There are two basic approaches to the construction of price indexes. The Base Weight (or Laspeyres) Index employs a base period 'basket' of goods and services to compare the current period value of the basket (using the current period prices of the goods and services in the basket) with the base period value of the same basket (using base period prices). The use of the same (base period) basket for both base and current periods ensures that any change in the index reflects *only* price changes between the two periods. The index for the base period must be equal to 100 since, in that period, base prices and current prices are identical. The value of the index for the current period indicates therefore the percentage increase in prices that has occurred between the base and current periods; that is, on our definition of inflation, the rate of inflation for that period. By contrast, the Current Weight (or Paasche) Index uses a current period basket of goods and services to compare the current period value of the basket to the base period value. As with the Base Weight Index, the value of the index in the base period is 100 and the current period index indicates the rate of inflation over the period. Unlike the Base Weight Index, however, which is a fixed basket index (until such time as the basket is revised), the composition of the basket of goods and services in the Current Weight Index changes each period—it is therefore a variable basket index.

Ignoring for the moment the coverage of the index, there are deficiencies in both Base Weight and Current Weight Indexes as measures of inflation. In Base Weight Indexes the composition of the basket of goods and services (the 'regimen') is revised periodically but remains fixed between revisions. Such indexes therefore tend to become less representative the longer is the time period between revisions, because changes in the pattern of demand induced by new products, changes in preferences and relative price changes are not reflected in the regimen. Current Weight Indexes are always representative of current period demand patterns; such indexes therefore not only measure the inflation rate but also reflect changes in the composition of goods and services.

As well as compositional changes, the quality of goods can vary over time. If these quality changes are associated with price movements, they will be reflected by variations in the particular price index being used. Strictly, such price changes should not be included in the price index. To the extent that this type of price change is present in the price index, the 'true' measure of inflation is distorted.

The Boskin Commission in the United States found that the US Consumer Price Index overstated the 'true' rate of inflation by 1.1 percentage points per year, of which 0.6 percentage points per year were attributable to new products and quality changes (Boskin et al. 1998, p.12). No comparable estimates have been made for the Australian CPI.

It is the broad coverage indexes that are relevant to the measurement of inflation. These include the Consumer Price Index (CPI) and the implicit price deflators for Gross Domestic Product (IGDPD) and for Domestic Final Demand (IDFDD). The CPI (a base-weighted index) is perhaps the best known measure of inflation. There are several reasons for its popularity: the CPI is usually published within one month of the end of the quarter to which it refers; it is widely (though incorrectly) regarded as an index of the 'cost of living'; it has been used as an input into wage and salary adjustments and was used as the basis for wage indexation and, until recently, for indexation of social security benefits. Notwithstanding its wide popular recognition as *the* measure of inflation, the CPI is somewhat limited in this regard, largely because of its coverage. The CPI measures quarterly changes in the prices of goods and services that represent a high proportion of the expenditure of metropolitan wage and salary earner households. This means that while the CPI includes price changes of all those domestically produced and imported consumer goods and services that form part of the basket, price changes of investment goods and exported goods are not explicitly included.

The various implicit price deflators (so named because they are not measured directly, but rather are derived from the current and constant price estimates of the National Accounting aggregates to which they apply) are also used as measures of the inflation rate. The implicit Domestic Final Demand deflator (IDFDD) reflects price changes for Domestic Final Demand, the components of which are current and capital expenditures by both private and public sectors, including expenditure on imported goods and services. By contrast, the implicit Gross Domestic Product deflator (IGDPD) captures movements in the prices of final goods and services, including exported goods, produced in Australia.

The preceding discussion suggests that, while several broad coverage price indexes are available, none can provide an estimate of *the* rate of inflation. Rather, they provide somewhat imperfect measures of the rate of change of the prices of goods and services that come within their ambit. This qualification partly explains why many economists, even those who argue that inflation imposes

**Figure 3.1  The path of Australia's inflation since 1960**

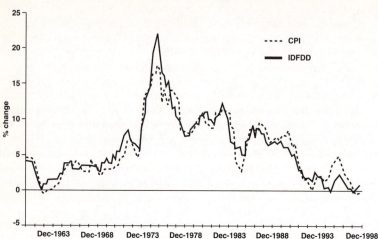

Source: ECONDATA

significant economic costs, stop short of arguing for zero inflation as a goal of macroeconomic policy.

## Australia's inflation experience—a broad brush

The path of Australia's inflation since 1960 is shown in Figure 3.1 by the rates of change of the Consumer Price Index and the implicit Domestic Final Demand deflator. In a comprehensive survey of inflation in Australia between 1950 and 1991, Stevens (1992) employed the implicit deflator for private consumption expenditure from the National Accounts in preference to the CPI. The latter series is rejected by Stevens (1992, p.183, n1) in order 'to avoid measurement difficulties . . . which have affected the short-term reliability of the published CPI as an indicator of prices for current consumption goods and services'. While it is true that the revised Medicare arrangements in 1984 and the introduction of mortgage interest charges in 1986 have given rise to 'measurement difficulties', it is also true that the CPI, despite its limitations, remains the most closely watched indicator of inflation. It is for this reason that a CPI-based inflation rate, together with one based on Domestic Final Demand (which is free of the particular limitations noted by Stevens), are employed here.

The time period chosen, from 1960 to the present, is sufficiently long for a wide range of inflation experiences to be observed.

The first point to be made is that although there have been

episodes when the two indexes have diverged, both when inflation was increasing and when it was decreasing, they have for the most part moved together. That is, notwithstanding the differences in coverage, these two indexes are telling essentially the same story about inflation over the period 1960 to 1998.

Second, three inflationary sub-periods can be discerned:

- the period 1961 to 1972 when inflation increased from an annual rate of less than 2 per cent in 1961 to around 4 per cent in 1964, stabilised at this level until the end of 1969, and then accelerated again to around 7 per cent;
- the period 1972 to 1986 which was characterised by marked volatility in inflation rates with peaks in 1975, 1982 and 1986, and troughs in 1978 and 1985. Inflation rates, as measured by the IDFDD, varied between a high of 21.6 per cent in 1975 and a low of 5.2 per cent in 1985;
- the period 1986 to the present which has seen inflation rates fluctuating around a downward trend, though with a sharp increase in 1995 followed by an equally sharp decline in the CPI-based rate, with this measure of inflation recording negative annual rates for the September and December quarters of 1997 and the March quarter of 1998.

Third, Carmichael (1990), using the growth of the CPI as his measure of inflation, characterised the 1970s as the decade of high inflation and the 1980s as the decade of steady inflation, and suggested that '[b]y mid 1988, hopes of a continuing steady decline in inflation . . . had been dashed'. With the advantage of an additional decade of data, we can see that Carmichael's pessimism was not warranted. Inflation, whether measured by the CPI or IDFDD, fell sharply after the March quarter 1990. However, as can be seen in Figure 3.1, the CPI-based inflation rate diverged from the IDFDD-based rate in 1986, and from the June quarter 1989 until the March quarter 1990 the two measures moved in opposite directions. Further, the spike in the CPI-based inflation rate in 1995 was not associated with a similar movement in the IDFDD-based rate. This suggests that Stevens' concern regarding the 'short-term reliability' of the CPI—arising in this instance from the inclusion of mortgage interest charges in the post-1987 regimen—may be well placed.

The impact of government policy changes on the CPI has focussed attention on the 'underlying' (or 'core') rate of inflation— the inflation rate corrected for the effects of these policy changes. However, the exclusion of particular items depends on whether the CPI is intended to serve as a general measure of inflation or as the basis for adjusting wages and social security benefits. In its 1992

**Table 3.1  The CPI (All Groups) and alternative measures of the 'underlying' inflation rate (percentage change December quarter over December quarter in previous year)**

|                                         | 1992 | 1993 | 1994 | 1995 | 1996 | 1997 | 1998 |
|-----------------------------------------|------|------|------|------|------|------|------|
| CPI (All Groups)                        | 0.3  | 1.9  | 2.5  | 5.1  | 1.5  | –0.2 | 1.6  |
| CPI (excluding interest charges and volatile items) | 2.1  | 2.9  | 2.4  | 3.9  | 2.2  | 1.7  | 1.7  |
| Privately-provided goods and services   | 1.9  | 2.5  | 2.0  | 4.1  | 2.0  | 1.3  | 1.5  |
| Treasury 'underlying rate'              | 1.9  | 2.1  | 2.1  | 3.2  | 2.1  | 1.4  | 1.6  |

*Source:* ABS, *Consumer Price Index*, Cat. No. 6401.0, various issues, Reserve Bank of Australia, *Bulletin*, various issues

review of the CPI, the ABS noted that income compensation has been the major traditional use of the CPI, and for this reason an All Groups index based on outlays was judged appropriate.

Several measures of underlying inflation, derived by excluding items from the All Groups regimen, are compiled for Australia. The ABS currently reports price changes for 'All groups excluding interest and volatile items'; the Reserve Bank of Australia reports changes in 'Prices for privately-provided goods and services'; and the Federal Treasury reports changes in an Underlying Inflation series which it compiles. These measures comprise, respectively, slightly less than 85 per cent, slightly less than 70 per cent, and about 51 per cent, of the All Groups regimen.

Table 3.1 shows these three measures of underlying inflation, together with the CPI (All Groups) inflation rate. Three features of these data might be noted. First, although the underlying inflation measures exhibit greater stability than the CPI inflation rate (which is to be expected given the way in which the underlying measures were derived), the All Groups measure is lower than the underlying rate measures in four of the seven years. Second, the three underlying inflation series provide similar values for the inflation rate and, with only one exception, show the same direction of change of the inflation rate. Third, the large increase in the inflation rate in 1995 suggested by the CPI (All Groups) measure is not fully reflected in the underlying measures, all of which suggest a rather smaller increase in the inflation rate in that year.

## A closer look at the CPI

One attraction of the CPI is that the ABS publishes a decomposition of the overall change in the inflation rate into rates of change for the various expenditure categories. Table 3.2 shows the quarterly percentage change in the CPI, expressed as the weighted average of the eight capital cities, for the eight major categories of expenditure.

**Table 3.2  Consumer Price Index-weighted average of eight capital cities (percentage change between current quarter and previous quarter)**

| Category | 1997 | | | | 1998 | | | |
|---|---|---|---|---|---|---|---|---|
| | March | June | Sept | Dec | March | June | Sept | Dec |
| Food | 0.7 | 0.5 | 0.0 | 0.2 | 0.8 | 0.8 | 1.3 | 1.0 |
| Clothing | −0.5 | 0.3 | −0.2 | 0.7 | −0.4 | −0.1 | −0.3 | −0.1 |
| Housing | −2.9 | −3.3 | −1.0 | −1.8 | −0.8 | 1.2 | 0.3 | 0.7 |
| Household equipment and operation | −0.1 | 0.4 | −0.4 | 0.4 | 0.0 | 0.2 | −0.1 | 0.2 |
| Transportation | 0.6 | −1.0 | 0.4 | −0.3 | −0.9 | −0.1 | −0.5 | −0.3 |
| Tobacco and alcohol | 0.3 | 0.2 | −0.1 | 1.5 | 0.7 | 0.8 | 0.5 | 0.2 |
| Health and personal care | 2.7 | 2.3 | −3.5 | 3.0 | 1.2 | 2.0 | 0.8 | −0.4 |
| Recreation and education | 1.9 | −0.1 | 0.9 | 0.3 | 2.0 | 0.2 | −0.3 | 0.9 |
| All Groups | 0.2 | −0.2 | −0.4 | 0.3 | 0.3 | 0.6 | 0.2 | 0.5 |

Source: ABS, *Consumer Price Index*, Cat. No. 6401.0, various issues

As might be expected when annual inflation rates (measured here by the CPI) range between −0.3 and 1.6, the quarterly percentage changes for the expenditure categories are a mixture of positive (increasing prices) and negative (decreasing prices) figures. A striking feature of Table 3.2 is the extent to which the relatively large changes, both positive and negative, for the individual categories are the *direct* result of the budgetary policies of the Commonwealth and State governments and of monetary policy. Categories most susceptible to these influences are Housing (via the monetary policy effect on housing interest charges), Tobacco and alcohol (via Commonwealth excise on tobacco and State licence and franchise fees) and Health and personal care (via changes to the Pharmaceutical Benefits Scheme).

Housing, with a weight of 15.90 per cent in the latest CPI, has been an important source of deflationary pressure over the period from the March quarter 1997 to the March quarter 1998, especially in the March and June quarters 1997 when this category reduced the inflation rate by nearly one-half of a percentage point in each quarter. By contrast, over the same period, Tobacco and alcohol, with a weight of 7.475 per cent, has been a modest contributor to inflationary pressure, especially in the last quarter of 1997 and the first two quarters of 1998.

Health and personal care, with a weight of 6.85 per cent, was an important source of inflationary pressure over the whole period, with the exception of the September quarter 1997, when this expenditure category led to a reduction in the inflation rate of around

**Figure 3.2   Annual rate of inflation for eight expenditure categories and for
All Groups, December quarter over December quarter in
preceding year**

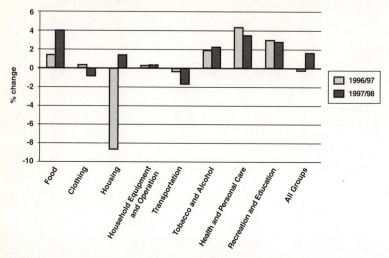

*Source:* ABS, *Consumer Price Index,* Cat. No. 6401.0, Various issues

0.24 of a percentage point. This was a one-off reduction as a result
of the introduction by the Australian government of the Private
Health Insurance Incentive Scheme in mid-1997.

Figure 3.2 shows the annual rate of inflation (measured as the
December quarter CPI over the December quarter CPI in the preceding year) for the eight expenditure categories and for All Groups
for the last two years. This reinforces the point made by Table 3.2,
that the main contributor to low inflation recently has been the
large fall in housing costs which is largely, but not entirely, the
consequence of falling interest rates.

## The causes of inflation

Economic theory suggests that both supply and demand factors
should be evaluated in seeking explanations for inflationary processes. Identifying the source of inflationary pressure is important
in the formulation of appropriate anti-inflation policies. Inflation
generated by demand factors might be expected to respond to
policies designed to reduce aggregate demand. If, on the other hand,
supply factors are the source of the inflation, then policies which
moderate demand, although leading to reduced economic activity,
may not have any direct impact on inflation.

Two competing explanations of the inflationary process can be

identified. The first nominates *excess demand* as the cause of inflation; the second nominates disturbances on the supply side which
lead to *cost increases* as the cause of inflationary pressures. Before
undertaking an explanation of the causes of inflation in Australia,
a brief discussion of these competing explanations is necessary. The
common feature of the various theories of inflation which come
under the general heading of demand-pull inflation is that the
general level of prices is 'pulled-up' by excess demand for goods
and services. What distinguishes these theories from each other is
the *cause* of the excess demand.

The Keynesian demand-pull theory of inflation attributes inflationary pressures to the existence of excess demand for goods and
services. This excess demand may originate from domestic sources
(private or government demand) or from overseas (export demand).

What is meant by 'excess demand'? One approach is to define
it by reference to the deviation of the actual rate of unemployment
(taken to be a proxy for the state of aggregate demand) from the
Non-Accelerating Inflation Rate of Unemployment (NAIRU). The
NAIRU is the unemployment rate at which supply and demand
pressures in the labour market are balanced and where, therefore,
there is an absence of upward (and downward) pressure on money
wages and prices. If the actual rate of unemployment is less than
the NAIRU then money wage rates will begin to increase, and the
associated increase in unit costs will put upward pressure on the
general level of prices. The lower is the actual rate of unemployment
relative to NAIRU (that is, the greater the excess demand), the
higher will be the rate of inflation.

A variant of the Keynesian demand-pull theory of inflation
divides the labour market into sub-markets for specific types of
labour (carpenters, electricians, clerks, etc.). For such segmented
labour markets it is likely that if aggregate demand increases, full
employment will be reached in some sectors prior to others. These
full employment sectors are described as bottleneck sectors since,
given limited mobility between sectors, money wages in these sectors
and, therefore, production costs, will begin to increase. The bottleneck sectors, therefore, will cause the *general* level of prices to
increase. In this version of demand-pull inflation, it is excess demand
for labour in particular sectors that leads to inflationary pressure,
not a general excess demand for labour.

Although Keynesian theory identifies excess demand as the
source of inflationary pressure, its policy prescriptions for *disinflation* (that is, for reducing the rate of inflation) include both
restriction of aggregate demand and some form of incomes policy
to moderate money wage growth.

An alternative theory of demand-pull inflation is the monetarist version based on the Quantity Theory of Money. This version holds that inflation is the consequence of the money supply growing faster than real output ('too much money chasing too few goods') and the inflation rate is simply the difference between the rate of growth of money supply and the rate of growth of output. If, for example, the money supply is growing at 20 per cent per year and the level of output corresponding with NAIRU (monetarists use the term 'natural rate output') is growing at 3 per cent per year, then the equilibrium rate of inflation will be 17 per cent per year. The monetarist policy prescription emerges directly from this. If, for example, a zero rate of inflation is desired, then the Reserve Bank should ensure that the money supply grows at a rate equal to the expected rate of growth of natural rate output (adjusted, if necessary, for any trend changes in the velocity of circulation).

Both the Keynesian and Monetarist explanations of the inflationary process are examples of *pure* demand-pull inflation; that is, the inflationary pressure emanates only from the demand side. These theories of inflation, where prices are pulled up by excess demand, may be contrasted with those where prices are pushed up by higher unit costs of production.

The essential characteristic of a pure cost-push inflation is that the upward pressure on the general level of prices is caused by supply-side disturbances, and *occurs in the absence of any excess demand for goods and services*. One or more of the following supply-side disturbances may give rise to cost-push inflationary pressure:

- growth of the general level of money wages in excess of labour productivity growth ('wage-push' inflation);
- an increase in producers' mark-up over their costs of production ('profit-push' inflation);
- an increase in the domestic price of imported inputs; and,
- an increase in government charges and taxation.

If money wage growth exceeds the growth of average labour productivity, then the wages cost of a unit of output will increase. If, further, prices are set by producers as a percentage mark-up over unit wage costs and if producers seek to maintain their percentage mark-up, then wage-push inflationary pressure will be generated. Similarly, profit-push inflation will be generated if, given constant unit wage costs, producers increase their percentage mark-up and prices rise.

To the extent that domestic economy trades with the rest of the world, then changes in the price of imported goods and services will impact on the domestic price level. Import price increases can occur because of inflationary pressures in the exporting countries, or as a result of a depreciation (devaluation) of the domestic exchange rate. If the imported good or service satisfies a final demand, there will be a *direct* impact on the domestic inflation rate; if, on the other hand, the imported good or service is an intermediate good, there will be an *indirect* impact as unit production costs increase.

Governments impose indirect taxes (and pay subsidies) which drive a wedge between output valued at its cost of production (which is not affected by these taxes and subsidies) and output valued at market prices (which is affected). It follows, therefore, that if indirect taxes are increased (or subsidies reduced), the market price of goods will increase. A similar argument applies to government charges for goods and services supplied by the public sector.

The general level of prices can, therefore, be pushed up as a result of both overseas and government influences, without regard to the level of domestic demand. A process of sustained inflation will result as firms seek to preserve profit margins in the face of cost increases, and wage earners seek to preserve real incomes in the face of price increases.

Another form of pure cost-push inflation, which combines elements of both wage and profit-push inflation, is the 'conflict' theory of inflation. This theory regards inflation as the result of conflict over the distribution of national income, when the sum of the shares of total income (wages share, profits share) sought by the competing groups (workers, producers) exceeds unity. Inflationary pressures will persist while ever the desired shares are inconsistent. The condition for zero inflation in this theory is therefore that the sum of the desired shares be equal to unity.

A third variety of cost-push inflation is 'inertial' inflation. This arises in situations in which workers and producers expect inflation to continue in future income periods. Thus, even if income claims are consistent, inflationary pressures will be generated if the *expectation* of future inflation causes economic agents to attempt to adjust their money wages and prices in order to *maintain* their current relative position. Such an inflationary process is regarded as inertial because the inflation arises from an attempt to maintain, rather than increase, relative shares. If workers and producers expect an inflation of 10 per cent per year, then, if they do not attempt to increase their wages and profits by the same amount (assuming zero labour productivity growth), they are willingly accepting an expected reduction in their relative share.

The discussion above has been concerned with 'pure' varieties of demand-pull and cost-push inflation. A focus on pure types of inflation is justified by the need to establish their essential characteristics. Two points, however, need to be made about such an approach:

- it is not suggested that hybrid inflation (mixed demand-pull and cost-push) does not exist. To the contrary, such an inflation type is likely to be the norm; and
- in practice, it is difficult (if not impossible) to classify any real-world inflation as either demand-pull *or* cost-push. The inflationary process will be associated with both money wages and prices rising; it will be difficult therefore to establish a causal link from wages to prices or from prices to wages. What can be done is to point to the various influences on inflation, without attempting to apportion any particular rate of inflation between these influences.

## Causes of inflation in Australia since 1960

When the inflationary pressures at work in Australia over the period from 1960 are observed, both supply and demand influences may be detected, although, for the reasons given above, it is not generally possible to disentangle their separate effects. Before proceeding to a closer examination of Australia's inflation experience, one general point should be made. This relates to the importance of foreign influences on Australia's inflation rate. Stevens (1992, p.186) points to the close correlation between Australia's inflation rate and the average inflation rate for the G7 economies, particularly over the period prior to the floating of the $A in 1983. This is not to argue that domestic influences, whether policy-induced or otherwise, have not been important. The contention is rather that, given that Australia is a small open commodity-exporting economy, foreign shocks and in particular terms-of-trade shocks are likely to be endemic.

The various influences on Australia's inflation rate over the period from 1960 to the present may be considered for the three sub-periods identified on page 31.

### *1961–1972*

Inflation was low from 1960/61 to 1971/72, but increased in the last two years of this period. The annual average growth rate of the IDFDD was 2.7 per cent between 1960/61 and 1969/70, increasing to an annual rate of 6.5 per cent in 1970/71 and 7.3 per cent in 1971/72.

Demand-side factors, and particularly those emanating from domestic sources, were an important contributor to inflationary pressures during this period. The economy grew strongly in the 1960s with real GDP growing at an annual average rate of just under 5.3 per cent, and real Domestic Final Demand growing slightly faster at just over 5.3 per cent. The unemployment rate, which had increased in 1961 as a result of the tight monetary and fiscal policies implemented in 1960, fell from 1961 to 1965 and then remained relatively stable in the range 1.4 to 1.7 per cent until 1972, when it rose to 2.5 per cent. Reflecting the tightness in the labour market, average weekly earnings (AWE) increased at an annual average rate of 5.6 per cent between 1960/61 and 1969/70, as a result of both award wage growth and wages drift. There was little impetus to inflation from overseas demand in this period; export prices rose from 1960/61 to 1963/64 but remained relatively stable for the rest of the period.

The end of this period—the first two years of the 1970s—present a slightly different picture. Domestic Final Demand grew more slowly than GDP in both years, the unemployment rate increased to 2.5 per cent in 1972, and growth of AWE increased to over 10 per cent per year. These data suggest that domestic cost pressures began to exert a greater influence on the inflation rate at this time. At the same time, import prices began to increase after being relatively stable for much of the 1960s. The import price deflator increased by 8.3 per cent in 1970/71 and by 6.4 per cent in 1971/72. Given the fixed exchange rate regime in place at the time, these import price increases fed directly into domestic inflation.

On balance, it seems that this period was one in which the predominant influence on inflation was domestic demand, with some domestic and foreign cost influences apparent in the last two years.

## 1972–1986

The period from 1972 to 1986 exhibited considerable volatility in inflation rates. Nevile (1979) observes that in each episode of increasing inflation during this period macroeconomic policy mistakes were, in part, responsible for these increases. In particular, Nevile notes (p.122) that the failure of the government to revalue the $A in 1971/72 'can be regarded as the start of Australia's inflationary problems in the nineteen-seventies'. An undervalued $A in the early 1970s induced significant capital inflow and coexisted with a boom in commodity prices. The export price index increased by 20.9 per cent in 1972/73 and by a further 19.8 per cent in 1973/74. Even an increase of 11.5 per cent in the import price index in 1973/74 could not prevent the terms of trade turning sharply in Australia's favour at this time, and in 1972/73 there was a surplus on the current account of the balance of payments.

An improving current account and large surpluses on the capital account in these two years, combined with increasing growth rates of Domestic Final Demand resulting largely from strong expansion of both private and public current expenditure and a fall in the unemployment rate to 1.8 per cent in 1973, increased demand pressures on the inflation rate. This was reflected in AWE which grew by 9 per cent in 1972/73 and 16.2 per cent in 1973/74. Notwithstanding these pressures the rate of inflation fell slightly in 1972/73, largely as a consequence of the revaluation of the $A in December 1972. A further revaluation in September 1973 also assisted in moderating the inflationary pressure, albeit in the face of external and domestic supply shocks which, overall, led to a marked increase in the inflation rate.

The external shocks were in large part the direct and indirect effects of OPEC oil price increase in late 1973. Import prices rose by 11.5 per cent in 1973/74 and 27.7 per cent in 1974/75, and not until 1978/79 did their annual rate of increase drop below 10 per cent. At about the same time, domestic supply shocks impacted on inflation. Money wage growth accelerated to 25.4 per cent in 1974/75, encouraged in part by the use of public sector wages as pacesetters and government endorsement of private sector wage demands. Money wage growth was reduced to 14.4 per cent in 1975/76 and 12.4 per cent in 1976/77. Although there was also an acceleration in inflation at this time, money wage growth in the mid-1970s exceeded the rate of inflation, and real wages and real unit labour costs both increased. Real demand growth fell away in the second half of the 1970s, averaging only 2.9 per cent per year over this period. Reflecting this fall in demand and the increase in real wages, the unemployment rate nearly doubled to 4.6 per cent in 1975, increased to a peak of 6.2 per cent in 1978, then settled in a 5 to 6 per cent range until it increased to 6.7 per cent in 1982 and to 9.9 per cent in 1983. In the light of this moderation in demand pressures and the importance of the supply shocks, it is reasonable to characterise this inflationary episode as predominantly cost-push in nature, though with strong demand elements in the period to 1975/76.

The acceleration in inflation to a peak, in 1974/75, of 20.8 per cent as measured by the IDFDD (and 16.7 per cent as measured by the CPI) was associated with a number of policy changes. The $A was devalued in September 1974 and again in November 1976; the motivation for these devaluations was the worsening current account position, but they also had the unwanted effect of increasing the inflation rate. The introduction of the Prices Justification Tribunal in August 1973 was an attempt to reduce inflation directly. Chapman and Junor (1981) offer indirect evidence of an average reduction in the inflation rate of about 0.5 per cent per year over the PJT's period of operation. Both fiscal and monetary policy settings were tightened in the second half of the 1970s and into the 1980s, although the experience of monetary targeting was somewhat mixed, with the targets being met in only one year.

Money wage growth, which had slowed to single digit figures in the latter part of the 1970s, increased to 13.4 per cent in 1980/81 and to 15.8 per cent in 1981/82 under the impetus of the resources boom. Domestic Final Demand grew strongly in these years—and somewhat faster than real GDP, particularly in 1981/82. At about this time, however, the world economy slipped into a policy-induced recession which was associated with falls in export prices and a modest deterioration in the terms of trade. Although inflationary pressures from the demand side were abating, the rate of inflation remained stuck at slightly more than 10 per cent per year, not falling until 1983/84 and 1984/85. In this latter year, with inflation at 5.9 per cent, it reached its lowest level since 1969/70.

The years 1983/84 and 1984/85 offer some interesting insights into the inflationary process. The Hawke government, elected in March 1983, embarked on a policy of fiscal expansion with the stated aim of reducing unemployment; the world economy was coming out of recession, although the terms of trade continued to deteriorate; and the domestic economy was growing strongly with real GDP increasing at 5.6 per cent in 1983/84 and 5.4 per cent in 1984/85. With the unemployment rate falling, these might be regarded as years in which demand factors would generate upward pressure on the rate of inflation. However, as noted above, the rate of inflation fell sharply. A number of economists have pointed to the wages policy introduced by the new government—the Prices and Incomes Accord—as playing an important role in this outcome. Chapman (1990) argues that a conservative estimate of the impact of the Accord is that it reduced the rate of money wage inflation by three percentage points per year below the rate that would otherwise have resulted, and reduced real wages by 10 per cent between 1983 and 1989. Similarly, the OECD (1990, p.21) noted in its 1989/90 economic survey of Australia, that the evidence is 'that the Accord, up to the present, has produced lower real wage outcomes as well as helping to lower strike activity'. This conclusion is supported by Table 3.3, extracted from Table 3.4 in OECD (1990, p.22), which shows annual average rates growth of money wages and several other relevant variables before and after the introduction of the Accord.

The impact of the Accord on real unit labour cost seems to be somewhat understated in this table, which reports only annual average changes. Large falls in real unit labour cost occurred in 1983/84 when the index fell by 4.6 per cent and in 1984/85 when a fall of 1.9 per cent was recorded. It is difficult to avoid the

**Table 3.3**   **Indicators of labour market performance before and after the Accord (% p.a. growth rates)**

|  | Pre-Accord 1978–83 | Accord 1984–88 |
|---|---|---|
| Wage rate | 9.5 | 6.3 |
| Real wage rate | –0.1 | –1.1 |
| Real unit labour cost | 0.5 | –0.5 |
| Employment | 0.7 | 3.2 |
| Unemployment rate (%) | 6.9 | 8.1 |

*Source:* Extracted from OECD (1990) Table 3.4

conclusion that the Accord was the key institutional change that permitted an expansion in demand and the associated reduction in the unemployment rate, while moderating money wage growth and inflation, and reducing real unit labour cost.

The Accord was introduced in the last three years of the second inflation period delineated above and arguably, by moderating money wage growth, set the scene for the reduction in inflation rates that marked the final period from 1986 to the present. Before considering the demand- and supply-side factors at work in this last period, one further institutional change requires consideration. The decision to float the $A in December 1983 had important implications for the conduct of macroeconomic policy in Australia, and also as an independent source of inflationary (and deflationary) pressures. Menon (1993) distinguishes three conduits by which exchange rate changes can feed through into domestic inflation—the direct and indirect effects discussed above, and an effect on the price of domestically produced goods that are close substitutes for imports. In his study of Australian imports of manufactured goods from 1981 to 1991, Menon finds that the 'pass-through' of exchange rate changes to the $A price of imported manufactures averaged about 70 per cent for final goods and a higher rate for intermediate goods. Further, he suggests that where domestically produced manufactures and imports are close substitutes, the price of the domestic good will track closely the $A price of the imported good. It would appear, therefore, that incomplete pass-through of exchange rate changes to the $A price of imports contributed to a moderation of inflationary pressures in Australia, although, to the extent that the third effect was important, even incomplete exchange rate pass-through would have had inflationary consequences. The modification of inflationary pressure was observable particularly during the period from 1984/85 to 1986/87 when the $A sharply depreciated and the average $A price of imported manufactures appears to have been smoothed relative to their full pass-through price (Menon 1993, p.42).

No simple characterisation of inflation in this period, or sub-periods, as demand-pull or cost-push, is possible. Demand elements were present at different times, emanating from external and policy-induced sources. The predominant influences on the rate of inflation during this period were from the supply side, although, as was noted, there were marked inter-temporal changes in the relative importance of the various supply-side shocks.

*1986–present*

Attention may now be directed to the final period from 1986 to the present, when the inflation rate, as measured by the IDFDD, fell from 8.5 per cent in 1985/86, levelled off at 6.6 per cent from 1987/88 to 1988/89, and then fell sharply to stabilise at around 2 per cent since 1991/92.

With the exception of 1986/87 when a growth rate of 0.8 per cent was recorded, real Domestic Final Demand grew by more than 4 per cent per year from 1985/86 to 1988/89. An improvement in the terms of trade in both 1987/88 and 1988/89 added external support to the overall growth, in demand. Although fiscal policy was tight, monetary policy was eased in the first half of 1987 and further eased after the stock market crash in October 1987. This was associated with a steady fall in the unemployment rate from 7.8 per cent in 1985/86 to 5.7 per cent in 1988/89. Despite the tightening labour market, money wage growth was relatively stable in a range between 5.9 and 7.4 per cent per year from the opening of this period until 1990/91. As in the previous period, this atypical behaviour of money wage growth, in the presence of an improving labour market, can be attributed to the operation of the Accord.

During 1988, in response to the rising current account deficit, monetary policy was progressively tightened and interest rates rose sharply. Real demand growth slowed in 1989/90 and became negative in 1990/91. The unemployment rate increased to 8.4 per cent in 1990/91 and continued to increase to 11 per cent in 1992/93; the modest growth of real domestic demand in 1990/91 and 1991/92 was insufficient to prevent the unemployment rate from rising. Money wage growth fell to 2.9 per cent in 1991/92 and to 0.7 per cent in 1992/93. Since this fall in money wage growth over 1991/92 and 1992/93 coincided with an increase in the unemployment rate, the disinflation can be attributed in part to the policy-induced reduction in demand. Since 1992/93, the rate of growth of real domestic demand has increased. This was associated with a fall in the unemployment rate to 8.2 per cent in July 1995; a tightening of monetary policy in 1994/95 has since caused a small increase in the unemployment rate. Money wage growth since 1992/93 has been less than 2 per cent per year, unit labour costs over this period have been relatively steady, and the IDFDD increased by 0.7 per cent in 1993/94 and 1.8 per cent in 1994/95.

Although demand pressures were present for the first half of this period, as well as towards the end of the period, they were not translated into increases in the inflation rate. Stevens (1992) suggests that flexible exchange rates, which led to falling $A import prices when a monetary policy-induced appreciation of the $A occurred in the late 1980s, and the Accord, which restrained money wage growth when the unemployment rate fell, are jointly responsible for this atypical outcome. The sharp fall in inflation in the 1990s is attributable to the policy-induced contraction in demand initiated in the late 1980s.

This discussion of the causes of inflation in Australia since 1960 has identified the presence of both supply and demand influences and has highlighted the vulnerability of the economy to overseas inflationary shocks, whether deriving from the supply-side or the demand-side. The depreciation of the Australian dollar as a consequence of the current crisis in the Asian economies is expected to lead to upward pressure on inflation via higher import prices; as noted previously the Reserve Bank expects that this supply-side shock will push the inflation rate to about 2.5 per cent per year by the middle of 1999.

### The costs of inflation and the costs and benefits of anti-inflation policies

The approach adopted by McTaggart (1992) to estimate the costs of inflation in Australia over the period 1970 to 1991 focuses on the impact of both the level and the variability of inflation on the level of output. McTaggart undertakes several 'back-of-the-envelope' type calculations based on empirical estimates of the effects of the level and variability of inflation on investment and output over the period 1962/63 to 1990/91 in Australia. His calculations suggest that a one percentage point increase in the inflation rate causes a reduction of approximately one-quarter of a percentage point in real GDP in the long run. Thus, if inflation were to be reduced to zero from its current annual rate of around 2 per cent (in underlying terms), then a permanent increase in GDP of one-half of one percentage point (equal, in 1997/98, to $2.82 billion) would result. Overseas studies advocating zero-inflation policies have suggested rather larger gains from disinflation than does McTaggart. For the USA, for example, Feldstein (1997) estimates that reducing inflation from 2 per cent per year to zero would produce an annual gain of between 0.76 per cent and 1.04 per cent of GDP, while at the same time noting that these estimates are subject to considerable uncertainty. Feldstein employs a different approach from McTaggart by attempting to estimate the welfare gains generated by the changes in household behaviour and tax revenue induced by the reduction in inflation.

Before concluding that, simply because inflation imposes costs, an anti-inflation strategy is justified, it is necessary to consider the costs of disinflation as measured by foregone output and unemployment.

The Natural Rate Hypothesis (NRH), formulated in the late 1960s by Milton Friedman and Edmund Phelps, has dominated thinking about anti-inflation policies for much of the subsequent period. In essence, the NRH states that there is a unique and stable rate of unemployment, the natural rate, at which the rate of inflation is also stable. If, therefore, the actual rate of unemployment coincides with the natural rate, then there are no forces acting to change the ruling rate of inflation, *whatever it happens to be*. Conversely, if the actual rate of unemployment is greater (less) than the natural rate, then the inflation rate will be falling (rising).

Reducing inflation in this framework requires that the policy authorities implement contractionary policies. In the New Classical version of the NRH, announcement of a credible policy (that is, a policy which economic agents believe will reduce inflation and expect the policy authorities to maintain) will reduce inflation without increasing unemployment above the natural rate. By contrast, in the Keynesian and monetarist versions, the actual rate of unemployment must exceed the natural rate for a period of time (though the precise length of this period is a matter of dispute between the two versions) in order to reduce the inflation rate. The common feature of all these versions of the NRH is that, when equilibrium is restored, the actual rate of unemployment will again be equal to the natural rate and inflation will be stable at a lower, though not necessarily zero, rate.

In the context of the NRH model, the costs of anti-inflation policies can therefore be evaluated in terms of the increase in unemployment caused by these policies; similarly, the benefits of such policies can be evaluated in terms of the induced decrease in the inflation rate. To compare the costs and benefits of anti-inflation policies, however, the outcomes of such policies must be expressed, not in terms of unemployment and inflation, but in terms of a single measure. Real output, as measured by GDP, can serve as this measure.

The argument that reducing inflation would increase real output has already been noted. McTaggart (1992) estimated that, for Australia, a one percentage point decrease in the inflation rate would cause real output to increase by one-quarter of a percentage point. But it is also the case that higher unemployment will be associated with a policy-induced reduction in real output. Junankar and Kapuscinski (1992) have attempted to estimate the output costs of unemployment in Australia from 1981/82 to 1991/92. They employ three different methods to estimate such output losses and conclude that, based on the mean values generated by the three methods, a one percentage point increase in the unemployment rate will be associated with a decrease of 1 to 1.2 per cent in the level of real output (equal, in 1997/98, to between $5.64 billion and $6.76 billion).

To form a judgment regarding the *net* benefit (or cost) of anti-inflation policies, in terms of real output, requires that we have evidence on (a) the percentage increase in unemployment required to generate a one percentage point fall in the inflation rate, and (b) the time period relevant to the reduction in inflation and to the unemployment increase. In this regard, Schelde-Andersen (1992, p.109) notes the existence of 'a general consensus that, while the benefits of lower inflation are permanent, the costs associated with reducing inflation are only transitory, so that a cost-benefit analysis would always come down in favour of adopting a policy of price stability'. Clearly this consensus is based on the NRH; contrary to his assertion, however, it is *not* the case that a cost-benefit analysis will *always* favour disinflation. If, for example, the output gains from lower inflation are small relative to the output losses from the temporarily higher unemployment and if equilibrium is restored only slowly, then it is quite possible for the discounted present value of the output gains to be less than the discounted value of the output losses. Further, even though the output gains from lower inflation are permanent, if the discount rate applied to these gains is high, their present value will be small.

Empirical estimates of the relationship between the increase in unemployment (output loss) and the decrease in the inflation rate are presented as 'sacrifice ratios'. The sacrifice ratio is defined as the ratio of the cumulative rise in the unemployment rate (or the cumulative output loss) to the decline in the inflation rate over the same period. Three recent studies by Ball (1993), Schelde-Andersen (1992), and Stevens (1992) have estimated sacrifice ratios for Australia in terms of both cumulative output loss and cumulative unemployment increase. The results of these studies are summarised in Table 3.4.

The three sets of results are not strictly comparable because (a) Stevens and Ball examine particular episodes of disinflation, whereas Schelde-Andersen uses the same time period for all the OECD economies, and in the case of Australia this period embraces *two*

**Table 3.4 Sacrifice ratios for Australia**

|  | GDP | Unemployment |
|---|---|---|
| Ball | 1.00 | — |
| Schelde-Andersen | –0.15 | 6.00 |
| Stevens | 1.30–2.70 | 1.10–6.40 |

*Sources:* Ball (1993), Schelde-Andersen (1992), Stevens (1992)

disinflation episodes; (b) the numerator in the sacrifice ratios of Stevens and Ball is the deviation of output (or unemployment) from trend, while Schelde-Andersen uses the deviations from the initial actual values; and (c) Ball truncates the output losses by assuming that output returns to its normal growth path one year after the end of the disinflation, and this may have the effect of understating the sacrifice ratio.

Notwithstanding these differences, one clear conclusion does emerge from consideration of these sacrifice ratios—the New Classical view that anti-inflation policy generates costless gains is not supported by Australian experience. Past episodes of disinflation *have* imposed output and employment losses.

The results of Ball and Stevens, based on a similar analytical approach, suggest that a reduction of one percentage point in the rate of inflation leads to a cumulative loss of real output of between 1 and 2.7 per cent. Stevens (1992, p.234) sets the output loss slightly higher at between 1.5 and 3 per cent. If these results are combined with those of McTaggart (1992), then a permanent real output gain of 0.25 per cent per year (as a result of a one percentage point reduction in the inflation rate) must be set against cumulative transitory real output losses of between 1 and 3 per cent of GDP. Without details of the size of the annual output losses in particular disinflation episodes and of the appropriate discount rate, it is not possible to estimate the net present value of these output gains and losses. However, it is likely that for output losses at the upper end of the range, the present value of these transitory losses would exceed that of the permanent output gains. This suggests that anti-inflation policy may impose net output losses—this is not consistent with the consensus view that a cost-benefit analysis would always favour lower inflation.

This conclusion is given further support when Stevens' estimates of the unemployment sacrifice ratio are combined with the findings of Junankar and Kapuscinski (1992) noted previously. Together these suggest that a permanent real output gain of 0.25 per cent per year should be set against cumulative transitory output losses of between 1.1 and 7.7 per cent of GDP.

Numerators in sacrifice ratios are usually calculated as deviations

of actual output (or unemployment) from their potential or equilibrium level (or rate). If these equilibrium levels and rates are
*themselves* affected by the anti-inflation policies, along with the
actual levels and rates, then this should be taken into account in
estimating the output costs of such policies. Consider an anti-inflation policy which causes the actual unemployment rate to rise; if
the natural rate of unemployment is influenced by the actual unemployment rate, then the natural rate will also increase. This
phenomenon, where the natural rate tracks the actual rate, is known
as hysteresis. To the extent that hysteresis is present, then anti-inflation policies will result in a *permanent* increase in unemployment
and therefore permanent, rather than transitory, output losses. Thus,
to the extent that there is hysteresis in the natural rate, this will
render the results of a cost-benefit analysis *less* favourable for any
given disinflation policy.

On balance, the evidence, for Australia at least, is inconclusive
on the relative output costs of inflation and unemployment, and
therefore on the desirability of anti-inflation policy, at least for low
to moderate rates of inflation. Interestingly, the advent of low and
relatively stable inflation rates in the world economy has been
associated with calls from both central bankers (for example, Melzer
1997) and academic economists (for example, Feldstein 1997) for
policy to pursue a zero inflation objective. This objective raises a
number of issues.

First, what is the appropriate measure of inflation? When the
policy objective is simply to lower the inflation rate, the measure
of inflation used is not important because, as was noted earlier, in
the medium term all of the measures tend to move in the same
direction. If *zero* inflation is the objective, then the precise measure
of inflation used becomes important. The deficiencies of the CPI,
and of the various measures of the underlying inflation rate derived
from the CPI, have previously been noted. The several implicit price
deflators derived from the quarterly National Accounts often
undergo significant revision and are, therefore, from a zero inflation
policy point of view, of limited use.

Second, what exactly is meant by *zero* inflation? Clark (1998,
p.5) suggests that zero inflation has been achieved 'when inflation
ceases to be a factor in the decision-making processes of businesses
and individuals'. The problem with this definition of zero inflation
is that it is the *actual* inflation rate that policy makers seek to
influence, while it is the *expected* inflation rate that impinges on
some decisions by businesses and individuals. Figure 3.3 shows the
CPI-based inflation rate and the Institute of Applied Economic and
Social Research measure of consumers' expected inflation rate one
year ahead.

**Figure 3.3  Actual and expected inflation in Australia**

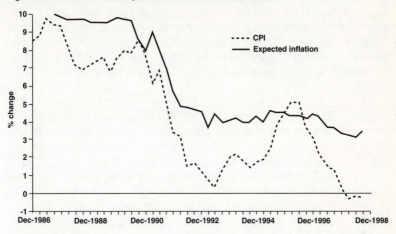

Source:  ECONDATA

What is notable about this graph is how resistant expected inflation has been to falls in the actual inflation rate. Thus while expected inflation initially tracked actual inflation when the latter began falling in early 1990, it settled at about 4 per cent per year in mid-1992 and it is only since mid-1996 that it has begun to trend downwards again. During this same period, inflation remained at least two percentage points below expected inflation, except for the spike in 1995/96. It is true that over this period the various under-lying inflation rates and the implicit deflators-based rates were both higher and exhibited greater stability than the CPI-based rate; it remains the case, nevertheless, that expected inflation has remained persistently above the actual rate, whatever measure of the latter is employed. Given such inertia in expected inflation, it is unlikely that the successful pursuit of zero inflation would give rise to zero expected inflation. In such circumstances, business and household decisions will continue to be influenced by inflation, contrary to Clark's definition.

Other advocates of zero inflation have adopted rather more pragmatic definitions. Feldstein (1997, p.2, n4) simply assumes that the official measure of the inflation rate overstates the true rate by two percentage points and then defines zero inflation as 2 per cent per year.

Third, what exactly is the case for zero inflation? Essentially, the case for zero inflation is a variant of the case for lower inflation. The argument runs as follows: inflation imposes costs, therefore any inflation rate above zero is sub-optimal because reducing inflation to zero will maximise the permanent gains from lower inflation, and these gains will swamp the temporary costs of disinflation.

As noted previously, the argument that the gains from lower inflation outweigh the costs of disinflation is still controversial and certainly it has *not* been decided generally in favour of disinflation; ultimately it is an empirical question which requires much more research.

Critics of the zero inflation proposal have also countered by arguing that low, positive rates of inflation may have beneficial effects. One such effect is that inflation can generate downward real wage adjustments where, for whatever reason, money wages are not cut, and that this will in turn produce lower unemployment rates (Akerlof et al. 1996). On this argument, if real wage reductions are necessary, zero inflation will require money wages to fall; given money wage rigidity, this will lead to higher unemployment. Another argument is that positive inflation allows real interest rates to become negative and that this improves the efficacy of expansionary monetary policy. Since the money rate of interest cannot be lower than zero, a zero inflation rate means that the real rate of interest also cannot be lower than zero, and this will limit the effectiveness of expansionary monetary policy.

For these reasons, the conclusion of Akerlof, Dickens and Perry (1996, p.17), 'We cannot say precisely what inflation rate best serves the people of the United States, but we are confident it is not zero' is likely to be, suitably amended, applicable to other economies including Australia.

## Current Australian anti-inflation policy

In order to maintain inflation at its current low level, the Reserve Bank of Australia introduced a target rate of inflation several years ago. The aim of this, according to Macfarlane (1995, p.11), is 'to achieve an average underlying inflation rate of somewhere between 2 and 3 per cent over the medium term'. The various pronouncements of the Reserve Bank and the tightening of monetary policy in 1994/95 were motivated in large part by a desire on the part of the bank to establish this inflation rate of 2 to 3 per cent as a credible target. To the extent that the bank is successful in establishing its credibility (that is, that economic agents *believe* that the bank will implement and maintain appropriately tight monetary policies if the inflation rate seems likely to exceed 3 per cent in the medium term), this should have a desirable impact on inflationary expectations and therefore on, *inter alia*, money wage outcomes. In the case of the Reserve Bank of Australia, the inflation target is an informal one and the bank faces no explicit sanctions if it fails to meet the target.

This raises the question of whether the Reserve Bank of Australia should be required to meet a formal inflation target of the New Zealand variant, with explicit sanctions for failure to achieve the target set by the government. The case for a formal target is that the credibility of policy makers is enhanced by an explicit, legislatively established target accompanied by sanctions against the policy makers that are triggered by failure to achieve the target. The case against such targets is that, by requiring the achievement of the target in the short run they are unnecessarily rigid, especially in small open economies subject to external shocks. By contrast, the informal target inflation rate for Australia is described by Debelle and Stevens (1995, p.3) as a 'thick point' and not a narrow 'target band' in the sense that 'it is not a range within which the Bank feels inflation must, or necessarily can, be maintained at all times and under any circumstances'.

At present, the underlying inflation rate in Australia is slightly above the corresponding rate in New Zealand. This suggests that the Australian informal inflation target approach has achieved inflation outcomes that are not notably inferior to the New Zealand formal inflation target approach—the real test for both approaches will come when the world economy moves away from its current low inflation norm.

# 4 The Australian unemployment experience
## T. Stegman

The ABS estimate of the seasonally adjusted unemployment rate for April 1998 of 7.9 per cent, represented the first time since 1992 that this rate had fallen below the 8 per cent barrier despite a six-year period of sustained economic growth and low inflation. Ominously, neither official, academic nor business commentators saw this as a harbinger of continuing falls in the unemployment rate and a return to sustainable lower rates. With the continuous economic growth of the past six years unlikely to continue in the face of the effects of the Asian financial crisis on Australia's balance of payments, the April 1998 result was viewed as just a favourable blip in the numbers—a freak patch of false light in a gloomy outlook for unemployment. A variety of estimates (based on analysis of time series statistics and a variety of assumptions about what constitutes 'steady state equilibrium' in the labour market) yield figures of between 7 and 8 per cent as the long-term or sustainable unemployment rate (see Borland 1997, p.393).

Neither did the Commonwealth Government Budget, brought down in May 1998, provide any reason for doubting that Australia was going to have to get used to an unemployment rate of around 7–8 per cent at best for the foreseeable future. The Budget, triumphantly brought into surplus, provided no general fiscal stimulus, nor any increased expenditures on targeted labour market programs.

Buttressed by the notion that 7–8 per cent was some sort of 'natural' rate of unemployment given structural factors in the economy, Government rhetoric has emphasised its programs of deregulation and microeconomic reform, as the route to future sustainable reductions in the unemployment rate. It does seem however that there is a lack of urgency and a lowering of the aims in unemployment policy—particularly with respect to macroeconomic policy. This might be seen as surprising given the enormous efficiency costs associated with a 7–8 per cent unemployment rate, in foregone national production alone, which dwarf the estimates for efficiency gains associated with successful microeconomic reform. (See the discussion of costs from unemployment below and Mitchell and Watts (1997) for some comparative estimates.)

It is useful to see macroeconomic policy as a juggling act of goals related to the three major national economic problems of unemployment, inflation and the balance of payments position. While this chapter addresses the problem of unemployment, it is important to appreciate that, from a macroeconomic perspective, the three problems are interdependent. The three problems are interdependent because (as is explained below) they are all related to the fundamental issue of macroeconomics: the level and rate of growth of the nation's aggregate production of goods and services (Gross Domestic Product, GDP). The nature of the interrelationships between the three problems, the causes and the appropriate policy responses, and the extent to which their interdependence requires policy trade-offs, are matters which provide the basis for much economic and political debate.

The aim of this chapter is to provide some analysis of the problem of unemployment in Australia—the economic costs and the measurement of unemployment; the nature and dimensions of the problem in Australia; and the relationship between economic growth and changes in the unemployment rate. This chapter also provides a brief summary of the theoretical and policy debate about causes and cures; and a consideration of recent unemployment policy.

## The costs and measurement of unemployment

Since the level of unemployment is a reflection of the extent to which we are failing to fully utilise the nation's labour resources, there is an obvious general cost from unemployment in terms of forgone output, lower per capita income and lower national living standards. The existence of unemployment means that aggregate production of goods and services is less than the potential output of the nation: aggregate economic activity, and hence aggregate output and national income, are less than the economy is capable of producing. (See Martin and Watts 1997 for estimates of these costs.)

In addition to this opportunity cost to the nation, there are well-known individual costs from unemployment borne by those who cannot find the paid employment necessary to provide for themselves and their families. Australian research points to unemployment being the major cause of poverty in this country (see, for example, Saunders 1992). Broader social costs linked to high levels of unemployment include rising crime rates, lower community health standards and social alienation.[1]

Transfers from those employed to those unemployed, through the taxation and social welfare systems, attempt to spread the costs of unemployment more evenly across society. However, rather than attempts to share out a reduced national economic 'cake' more fairly, the desirable solution is to raise the level of employment, increase the level of productive activity of the nation up closer to its full-employment potential, and have a bigger national economic cake.

The level of unemployment is usually measured as a rate: the unemployment rate is the percentage of the labour force unemployed—that is, not in employment for pay or profit. The labour force is defined as those of working age (15 years and older) willing and able to work.

While this definition of the unemployment rate seems clear, its measurement in practice provides many difficulties.

The official unemployment figures come from a monthly survey of around 30 000 households by the Australian Bureau of Statistics (ABS).

According to the ABS definitions, a person is counted as employed if either they did at least one hour of work for pay or profit ('employed' includes 'self-employed') or they worked at least one hour unpaid in a family business or farm in the survey week. Those not counted as employed are classified as 'unemployed' only if they actively sought, and were willing and able to start, employment in the survey week. The remainder are classified as 'not in the labour force'.

Thus the ABS definition of unemployment is very strict, and may significantly understate the 'true' level of unemployment for two main reasons:

• **Underemployment**

The measured unemployment rate makes no allowance for workers who worked part-time in the survey week but would prefer more hours, or who would prefer full-time employment and were unable to find it. Neither can the official measure make any allowances for employed workers whose skills are currently under-utilised because they are unable to find employment in jobs where their skills would be more productively used.

• **Discouraged workers**

Since those out of work are not officially counted as unemployed if they have not actively sought work in the survey week, the ABS unemployment figures may omit many people who should be considered as genuinely unemployed. These are people who, although they want employment and are willing and able to start, have not actively sought work in the current week because they perceive that their chances of finding a job are currently poor. Because actively seeking work incurs costs in terms of time, effort and money, some genuinely unemployed may become discouraged from job-seeking until they perceive that the probability of being successful has improved. In the ABS figures these 'discouraged workers' will be counted as 'not in the labour force' rather than as unemployed.

When there is a downturn in the labour market and demand for labour falls, the 'discouraged worker effect' will mean that the official unemployment figures understate the extent of the deterioration, since those who give up actively looking for work, even temporarily, will be considered as having dropped out of the labour force.

On the other hand, when the labour market recovers and demand for labour picks up, increased job opportunities will draw many people who were not actively seeking employment back into the labour force. This will weaken the impact of the recovery in demand for labour on reducing the official unemployment figures.

The extent to which the official figures underestimate 'true' unemployment (the degree to which the nation's labour resources are under-utilised) is difficult to measure. Labour market research suggests that not only is hidden unemployment a significant problem, but that it increases substantially when there is a recession in the labour market and demand for labour is depressed.[2]

The official figures for employment and unemployment are released on a monthly basis, but it is unwise to place too much emphasis on month-to-month variations, for two reasons: seasonality and sampling error.

The factors that determine changes in the unemployment rate (the size of the labour force and the number of people in employment) are subject to strong seasonal influences. For example, there is a surge of school leavers into the labour force in the period from December to February, and there is an increase in temporary and part-time employment opportunities in the retail industry in December. To take account of seasonal factors the ABS publishes estimates of 'seasonally adjusted' figures, but like all estimates these have a degree of imprecision. Alternatively, we may simply compare the figure for a particular month in successive years, in trying to measure the trend movement in the unemployment rate.

The second reason we should not read too much into month-

**Table 4.1  The Australian unemployment record**

| At August | % of LF | persons ('000) | Average duration (weeks) |
|---|---|---|---|
| 1973 | 1.8 | 106 | 9 |
| 1974 | 2.4 | 141 | |
| 1975 | 4.6 | 278 | 13 |
| 1976 | 4.7 | 293 | |
| 1977 | 5.7 | 359 | |
| 1978 | 6.2 | 396 | 26 |
| 1979 | 5.9 | 374 | |
| 1980 | 5.9 | 392 | |
| 1981 | 5.6 | 377 | 35 |
| 1982 | 6.7 | 459 | |
| 1983 | 9.9 | 684 | 42 |
| 1984 | 8.5 | 605 | |
| 1985 | 7.9 | 571 | |
| 1986 | 8.0 | 597 | 49 |
| 1987 | 7.8 | 602 | |
| 1988 | 6.8 | 539 | |
| 1989 | 5.7 | 469 | 44 |
| 1990 | 7.0 | 587 | |
| 1991 | 9.5 | 806 | |
| 1992 | 10.6 | 906 | 51 |
| 1993 | 10.7 | 924 | |
| 1994 | 9.2 | 798 | |
| 1995 | 8.1 | 722 | |
| 1996 | 8.5 | 771 | 50 |
| 1997 | 8.4 | 765 | 55 |
| 1998 | 7.9 | 728 | 60 |

(Average unemployment rate for 1962–1972 = 1.6%).
*Source:*  ABS Cat. Nos 6202.0, 6203.0

to-month variations in the unemployment rate is that the figures are population estimates based on a sample. The sample is chosen to be representative and is relatively large. However, in assuming that the labour market experience of the people in the sample gives unemployment rates that can be applied to the population as a whole, we can only be reasonably confident that the resulting estimates are 'about right'. Small variations in the official monthly unemployment rate may well be due to experiences peculiar to the people in the sample rather than indicative of some general trend in the labour market.

## Australia's unemployment experience

Table 4.1 presents the ABS figures for the unemployment rate for the last 25 years (measured at August in each year).

Australia's unemployment experience can be summarised as follows:

**Figure 4.1 Unemployment: % of labour force**

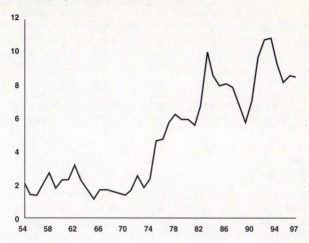

- From a fairly stable rate averaging around 1.6 per cent for the decade 1962–1972, the unemployment rate rose significantly in the mid-1970s.
- The unemployment rate appeared to stabilise at the higher level from 1979 to 1982, but rose sharply again in 1982 and 1983.
- The unemployment rate fell slowly but steadily from 1984 to 1989 before climbing sharply again from 1989 to 1993, to peak at just under 11 per cent.
- 1994 and 1995 evidenced a recovery in the labour market with the unemployment rate falling to just over 8 per cent by the middle of 1995 but the rate rose again in 1996 to 8.5 per cent, appearing to be stuck around this level over 1997.

This pattern is depicted in Figure 4.1.

Table 4.1 also provides the average duration in weeks of unemployment for selected years. It is significant that with the increase in the unemployment rate, the average duration of unemployment has also increased substantially. This is a reflection of the unequal incidence of unemployment, as can be explained by the following example:

Suppose the unemployment rate is constant over a year at 1/12th of the labour force (8.33 per cent—the Australian unemployment rate was around this level in 1986). If everyone in the labour force had an equal share of unemployment over the year then we would expect the average duration to be about 1 month. (Since 1/12th of the labour force is unemployed over the year, equal incidence would

Table 4.2  Unemployment rates by age and sex (August)

|      | 15–19 years | | | 20 + years | | |
|------|------|------|------|------|------|------|
|      | M | F | P | M | F | P |
| 1973 | 4.6 | 4.9 | 4.7 | 1.0 | 2.3 | 1.4 |
| 1983 | 23.0 | 22.2 | 22.6 | 8.7 | 7.9 | 8.4 |
| 1985 | 19.3 | 17.1 | 18.2 | 6.8 | 6.7 | 6.7 |
| 1990 | 16.6 | 16.5 | 16.5 | 6.0 | 6.0 | 6.0 |
| 1992 | 25.1 | 24.8 | 25.0 | 10.2 | 7.9 | 9.3 |
| 1995 | 19.7 | 20.2 | 20.0 | 7.7 | 6.2 | 7.0 |
| 1996 | 20.3 | 18.6 | 19.5 | 8.0 | 6.9 | 7.5 |
| 1997 | 20.2 | 18.4 | 19.3 | 7.8 | 7.1 | 7.5 |
| 1998 | 20.6 | 16.9 | 18.8 | 7.4 | 6.3 | 7.0 |

Source:  ABS

mean everyone would get a spell of 1/12th of the year in unemployment.) The fact that the average duration in 1986 was much higher, at 49 weeks, means that the burden of unemployment has fallen on only a minority of the labour force—the majority of workers have been sheltered from experiencing unemployment.

The substantial increase in the average duration of unemployment, and the unequal incidence on particular social groups, also points to an increasing problem of long-term or 'hard-core' unemployment.

In August 1992 the proportion of the unemployed who had been unemployed for 12 months or more was 33.4 per cent (around 300 000 persons). By comparison, the figure in August 1981 was 20 per cent (around 70 000 persons). In August 1996 the proportion had fallen to 28.4 per cent (perhaps as a result of Working Nation targeted policies—discussed below) but by August 1997 it was back up to 30.8 per cent.

Research clearly shows that the probability of finding employment falls with the length of unemployment (see, for example, Foster and Gregory 1983). With increases in the general unemployment rate comes an increase in the number of workers who have been unemployed for a long period of time and whose prospects of leaving the unemployment pool are poor. Even with a recovery in labour market conditions, the erosion of job skills and attractiveness to potential employers that results from a prolonged spell of unemployment means that these people remain disadvantaged. The new job opportunities are likely to be taken by new entrants to the labour force and by those with only a brief spell in unemployment.

Even with a recovery in conditions generally, the problem of long-term unemployment is likely to require special targeted policies to offset labour market disadvantages.

The unequal incidence of unemployment, and the possible need for targeted assistance programs, has led to considerable research into the labour market experience of particular social groups such as migrants, women, youth and middle-aged males.

Table 4.2 presents the unemployment rates by sex and age for some selected years. While the main feature of this table is the much higher rates of unemployment for youth than for adults (in August 1992 the adult unemployment rate was 9.3 per cent, but the youth rate was 25 per cent), a number of points about the youth unemployment rate need to be understood.

Firstly, in 1992 for example, only 51 per cent of the population aged 15–19 years were participants in the labour force—nearly half of the working age youth population are in full-time education and are not counted as either employed or unemployed.

Secondly, although youth has many inherent disadvantages in the competition for jobs (e.g. lack of experience, 'last in, first out' retrenchment policies), many first-time youth jobs are of short duration, interspersed with frequent, very short spells of unemployment, and represent job-sampling behaviour.

Thirdly, although the youth unemployment rate in the current recession is about three times the adult rate, a comparison with previous periods reveals that the youth rate is always about three times the adult rate. For example, in the buoyant conditions of 1973 the adult rate was 1.4 per cent and the youth rate was 4.7 per cent. This suggests that the current high level of youth unemployment is not the result of some factor peculiar to the current youth labour market (such as current youth wage levels), but is the result of the high level of general unemployment and the perennial labour market disadvantages of youth. The best way to get youth unemployment down is to get the general level of unemployment down.

These qualifications should not decrease our concern about high youth unemployment. High youth unemployment today will mean future shortages of the labour skills acquired through on-the-job training. Future recovery in labour demand may run into shortages of skilled labour and result in inflationary pressure rather than reductions in unemployment.

While special targeted labour market programs to assist particular groups may be justified on the grounds of equity and efficiency, it must be remembered that if the economy does not generate sufficient growth in aggregate employment to more than match increases in the size of the labour force, such programs will do no more than redistribute unemployment. The relationship between unemployment, employment, labour force growth and GDP growth can be appreciated with the use of some simple arithmetic:

If we express the definitional equation for unemployment,

$$U = LF - E$$

in terms of changes, then

$$\Delta U = \Delta LF - \Delta E.$$

We can appreciate that unemployment will increase if employment falls (a negative change in E), or if employment increases, but the increase in employment is insufficient to match any increase in the labour force.

To stop unemployment and the unemployment rate from increasing we need to generate sufficient growth in employment to match labour force growth.

The size of the labour force is determined by the size of the working age population and the participation rate—the proportion of the working age population which is considered as being in the labour force, i.e. counted as employed or as unemployed.

Population growth depends upon natural increase and net immigration. Changes in the age-mix of the population will determine the proportion that are of working age. Australian research finds no strong relationship between these factors and short-run economic conditions, although the level of immigration has appeared to respond to the state of the economy, largely because of changes in government targets (see Kelley and Schmidt 1979).

Economic factors are much more significant in affecting the participation rate. Trends in the participation rate largely reflect such factors as the workforce behaviour of married women and students, school retention rates, and the average retirement age.

In Australia over the last two decades there has been a long-term trend of increased participation by married women which has been partially offset by longer school retention for teenagers and earlier male retirement. Over the last seven years the male participation rate has stabilised, while the female participation rate for females aged 30 years and over has continued to increase strongly.

In the short run the participation rate is strongly influenced by economic conditions. When the economy goes into a recession the participation rate falls due to the discouraged worker effect. When the economy recovers discouraged workers and other non-participants are drawn back into the labour force. Therefore the participation rate typically moves pro-cyclically in the short run.

Table 4.3 presents estimates for the last decade and a half of the changes in the number of people unemployed, disaggregated into labour force and employment changes. Changes in the labour force are further disaggregated into changes resulting from the increase

**Table 4.3 The composition of changes in unemployment (all figures in '000 persons)**

| Year | ΔU | = | ΔLF | | | − ΔE |
|------|-----|---|--------------------|---|--------------------|------|
| | | | From ΔPop (*) | + | From ΔPR | |
| 1982 | 81 | | 145 | + | −73 = 72 | −9 |
| 1983 | 225 | | 144 | + | −34 = 110 | −115 |
| 1984 | −79 | | 126 | + | 20 = 146 | 225 |
| 1985 | −34 | | 142 | + | 36 = 178 | 210 |
| 1986 | 25 | | 157 | + | 111 = 268 | 243 |
| 1987 | 5 | | 152 | + | 26 = 178 | 173 |
| 1988 | −63 | | 160 | + | 38 = 198 | 261 |
| 1989 | −70 | | 162 | + | 143 = 305 | 375 |
| 1990 | 118 | | 139 | + | 76 = 215 | 97 |
| 1991 | 219 | | 146 | + | −83 = 63 | −156 |
| 1992 | 100 | | 128 | + | −18 = 110 | 10 |
| 1993 | 16 | | 54 | + | −31 = 23 | 7 |
| 1994 | −126 | | 46 | + | 28 = 74 | 200 |
| 1995 | −76 | | 122 | + | 134 = 256 | 332 |
| 1996 | 49 | | 136 | + | 15 = 151 | 102 |
| 1997 | −6 | | 133 | + | −143 = −10 | −4 |

(*)    This is the estimated change in the labour force that would have occurred if there had been no change in the participation rate from the previous year.
*Source:*  ABS

in the working age population and changes resulting from a change in the participation rate.

The pro-cyclical movement in the participation rate is clearly evident. For example in 1982, 1983 and 1991, falls in employment were accompanied by falls in the participation rate which moderated the impact on unemployment. On the other hand, in 1986 there was very strong growth in employment (243 000 additional jobs) but increased participation added 111 000 persons to the labour force; together with the natural increase in the working age population this meant that the employment growth was not enough to match labour force growth and the number unemployed actually rose (by 25 000). In 1995 strong growth in employment encouraged increased participation which lessened the fall in unemployment.

Over the 12 months to August 1997, the unemployment rate fell marginally but only because the natural increase in the labour force was more than completely offset by a dramatic fall in participation—employment actually fell by 4000.

The data of Table 4.3 also indicate that Australia's dramatic increases in unemployment over the last two decades cannot be attributed to any abnormal labour supply factors. We cannot blame an influx of married women or migrants into the labour force for the substantial increases in unemployment. In all the years that unemployment increased significantly, employment either fell or, compared to what might be considered normal labour force growth, the increase in employment was inadequate. We may conclude that Australian unemployment has increased so dramatically because the economy has failed to generate adequate growth in employment.

Since a growing labour force requires growth in employment to avoid any increase in unemployment, growth in aggregate production of goods and services in the economy (GDP) must be strong enough to create sufficient employment opportunities.

The rate at which GDP needs to grow to stop the unemployment rate from increasing depends on labour force growth and productivity growth.

Each year the labour force grows (due to population growth and any changes in the rate of participation of the population in the labour force, as discussed above). So we need sufficient economic growth to generate sufficient extra jobs to provide for the increase in the labour force.

Additionally, output per person employed, a measure of average labour productivity, tends to increase over time (due to the increased quantity and quality of the capital goods with which labour works, i.e. technological progress).

Therefore, to stop unemployment increasing we need sufficient economic growth to cover increases in both the labour force and in productivity.

The rule relating required output growth (for no increase in the unemployment rate) to labour force and productivity growth rates is referred to as 'Okun's Law':

> *To maintain a constant unemployment rate, output must grow at a rate equal to the sum of the growth rates in the labour force and in the average productivity of labour.*

Growth in aggregate production of goods and services must be sufficient to generate enough extra jobs to provide for a growing work force, and to provide for the fact that each worker can produce a higher volume of output. (This is not to imply that an appropriate cure for unemployment is to reduce productivity growth. The point is, that to avoid increased unemployment, productivity growth must be used to *increase production of goods and services*, rather than to *save on the number of jobs*.)

If output growth falls below the Okun's Law benchmark, the unemployment rate will increase. For a reduction in the unemployment rate, output growth is required to be greater than the benchmark rate.

Although both labour force and productivity exhibit trend

**Figure 4.2 Real GDP: % change on previous year**

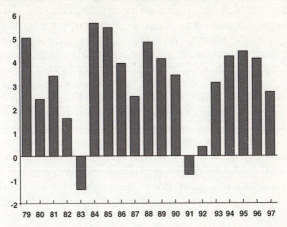

increases over the long run, in the short term both are affected by current economic conditions. For example, as we have discussed above, the participation rate will fall in times of low aggregate economic activity if job-seekers become discouraged and drop out of the workforce.

Average labour productivity, measured simply as output per person employed, is affected by changes in average working hours (say from a shift from full-time to part-time jobs), and by changes in the industrial composition of aggregate output (an increase in the relative contribution of capital-intensive industries like mining, at the expense of labour-intensive industries, would increase the average measure of labour productivity). Therefore the Okun's Law benchmark, while a useful rule of thumb, is subject to fluctuation.

On average, over the last decade or so, the Australian labour force has grown by approximately 2.5 per cent p.a.

Productivity growth has been slow by historical standards (due mainly to an increased proportion of part-time employment and the relative growth of labour-intensive service sectors), averaging only approximately 1 per cent p.a. On the basis of these figures the Okun's Law benchmark for GDP growth is approximately 3.5 per cent p.a.

Figure 4.2 depicts output growth for Australia for the period 1979 to 1994. Drawing an approximate Okun's Law benchmark at about 3.5 per cent, the correspondence between inadequate GDP growth in Figure 4.2, and the changes in the unemployment rate of Table 4.2 and Figure 4.1, is clear. In Figure 4.2, a line drawn across the graph of GDP growth generally identifies years in which the unemployment rate increased (GDP growth less than 3.5 per cent) and years in which the unemployment rate decreased (GDP growth greater than 3.5 per cent).

The fact that strong, consistent GDP growth is required just to stop the unemployment rate from increasing and, on present estimates, GDP growth well in excess of 3.5 per cent is necessary to make any substantial reduction in unemployment, highlights the main problems for unemployment policy. There are two constraints on the ability of the economy to sustain such growth rates. The first is the danger of inflationary pressures arising if policy seeks to generate increased growth through expansionary demand policies. In the face of shortages of particular types of skilled labour, and supply bottlenecks in particular industries, such policies may have their main effect as higher prices rather than higher employment.

The second constraint on growth concerns the balance of payments. The GDP growth required for reducing unemployment might result in a growth rate in imports (both consumer imports and imported inputs into production) which is not matched by adequate growth in Australia's exports. In these circumstances concern for the balance of payments, and the effect of current account deficits on the level of external debt, may mean that Australia cannot afford the GDP growth rates necessary to reduce unemployment significantly.

## The causes of unemployment

The causes of unemployment have long been a matter of controversy in both economic theory and policy debates. A full consideration of what economic theory has to say about the causes of unemployment is beyond the scope of this chapter. In this section we provide a brief summary of three main causal factors.

### Depressed levels of aggregate demand for goods and services

Since the demand for labour is derived from the demand for the goods and services that labour produces, if growth in aggregate demand expenditure is too low to provide sufficient growth in employment, unemployment will result. Thus one principle of national economic management is to try and ensure an adequate, stable rate of growth in aggregate demand expenditure, through appropriate fiscal and monetary policy, to maintain a high level of employment.

However, government policy often finds it necessary to restrict the level of demand expenditure to counter inflationary pressures, or because the economy is growing too quickly for the balance of payments constraint. This dilemma for macroeconomic demand management policy may require a trade-off between the goal of low unemployment and other policy goals.

## Frictional and structural unemployment

Frictional unemployment consists of 'job-searchers' temporarily unemployed between jobs. Although temporary for the individual, there will be an aggregate level of frictional unemployment determined by the amount of labour turnover (the number of people changing jobs) and the time taken to match the appropriate worker with the appropriate job.

Structural unemployment is a more serious concern. It is a reflection of the extent to which those unemployed are inadequately or inappropriately skilled to take advantage of any employment opportunities. Structural unemployment arises because the composition of the demand for labour does not match the composition of the available supply of labour.

The level of unemployment resulting from frictional and structural causes is referred to by some economists as the 'natural rate' of unemployment, or alternatively as the 'non-accelerating inflation rate of unemployment'. Note that to refer to frictional and structural unemployment as comprising the natural rate of unemployment does not imply that this rate of unemployment is incapable of responding to policy initiatives. Policies can be put in place to influence the levels of frictional and structural unemployment, e.g. improvements to job information networks, re-training and re-skilling schemes.

The point is that natural rate unemployment does not represent an excess supply of labour to put downward pressure on wages (since those unemployed are either voluntarily unemployed or do not have the appropriate job characteristics). Furthermore, general increases in aggregate demand for goods and services will not have much impact in reducing unemployment if it is structurally based, and may lead to a surge in inflation due to skill shortages.

The extent to which Australia's high unemployment is caused by structural factors is difficult to quantify.

Since productivity growth has been relatively low, it appears that technological unemployment has not been a major cause. Unemployment is not just the result of machines having replaced people in producing goods and services. If this had been the case, output per worker would have increased significantly.

A crude measure of the mismatch in the labour market, and the extent of structural unemployment, can be provided by the survey data that the ABS collects on unfilled vacancies.[3]

If U is the number unemployed, and V is the number of unfilled vacancies, then the ratio U/V is a rough indication of the extent of

**Figure 4.3  The Australian Beveridge Curve: 1979:3–1997:3**

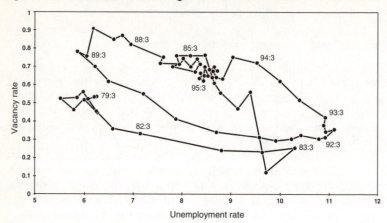

structural unemployment. If U/V is less than or equal to 1, then all unemployment can be considered as structural: there are sufficient job vacancies and the unemployed must therefore have inappropriate skills and characteristics for the available jobs. The higher the U/V ratio, the less important are structural imbalances in causing unemployment. The vacancy figures are notoriously unreliable, since many employers use informal networks in seeking labour, but taken at face value they imply U/V ratios which have been consistently much greater than 1 over the last decade in Australia. (In 1983 the U/V ratio was around 21. This would imply that even had we been able to wave a magic wand over the labour force to make everyone appropriately skilled, for every person placed in a job there would still be twenty left over as unemployed.)

Despite the unreliability of the vacancy figures, the U/V ratio has been so high that it can safely be concluded that the main cause of Australia's increased unemployment has been 'not enough job opportunities' rather than 'inappropriately skilled workers'.

An alternative way of using the relationship between unemployment and vacancies to measure structural inflexibility in the aggregate labour market is to plot the vacancy rate against the unemployment rate over time to derive a Beveridge Curve. Solow (1997) uses shifts in the Beveridge Curve to examine changes in labour market flexibility in the USA and Europe.

Figure 4.3 depicts the Beveridge Curve for Australia 1990 to 1997.

Movements north-west and south-east reflect cyclical effects on the labour market as upswing generates falls in unemployment and increases in vacancies, and downturn generates increases in unemployment and falls in vacancies.

Movements north-east reflect a deterioration in matching (unemployment and vacancies both rise), and movements south-west reflect an improvement in structural unemployment.

The cyclical movement associated with the 1990–91 recession is clear, as is the shift out of the Beveridge Curve as the economy recovered.

This seems clear evidence of the increase in structural imbalances that occurs after a recession due to lack of on-the-job training and the erosion of skills for the unemployed—the hysteresis effect.

## Inappropriate wage levels

The relationship between wages and unemployment is the most controversial issue in macroeconomics.

Simple supply and demand analysis would imply that if unemployment reflects an excess supply of labour over demand for labour, then, in the familiar supply and demand cross diagram, the current price of labour must be above its equilibrium. With normally sloped supply and demand curves, the cure is a fall in the price so as to equate supply and demand. Such simple analysis, however, can be quite misleading when applied to the aggregate economy and the question of general unemployment.

Since the demand for labour depends upon the demand for goods and services, and expenditure on goods and services is largely financed by the wage-income of labour, it is not clear that a reduction in wages would increase the demand for labour. Lower wages might mean lower expenditure on goods and services. Employers would hardly increase their demand for labour if their sales of products were falling.

In analysing the relationship between wages and unemployment, it is useful to distinguish three concepts of wages (the 'price' of labour):

- **Money wages** (also referred to as nominal wages) The general level of money wages is the average money wage per employee (per period, e.g. per week).
- **Real wages** This is the ratio of the average money wage to some measure of the average or general level of prices.
- **Relative wages** This is the ratio of the average money wage for one labour market group to the average money wage of other groups.

Changes in the level of money wages reflect movements in wages generally. If money wages rise, and the increase is greater than the increase in labour productivity (output per employee), then the labour cost of producing a unit of output will increase—unit labour costs increase. Businesses could be expected to pass on this cost increase in higher prices—the result is inflation. Since inflation results in a loss of international competitiveness, and consequently less demand for domestically produced goods and services in relation to overseas produced goods and services, the result is unemployment. Additionally, wage based inflation may provoke governments into imposing contractionary demand management policy, in the belief that increased unemployment will cause a moderation in wage demands.

If employers are not able to pass on increases in money wages by raising prices, and *real* wages rise faster than labour productivity, then the result is a squeeze on profit margins and a fall in business profitability. The experiences of 1974/5 and 1982/3 in Australia have shown that when a squeeze on business profitability occurs, the consequence is a fall in business investment, a fall in economic growth, and a resulting rise in unemployment (see Stegman 1985, 1990).

On the other hand it is not necessarily the case that a fall in real wages and a consequent increase in business profitability will reduce unemployment. Reduced real wages may mean reduced aggregate consumption expenditure which may deter business from increasing employment levels or investment expenditure. The Australian experience of the late 1970s and mid-1980s demonstrates that increased business profitability does not necessarily lead to investment in appropriate employment generating areas.

With regard to the relationship between relative wage levels and unemployment, most interest in Australian economic debate has centred on youth–adult and male–female relativities.

We have seen that youth unemployment rates in Australia are around three times the rate for adults. Whether a fall in the wages of youth relative to adults would do much to reduce the natural disadvantage youth has in the labour market is open to question. Additionally, such a change in wage relativities may only provide a substitution of youth for adults in employment without increasing total employment.

With regard to male–female relativities, the years following the equal pay legislation of the mid-1970s have seen an increase in average female earnings relative to average male earnings (although average female earnings are still only around 80 per cent of average male earnings). Contrary to what simple economic theory would predict, female employment has grown more strongly than male

**Figure 4.4  Labour market flows**

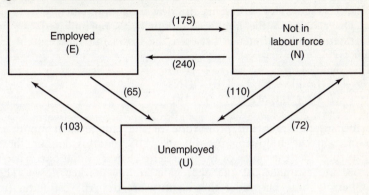

Notes:   Figures in parentheses for Jan–Feb 1989, '000 persons.
△U = EU + NU -- UE -- UN
In recession:
EU decreases from fall in voluntary quits, increases from retrenchments.
UN increases from 'discouraged workers' effect.
NU increases due to lack of employment opportunities for new entrants.
UE decreases from lack of new jobs to replace short-tenure jobs.
Probability of UE transition decreases with length of unemployment spell.

employment over this period (although much of the growth has been in part-time female employment).

Whatever the contribution of inappropriate relative wage levels to the relative unemployment rates of different labour market groups, one thing is clear. If the economy does not grow sufficiently to generate adequate growth in aggregate employment, changes in relative wages can do no more than shuffle around the incidence of unemployment. While an equitable sharing of the incidence of unemployment is a valid policy aim, reductions in the aggregate level of unemployment require policies that lift the constraints on economic growth.

## Labour market flows

Some useful insights into the dynamics of changes in unemployment can be gained by modelling the aggregate labour market in terms of labour market flows.

If we define the three possible labour market states: 'not in the labour force' (N), 'employed' (E), and 'unemployed' (U), then, as individuals change their status, we can define the six labour market flows: NE (from 'not in the labour force' to 'employed'), EN (from 'employed' to 'not in the labour force'), and (similarly) UE, EU, UN, NU. Figure 4.4 represents the flows diagrammatically.

The change in the number of individuals unemployed can be expressed as the difference between the flows into and out of U. That is:

$$\Delta U = EU + NU - UE - UN.$$
$$(-10)\ (103)\ (122)\ (117)\ (118)$$

Because a significant proportion of the sample each month is retained in the following month, the ABS monthly labour force survey provides estimates of the aggregate changes in labour market status, i.e. estimates of the aggregate labour market flows. The numbers in brackets under this identity are the ABS estimates (in thousands) of the flows between July 1997 and August 1997.

The numbers in brackets in Figure 4.4 are the estimates for the changes in labour market status between January 1989 and February 1989. This period is selected as an example because it illustrates a significant characteristic of the Australian labour market—its dynamism. For although there was no change in the total number of people unemployed between the two surveys, 765 000 individuals experienced a change in their labour market status—the net flows into and out of unemployment were offsetting.

The picture of the Australian labour market that emerges from these and other data on employment experience collected by the ABS is one where although the majority of workers are in long-tenure employment, a significant minority of the work force changes jobs frequently. Many workers have jobs with short duration or quit voluntarily and experience brief spells of unemployment before commencing their next short-tenure job. That is to say, a significant minority of workers have short-tenure, high turnover jobs—jobs with secondary labour market characteristics.

The behaviour of the various labour market flows over the business cycle provides insights into the characteristics of labour market recessions and the sources of increased unemployment. Despite the popular conception that dramatic increases in unemployment are the result of large-scale retrenchments and plant closures, these phenomena are more closely related to structural change than to cyclical downturns in the economy. Indeed, the EU flow may actually decrease in a labour market recession: if the fall in voluntary quits (because workers are pessimistic about finding a new job) dominates any increase in lay-offs and retrenchments. The UN flow is likely to increase in a labour market recession because of the discouraged worker effect. The main reasons for cyclical increases in unemployment are typically:

- increases in the NU flow (as employment opportunities for new entrants disappear); and
- decreases in the UE flow (because of the lack of new jobs to replace completed short-tenure jobs).

Rather than brief, between-jobs spells of unemployment, secondary market workers have increased difficulty in finding a new job. And, as has been emphasised above, the probability of a worker experiencing a UE status-change decreases with the length of unemployment.

Although the flows in previous recessions in Australia have tended to follow this cyclical pattern, the labour force survey statistics for the recession of the early 1990s suggest some atypical characteristics. Because the downturn in aggregate economic activity has coincided with a period of enormous structural change involving much labour-shedding, plant closures and retrenchments appear to have played a much more significant role in the increase in unemployment than is typical of a cyclical downturn. This is evidenced by the high EU flows and the significant numbers of middle-aged, male, white collar and long-tenure workers (i.e. primary labour market workers) going into the unemployment pool. Additionally, in the recent recession there has been an increase in the UE flows (although obviously not sufficient to offset the increase in NU and EU flows). What appears to be occurring in the Australian labour market is some casualisation of the work force (see Campbell and Webber 1996), with significant numbers of workers (mainly middle-aged males) being retrenched from full-time permanent jobs and forced to take a succession of short-tenure casual or part-time jobs. The countercyclical movement in the UE flow over the last cycle is a result of adult male flow behaviour (see Leeves 1996).

## Recent unemployment policy

In December 1993 the Labor Government released a detailed discussion paper, 'Restoring Full Employment' (hereafter referred to as the Green Paper). The Green Paper provided an assessment of recent unemployment policy and recommendations for future policy.

The Green Paper saw Australian government policy as providing a two-pronged attack on the problems associated with unemployment:

(i) Firstly, policy aimed to provide the capacity for, and achievement of, high rates of growth in aggregate activity. The necessity of high GDP growth rates for reductions in unemployment has been discussed above.

(ii) Secondly, since overall reductions in the level of unemployment will be only slowly achieved (even assuming the most
optimistic growth outcomes), policy also has to be directed
towards achieving an equitable sharing of the burden of
unemployment. This requires social service benefits systems
and labour market schemes which address the problems of
the long-term unemployed and other disadvantaged groups.

With regard to (i), the aims of policy are to provide macroeconomic policy settings (fiscal, monetary and wages policies), and to
instigate microeconomic reforms so as to allow a high rate of growth
in aggregate economic activity. The twin constraints on the pursuit
of pro-growth demand policies (expansionary fiscal and monetary
policies) are the balance of payments constraint and the extent
to which the supply side of the economy can respond in a non-
inflationary way to increases in demand. Thus the importance given
to microeconomic reform by the Labor Government in its unemployment strategy. Whereas in the 1980s policy relied on a
centralised wages policy and currency devaluation to provide for
non-inflationary growth within the balance of payments constraint,
the emphasis was now on reforms to product and labour markets
(with a decentralised approach to wage determination), in the pursuit of allocative and cost efficiencies and gains in international
competitiveness. Successful microeconomic reforms will raise the
potential 'speed limit' of the economy—by containing the threat of
inflation and easing the balance of payments constraint.

The Green Paper was optimistic in its assessment of both the
gains already achieved and the prospects for further gains from
microeconomic reform in easing the twin constraints on GDP
growth. It suggested that 'it should be possible to increase the annual
average rate of economic growth achievable over the remainder of
the decade to between 4.5 and 5 per cent' (p.70). A less optimistic
assessment might doubt whether the Australian economy is yet
capable of sustaining such a growth rate without a re-awakening of
inflationary pressures and a deterioration of the Current Account
on the Balance of Payments. Even with increased productive efficiency and lower inflation in relation to our trading partners, these
gains may well be translated into a higher valued exchange rate
with no consequent gain in international competitiveness. Without
more significant structural changes in the composition of its exports
and imports than has so far been achieved, Australia's 'affordable'
growth rate remains dependent on the vagaries of the world trading
environment and international commodity markets. Such restructuring may require a more pro-active industry policy with a strategy

for the *composition* of Australia's investment expenditure in productive capacity (see Stegman 1990).

Policy with regard to (ii) was seen by the Green Paper as needing to provide labour market programs targeted at retraining and the alleviation of labour market disadvantages, and seeking to ensure that the benefits system recognises current social conditions and does not penalise the taking up of employment opportunities at the margin.[4]

Since much of the microeconomic reform which has occurred has involved labour-shedding and restructuring through plant closures, thus exacerbating the problems of structural and long-term unemployment, the Green Paper recommended substantially increased expenditure on targeted labour market programs.[5]

In May 1994 the Government presented a major policy statement on unemployment and industry policy—the White Paper entitled 'Working Nation'. The White Paper, in accordance with Green Paper recommendations, placed a heavy emphasis on targeted labour market programs to improve the relative position of long-term unemployed and other disadvantaged groups. The main elements in this regard were a 'Jobs Compact' guaranteeing an employment placement of between 6 and 12 months to those who had been without work for more than 18 months, wage subsidies for the employment of long-term unemployed, and the implementation of a National Training Wage (at 80 per cent of the relevant award) in return for the facilitation by employers of on-the-job or off-the-job accredited training.

By August 1995 there was some evidence of a degree of success in achieving a more equitable sharing of the employment opportunities generated by the strong GDP growth of 1994/95. In the 12 months to August 1995 the level of long-term unemployment (52 weeks or more) had declined by 21.7 per cent (a fall of 64 800), compared with the fall of 10.6 per cent (−88 300) for all unemployed persons.

The election of a new Coalition Government in March 1996 saw the abandonment of the 'Working Nation' labour market programs. The new government's policy for unemployment had the creation of a more flexible labour market and a more competitive and efficient economy as its basis. If these policies are successful in lifting the 'speed limits' on GDP growth (in terms of inflation and the balance of payments constraint) then improvements in the unemployment rate could be expected—although progress may be slow and incidence and equity issues would remain.

Some aspects of the Government's policy approach serve to dampen optimism, however. Microeconomic reform and deregulation have meant a commitment by the Government to continued fiscal restraint and substantial public service employment reductions. The shift to the private sector of the employment matching services of the Commonwealth Employment Service provides no obvious source of improvement in structural or frictional unemployment problems and may worsen the position of the long-term unemployed, since the market incentives for private agencies are to match the most easily placed persons with the easiest-to-fill jobs.

Finally, the continued shift to unregulated enterprise bargaining in wage determination, and the erosion of the control of the Australian Industrial Commission over the general wage outcome, means that anti-inflation wages policy is now in the hands of the Reserve Bank through its statements as to what it sees as acceptable wage outcomes, and its threat to raise interest rates to deter and punish if the combination of award and bargained increases generate increases in the general level of wages which the bank regards as inflationary.

Without any central institutional arrangements for monitoring and containing aggregate wage outcomes, any situation of improving employment growth will generate fears of wage based inflation. In any pre-emptive role to control wage based inflation, the RBA will have to threaten rises in interest rates. Moreover, the threat will sometimes have to be made good. This approach to wages policy does not seem compatible with strong economic growth and high aggregate employment. (See Stegman 1997 for more detail on this issue.)

# 5 The Asian financial crisis and Australia's balance of payments

*Elaine Hutson and*
*Colm Kearney*

Australia is an open economy; that is, it is open to international trade in goods and services and in financial assets. Some of Australia's production is exported to foreign countries, while some goods and services that are consumed or invested in Australia are produced overseas and imported. Australian individuals and public and private institutions can hold either local assets such as Treasury bills or corporate bonds, or financial assets issued in foreign countries such as Britain, Canada or Japan. Most Australian individuals actually hold Australian assets, but that is certainly not true for banks, fund management institutions and large corporations. For example, portfolio managers will usually search around the world for the most attractive yields, and they may well decide at a particular time that holding German or Japanese government bonds, or Swiss bank deposits, offer a better yield than Australian securities. Overseas investors will do likewise and may decide to purchase Australian securities. The actions of international investors, seeking the best return on funds invested, have fundamental effects on Australia's exchange rate. This international movement of capital also affects the Reserve Bank of Australia's (RBA) ability to enact monetary policy by manipulating interest rates, and the level of national income and employment.

There are important links between international economic and financial developments and real economic activity in Australia. A potent example of the power of these links can be found by examining the origins of the recession in the early 1990s. During the late 1980s Australia's current account balance deteriorated very sharply.

It went from a deficit of $10.2 billion (3.8 per cent of GDP) in 1987/88 to $17.6 billion (5.5 per cent of GDP) in 1988/89, and it further deteriorated to a deficit of $21.6 billion (6.0 per cent of GDP) in 1989/90. The government became alarmed at this situation and responded by implementing tight fiscal and monetary policies. There were four consecutive years of fiscal surplus beginning in 1987/88, and the interest rate on 90-day bank bills was pushed up from 13.15 per cent in 1987/88 to 18.30 per cent in 1988/89. This policy mix succeeded in reducing the current account deficit to $15.4 billion (3.8 per cent of GDP) in 1992/93. But the cost of this policy stance was that it contributed significantly to the depth of the recession. The economy is still paying the price for this, in terms of continued high levels and duration of unemployment.

The purpose of this chapter is to provide an overview of the external financing requirements of the Australian economy and to describe the implications of the recent Asian financial crisis. This is achieved by first outlining the balance of payments accounts and their recent developments. The next section is an overview of Australia's external indebtedness. The last section presents an overview of the recent financial crisis in Asia and points to the lessons that may be learned from it. The final section summarises the chapter and draws together the conclusions.

## The balance of payments accounts

The *balance of payments* is a record of all transactions of the residents of a country with the rest of the world. There are two main accounts in the balance of payments: the *current account* and the *financial account*.

The current account records trade in goods and services, as well as other net incomes and transfer payments. Adding these together we arrive at the current account balance. The current account is in *surplus* if the sum of payments into Australia exceeds the sum of payments out of Australia in the current account. It is in *deficit* if the opposite situation obtains. The financial account records purchases and sales of assets, such as stocks, bonds and land. There is a financial account *surplus*—also known as a net capital inflow—when receipts from the sale of Australian assets exceed our payments for purchases of foreign assets. There is a financial account *deficit*—also known as a net capital outflow—when the opposite situation occurs on the financial account. As we shall see, the usual situation in Australia is a current account deficit and a financial account surplus.

**Table 5.1 The current account: 1996/97**

|  |  | $m |
| --- | --- | ---: |
| (1) | Merchandise trade: |  |
|  | Exports of goods | 80 682 |
|  | Imports of goods | −79 246 |
|  | Merchandise balance | 1 436 |
| (2) | Services balance | −1 |
| **(3)** | **Balance on goods and services** | 1 435 |
| (4) | Net income and transfers | −19 310 |
| **(5)** | **Current account balance** | **−17 875** |

*Source:* RBA

## The current account

Table 5.1 presents the format of the current account of the balance of payments. The figures provided are for the year 1996/97. The current account consists of (1) the merchandise trade balance and (2) the services balance, which together add up to (3) the goods and services trade balance. To this we add (4) the net income and net transfer balance to get (5) the overall current account balance.

The merchandise trade balance consists of exports (entered with a positive sign) less imports (entered with a negative sign). The word 'merchandise' refers to physical commodities; those you can see packed up at the docks to be loaded onto or unloaded from ships, or at the airports to be airfreighted into or out of the country. Services include, for example, freight and tourism. Adding these together gives the balance of trade in goods and services. The net income and transfers category refers to income earned by domestic residents from non-residents (credits) less the income earned by non-residents from residents (debits). It also includes transfer payments, which are payments made or received that are not in return for some economic service, such as migrant remittances and foreign aid donations. In general terms, net income refers to the net returns payable to the owners of assets and/or resources. In the current account, net income is further divided into (i) investment income, (ii) other property income and (iii) labour and other income.

In 1996/97, Australian residents exported almost $80.7 billion worth of merchandise and imported just over $79.2 billion worth, giving a merchandise trade balance surplus of $1.4 billion. The net services balance was in deficit by $1 million. Adding these together yielded a goods and services surplus of $1.4 billion. With a net income and transfers deficit of $19.3 billion, the overall current account deficit for the year was $17.9 billion.

**Table 5.2  The financial account 1996/97 ($ million)**

| Official | | | Non-official | | | | | | |
|---|---|---|---|---|---|---|---|---|---|
| General government | | Reserve Bank | Direct investment | | Portfolio and other investment | | | Financial account balance | Balancing item |
| Borrowings | Total | | Borrowings | Other | Borrowings | Other | Total | | |
| −2426 | −2426 | −5209 | 491 | 4724 | 17125 | 362 | 22 702 | 15 067 | 2808 |
| A | B<br>(=A) | C | D | E | F | G | H<br>(D+E+<br>F+G) | I<br>(B+C+H) | |

Source: RBA *Bulletin*, December 1997, Table H.2. See September 1997 issue for old format

## The financial account

Table 5.2 presents the format of the financial account of the balance of payments. Prior to the December 1997 issue of the RBA *Bulletin*, this table was known as the capital account of the balance of payments. From this table it can be seen that the financial account comprises an official and a non-official component. The official component comprises general government and Reserve Bank. The non-official component comprises two elements, direct investment, and portfolio and other investment, each of which is further classified as either borrowings or other. The total of the non-official components is provided before the summation of the official and non-official components to reach a financial account balance. The balancing item records the sum of unidentifiable transactions—this amount is equal to the difference between the current account and the financial account balance.

In 1996/97, the general government sector decreased its net reliance on foreign funds by $2.4 billion and the RBA raised its foreign reserve assets by just $5.2 billion. This was accompanied by a non-official (private sector) net capital inflow of $22.7 billion, made up mostly by a $17.1 billion increase in portfolio and other investment into Australia. Overall, therefore, Australia recorded a financial account surplus of $15.1 billion. If we add the financial account balancing item of $2.8 billion to the financial account balance of $15.1 billion, we see that it equals the $17.9 billion current account deficit in Table 5.1.

Let us now focus on the relation between the current account and the financial account. Suppose Australia runs persistent balance of trade deficits, which means that it imports more than it exports. The country is then living beyond its means. Suppose in addition that the country runs a persistent financial account surplus of equal magnitude to the balance of trade deficit. This means that overseas residents are accumulating Australian assets at a greater rate than

**Table 5.3 Australia's historical balance of payments (A$m, annual averages)**

|  | 1959/60 –1968/69 | 1969/70 –1978/79 | 1979/80 –1988/89 | 1989/90 –1996/97 |
|---|---|---|---|---|
| Goods and services balance | 61.5 | 1 003.70 | –1 370.40 | –2 784.4 |
| Current account | –620.4 | –1 508.20 | –10 819.30 | –19 292.5 |
| Financial account | 525.7 | 1 260.40 | 8 972.30 | 17 140.1 |

*Source:* RBA

domestic residents are accumulating foreign assets. In other words, foreigners are financing Australia's current trade deficit by acquiring domestic assets such as bonds, stocks, businesses and land. These foreign investors will require a return on their investments in the form of interest, dividends, profits, rent and possibly capital gains. The return that they earn appears in the balance of payments accounts as a negative entry in the net income component of the current account. This acts to worsen the current account balance and in turn imposes a greater need to attract foreign investment.

### Australia's foreign indebtedness

The process described above determines the country's external debt position. Persistent current account deficits require persistent financial account surpluses to finance them. Unless these financial account surpluses are generated by foreigners buying Australian land (that is, Australia 'sells off part of the farm' to finance its deficits), the country's level of international indebtedness will continually rise.

Table 5.3 presents a summary of Australia's balance of payments performance over the past 37 years. In the 1960s and 1970s, Australia's trade balance on goods and services was in surplus, but the current account was in deficit. In the 1980s and 1990s, the goods and services trade balance deteriorated into deficit and the current account deficit worsened. The deteriorating current account deficit was financed by increasing financial account surpluses. This means that foreign residents have financed Australia's current account deficits by acquiring more Australian assets than domestic residents have acquired foreign assets.

Can this situation continue indefinitely? The answer is yes, as long as foreigners are willing to continue to lend to Australia under similar arrangements, that is, as long as they retain confidence in our economy and in our continuing ability to pay the required return on their investments. If for some reason foreign investors lose confidence in the Australian economy, either our exchange rate will collapse or we will have to dramatically raise interest rates (or both). As we shall see in the next section, this is precisely what has

**Table 5.4  Australia's foreign indebtedness**
**$billions: 1980/81–1996/97**

|  | Official debt (1) | Official assets (2) | Official net debt (3) | Non-official debt (4) | Non-official assets (5) | Non-official net debt (6) | Total debt (7) | Total assets (8) | Total net debt (9) |
|---|---|---|---|---|---|---|---|---|---|
| 1980/81 | 4.8 | 5.7 | –0.9 | 10.4 | 0.9 | 9.5 | 15.2 | 6.6 | 8.6 |
| 1981/82 | 5.7 | 6.5 | –0.8 | 18.7 | 1.3 | 17.4 | 24.4 | 7.8 | 16.6 |
| 1982/83 | 7.7 | 10.8 | –3.1 | 28.2 | 1.8 | 26.5 | 35.9 | 12.6 | 23.4 |
| 1983/84 | 8.9 | 12.4 | –3.5 | 35.2 | 1.8 | 33.4 | 44.1 | 14.2 | 29.9 |
| 1984/85 | 14.9 | 13.6 | 1.3 | 52.6 | 2.6 | 49.9 | 67.5 | 16.2 | 51.2 |
| 1985/86 | 23.6 | 13.2 | 10.4 | 68.9 | 3.8 | 65.1 | 92.5 | 17.0 | 75.5 |
| 1986/87 | 30.4 | 18.0 | 12.4 | 77.1 | 3.3 | 73.7 | 107.5 | 21.3 | 86.1 |
| 1987/88 | 33.1 | 20.6 | 12.5 | 90.0 | 6.2 | 83.8 | 123.1 | 26.8 | 96.3 |
| 1988/89 | 36.8 | 21.1 | 15.7 | 109.9 | 8.3 | 101.5 | 146.7 | 29.4 | 117.2 |
| 1989/90 | 39.4 | 22.6 | 16.8 | 123.3 | 8.5 | 114.9 | 162.7 | 31.1 | 131.7 |
| 1990/91 | 41.9 | 24.5 | 17.4 | 136.8 | 12.2 | 124.6 | 178.7 | 36.7 | 142.0 |
| 1991/92 | 46.3 | 22.4 | 23.9 | 145.9 | 15.7 | 130.1 | 192.2 | 38.1 | 154.0 |
| 1992/93 | 60.7 | 21.0 | 39.7 | 149.9 | 20.4 | 129.4 | 210.6 | 41.4 | 169.1 |
| 1993/94 | 62.6 | 21.3 | 41.3 | 144.3 | 21.3 | 123.0 | 206.9 | 42.6 | 164.3 |
| 1994/95 | 75.0 | 20.2 | 54.8 | 148.6 | 22.0 | 126.7 | 223.6 | 42.2 | 181.5 |
| 1995/96 | 78.3 | 19.1 | 59.2 | 157.8 | 29.4 | 128.4 | 236.1 | 48.5 | 187.6 |
| 1996/97 | 82.7 | 22.9 | 59.8 | 172.0 | 29.8 | 142.2 | 254.7 | 52.7 | 202.0 |

*Source:* RBA

occurred in a number of Australia's Asian trading partners. Neither of these scenarios—a collapsing exchange rate or dramatically high interest rates—is conducive to achieving strong output and employment growth.

Tables 5.4 and 5.5 present developments in Australia's international indebtedness and debt servicing ratios since the beginning of the 1980s. The information in Table 5.4 is useful insofar as it allows us to determine whether the private sector or the government sector is responsible for the majority of our net external debt. Table 5.5 presents information about the size of the servicing burden which Australia's overall debt position imposes on the economy.

Turning first to Table 5.4, which shows official, non-official and total gross external debt, external assets and net external debt in billions of dollars: column 3 shows that official net external debt rose from –$0.9 billion in 1980/81 to $59.8 billion in 1996/97, while column 6 shows that non-official net external debt rose from $9.5 billion in 1980/81 to $142.2 billion in 1996/97. Overall, therefore, as column 9 reveals, the economy's total net external debt rose by $193.4 billion from 1980/81 to 1996/97. This was made up of a $60.7 billion rise in official net external debt and a $132.7 billion rise in non-official net external debt. In summary,

**Table 5.5 Australia's debt service ratios**

| | Total net external debt as % of GDP | Official interest payments ($b) | Non-official interest payments ($b) | Total interest payments ($b) | Total interest payments as % of exports |
|---|---|---|---|---|---|
| 1981/82 | 10.6 | 0.2 | 1.4 | 1.6 | 6.7 |
| 1982/83 | 13.8 | 0.1 | 2.2 | 2.3 | 9.0 |
| 1983/84 | 15.5 | 0.0 | 2.9 | 2.9 | 10.0 |
| 1984/85 | 23.7 | 0.1 | 4.3 | 4.4 | 12.3 |
| 1985/86 | 31.3 | 0.8 | 5.1 | 5.9 | 15.0 |
| 1986/87 | 32.5 | 1.7 | 5.5 | 7.2 | 16.3 |
| 1987/88 | 32.1 | 2.2 | 5.6 | 7.8 | 15.1 |
| 1988/89 | 35.0 | 2.1 | 7.4 | 9.5 | 17.2 |
| 1989/90 | 35.9 | 2.7 | 9.8 | 12.5 | 20.5 |
| 1990/91 | 37.6 | 2.2 | 10.4 | 12.6 | 19.0 |
| 1991/92 | 39.3 | 2.3 | 8.7 | 11.0 | 15.7 |
| 1992/93 | 41.1 | 2.1 | 7.1 | 9.2 | 12.0 |
| 1993/94 | 37.9 | 3.2 | 6.0 | 9.3 | 11.2 |
| 1994/95 | 39.9 | 3.0 | 6.8 | 9.8 | 11.2 |
| 1995/96 | 38.5 | 4.0 | 7.1 | 11.0 | 11.1 |
| 1996/97 | 40.0 | 3.7 | 7.4 | 11.1 | 10.6 |

*Source:* RBA

during the period under consideration, Australia's net foreign debt rose very markedly, with the private sector's net foreign indebtedness rising at more than twice the increase in official net foreign indebtedness.

Looking now at Table 5.5, column 1 reveals that the economy's total net external debt rose very markedly over the period from 10.6 per cent of total GDP in 1981/82 to 40 per cent of GDP in 1996/97. During this period, total net interest payments rose from $1.6 billion to $11.1 billion, with non-official net interest payments rising, as expected, to higher levels than official net interest payments.

The last column of Table 5.5 shows how the economy's total net interest payments as a percentage of exports have evolved over the period being discussed. This measure shows the extent to which the economy can finance its net interest payments by export earnings. Over the period 1981/82–1996/97, Australia's total net interest payments as a percentage of exports rose from 6.7 per cent to 10.6 per cent, peaking at 20.5 per cent in 1989/90. In summary, during the period under consideration, Australia's debt to GDP ratio rose almost fourfold while its debt service ratio, measured by total net interest payments as a percentage of exports, rose by over two-thirds. The latter rose at a slower rate than the former due to declining world interest rates in the 1990s and to good export growth.

## The recent Asian financial crisis

It is widely agreed that the causes of the 1997 Asian crisis are multiple and complex in nature. It is not our intention to identify each of the causes and attach weights to them. Not only is such a task beyond the scope of this book, but the international economic and financial community is still in the process of gaining a complete understanding of this issue. Our purpose is to detail the main lessons that can be learned from the Asian crisis. Unfortunately, many of these lessons have not been adequately learned by some of the countries involved. This is a matter of ongoing concern, and may delay these countries' recovery from the crisis.

Before discussing the lessons that can be learned, we present a brief history of the emergence of the Asian crisis. It illustrates the speed with which economic crises can descend in the modern world financial system, and also how quickly 'contagion' occurs.

### The emergence of the crisis

#### 1997

*14–15 May:* The Thai baht is hit by a massive speculative attack based on poor economic performance and political instability. The central bank raises interest rates to 13 per cent and intervenes to support the baht. The Singapore central bank assists and speculators move on to the Filipino peso.

*19 June:* The Thai finance minister resigns and contagion spreads further to the Philippines where short-term interest rates rise to 15 per cent.

*27 June:* The Thai central bank suspends operations of 16 illiquid finance companies and orders them to consolidate or merge.

*30 June:* The Thai Prime Minister announces in a televised broadcast that there will be no devaluation of the baht.

*2 July:* The Thai central bank introduces a managed float and seeks IMF assistance. This amounts to a 15–20 per cent devaluation of the baht to a record low of almost 29 to the US dollar.

*3 July:* Speculators attack the Filipino peso and the central bank defends it by intervention and by raising interest rates from 15 to 24 per cent.

*8 July:* Speculators attack the Malaysian ringgit and the central bank successfully defends the currency through intervention.

*11 July:* Speculators attack the Indonesian rupiah. The Indonesian authorities respond by intervention and by widening the trading band of the rupiah vis-à-vis the US dollar from 8 per cent to 12 per cent. The Philippine central bank also widens its trading range for the peso against the US dollar.

*14 July:* The Philippines obtains US$1.1 billion from the IMF.

*24 July:* Speculators attack the Malaysian ringgit and drive it to a three-year low of 2.653 ringgits per US dollar. Prime Minister Mahathir Mohammed criticises the role of speculators. Speculators also attack the Hong Kong dollar which is defended by US$1 billion intervention during an unspecified two-hour period.

*26 July:* Malaysian Prime Minister Mahathir Mohammed accuses fund manager George Soros of being responsible for the demise of the ringgit and calls him a 'moron'.

*11 August:* The Thai central bank suspends 48 finance firms and announces a revamping of its finance sector in line with the IMF rescue package.

*11 August:* Thailand obtains a rescue package of US$16 billion from the IMF.

*14 August:* Speculators attack the Indonesian rupiah, which is initially defended by intervention, but the central bank eventually abandons the managed exchange rate and allows the rupiah to fall to an historic low of 2755 rupiah to the dollar.

*20 August:* Thailand obtains a further US$3.9 billion rescue package from the IMF. Thailand's total rescue package now amounts to US$17.2 billion.

*4 September:* Speculators attack the Filipino peso and the Malaysian ringgit. The peso falls to a record low of 32.43 to the dollar and the ringgit crashes through the 3 per US dollar barrier.

*16 September:* The Indonesian government postpones 39 trillion rupiah worth of projects in order to reduce its budget deficit.

*20 September:* Malaysian Prime Minister Mahathir Mohammed states that currency trading is immoral and ought to be stopped.

*21 September:* Fund manager George Soros states publicly that 'Dr Mahathir is a menace to his own country'.

*1 October:* Dr Mahathir repeats his criticism of currency speculation and suggests a total ban on currency trading. Speculators attack the Malaysian ringgit which declines by 4 per cent in under two hours of trading to an historic low of 3.4 per US dollar.

*6 October:* Speculators attack the Indonesian rupiah and drive it to an historic low of 3845 per US dollar.

*8 October:* Indonesia seeks IMF rescue package funding.

*17 October:* The Malaysian government hands down a tight budget in an attempt to ward off further speculative attacks on the ringgit.

*20–23 October:* Hong Kong's Hang Seng index declines by 25 per cent in four days due to expectations of exchange rate depreciation and escalating interest rates.

*27 October:* After a slight recovery the Hang Seng declines by another 6 per cent. Contagion becomes worldwide. The Dow Jones declines by over 7 per cent and trading is suspended.

*31 October:* The IMF grants Indonesia a $23 billion financial support package.

*7 and 8 November:* Contagion spreads to South Korea where the stock market falls 11 per cent.

*17 November:* The South Korean won falls through the psychologically important 1000 to the dollar level; the stock market falls another 4 per cent.

*19 November:* Japan's Nikkei 225 index falls 5.3 per cent—the largest fall this year.

*20 November:* The Korean won falls 10 per cent after the government increases the allowable trading band from 2.25 per cent per day against the US dollar to 10 per cent per day. Other currencies in the region follow, falling sharply.

*21 November:* The won recovers, increasing by 7.9 per cent, after the South Korean government announces it will seek an IMF rescue package.

*25 November:* The yen plunges to its lowest level in five years; the Nikkei falls 5 per cent.

*3 December:* Concerns about South Korea's signing of the IMF loan agreement send markets down. The rupiah, baht and ringgit follow the won to all-time lows against the US dollar.

*4 December:* Agreement on the IMF's $57 billion South Korea bailout calm market jitters. The IMF revises its forecast for world economic growth, to 3.5 per cent (from 4.3 per cent three months ago).

*11 December:* As the South Korean crisis deepens with the won falling to an all-time low, contagion affects all regional stock markets, with Hong Kong falling 5.5 per cent, Indonesia 4.8 per cent,

Malaysia 7.4 per cent, the Philippines 4.9 per cent, Singapore 2.3 per cent, Thailand 4.9 per cent and Japan 2.6 per cent.

## 1998

*7 January:* Regional currencies again hit record lows, as Indonesia's budget fails to convince investors that countries in the region are committed to reforming their economies.

*8 January:* The ringgit and Indonesian stocks hit record lows, raising the spectre of civil unrest. Reports surface that the IMF has written a sharply-worded letter to Indonesia in response to the recent budget that was widely condemned as insufficiently austere.

*15 January:* Indonesia's signing of an agreement with the IMF fails to impress markets which need more proof that the government will really enact the tough measures required.

*22 January:* The rupiah falls to an all-time low, with other regional currencies following. The rupiah has fallen 60 per cent this year, and 80 per cent since July 1997.

*29 January:* South Korea announces a debt deal with global creditors: the exchange of short-term debt with government-guaranteed loans with maturities of one, two and three years. The Seoul stock market rebounds on this news.

*6 February:* The Japanese government has declared the economy stagnant in a report which surprises markets for its pessimism.

*16 February:* The rupiah plunges after reports that the IMF has threatened to withdraw support if Indonesia adopts a currency board (that is, a fixed exchange rate regime).

*23 February:* The yen plunges on news that the Group of Seven industrialised countries (G7) urges Japan to get its financial system in order.

*2 March:* Indonesia is on the brink of hyperinflation, with inflation at 32 per cent. Food price rises have been the main cause of ongoing civil unrest.

*6 March:* Continuing signs that Indonesian president Suharto is unwilling to implement reforms worries currency markets, with the rupiah down 25 per cent in the last three days. This devaluation exacerbates unemployment and the huge private debt overhang. Riots in the towns continue.

*16 March:* Confidence seems to have been restored in South Korea.

Foreign creditor banks have rolled over $22 billion of short-term debt into two- and three-year maturity loans.

*2 April:* Stocks throughout the region are sharply lower following the release of a Bank of Japan survey indicating that corporate confidence in the Japanese economy has sunk to a new low. The Nikkei falls 3.32 per cent. The yen falls later in the day after the chairman of Sony says that Japan's economy is verging on collapse.

*9 April:* Japan announces that as part of an economic stimulus package the government will cut income taxes by a total of 4 trillion yen (US$30.5 billion).

*13 May:* The Indonesian stock market slumps 8 per cent and the rupiah sinks below 10 000 to the dollar after six students are killed at a protest rally in Jakarta. Markets in bordering nations Singapore and Malaysia also experience large slumps of 4.86 and 3.66 per cent respectively.

*14 May:* Rioting and looting in central Jakarta sends the rupiah to 11 700 to the dollar, more than 25 per cent below the level two days ago.

*15 May:* Indonesian markets are virtually abandoned in the aftermath of four days of rioting, arson and looting in Jakarta. Banks are closed and most offices deserted. Overseas corporations start closing down operations and evacuating staff. Demands that President Suharto step down intensify. The death toll stands at more than 500.

*19 May:* Suharto promises new presidential elections in which he will not run. Jakarta stocks surge 6.4 per cent on this news, and the rupiah recovers to 11 000 after hitting a low of 16 000 to the dollar earlier in the day.

*21 May:* Suharto announces his resignation, handing over to Vice-President Jusuf Habibie. Regional markets rally on this news.

### Lessons from the Asian crisis

The above account of the emergence of the Asian crisis is not complete, and the situation continues to unfold. While economic and financial analysts continue to search for a complete understanding of the causes, the following lessons can be learned.

**Mahathir vs Soros: did predatory speculation cause the crisis?**
To blame speculators for the Asian crisis is to confuse the symptom with the disease. It is widely agreed that the crisis is due to the region's fundamental economic flaws such as bad economic

management, poor bank lending practice, crony capitalism, inadequate legal and regulatory infrastructure, and lack of complete global integration.

The crisis became manifested as a 'currency crisis' as investors—hedgers, fund managers and institutional investors as well as speculators—sold their holdings of Asian securities. In the process of liquidating their holdings, investors had to sell local currencies to convert their money back into US dollars or the currency of the country of origin. Foreign exchange speculators contributed to the sell-off as they saw the Asian currencies falling in value.

Speculators, as well as investors generally, perform an important function in financial markets. They provide liquidity to the markets allowing a well-functioning price discovery mechanism. This is crucial to the efficient allocation of resources in an economy. The widespread currency sell-off was the market's recognition of the massive fundamental problems in many of these Asian economies. Had the Asian economies been in perfect health, an attempted 'attack' by speculators would not have succeeded, as there would have been plenty of investors and speculators with confidence in the fundamentals to buy the currency and counter the sell-off.

## The need for improved bank lending practice

Since the start of the Asian crisis, multiple instances of poor lending practice have been documented as one of the causes of the bank and financial institution failures which occurred in the wake of the crisis. Inadequate risk assessment and overweighting by lending institutions in certain asset classes were common in Asian financial institutions. For example, in Thailand large proportions of bank funds were poured into speculative property developments. Overexposure to specific economic sectors is obviously very risky, as a downturn in one sector can precipitate an excess of non-performing loans and bad debts, which may lead to bank failure. There are a few lessons to be learned here. First, financial institutions must ensure adequate diversification of their loan portfolios. Second, they must establish rigorous risk assessment and pricing procedures. To achieve both of these objectives, financial institutions must ensure that they employ appropriately qualified and experienced staff. The third lesson is one that must be learned by governments in the region. In many cases the inadequate diversification of bank assets was due to the allocation of funds being based on government directives, rather than being market-determined. Economic history is littered with examples of the failure of government intervention in resource allocation, leading to serious inefficiencies.

## An adequate legal and regulatory infrastructure for business must be established

The dramatic and sudden withdrawal of international capital from a number of Asian countries during the second half of 1997 can be interpreted as a capital strike by investors in the West. This strike occurred because the suppliers of capital became impatient with the lack of transparency, poor allocation mechanisms, crony capitalism and maintenance of outdated monopolistic practices—problems which continue to pervade many economies in the region. These practices have had the effect of denying overseas investors the ability to earn their investments' full marginal revenue product. In other words, the capital was not being used optimally and efficiently.

The lesson for Asian countries is that governments and institutions in the West will be reluctant to embrace the Asian economies in a fully integrated global economic and financial system until they have in place appropriate legal and regulatory infrastructure. Many Asian economies lack such basic infrastructure, whose purpose it is to allow free and fair contracting and transparency of business transactions, and to promote the widespread dissemination of accurate information. For example, the companies in many of these countries are not required to adhere to a common set of accounting standards. Other examples of inadequate legal infrastructure are poorly developed bankruptcy laws and absence of risk management standards.

Further, bank regulation is inadequate in the region. Many Asian governments have not adopted the Bank of International Settlements' (BIS) recommendations on regulations pertaining to such issues as capital adequacy and risk management, which were established to protect the integrity of both national and international banking systems, and have had widespread acceptance in OECD countries. This absence of adequate bank regulation contributed to the widespread problems in banks and financial institutions documented above.

There is also a lesson here for Western countries. Given that there is widespread recognition of the importance of Asia in the sustainability of a healthy world economic system, it is in everyone's interest that the countries involved in the crisis get all possible assistance. The West must assist these countries to develop the legal and regulatory infrastructure that will be crucial to their continued survival and prosperity.

## Better exchange rate management is required

Table 5.6 documents the exchange rate management policies of the main countries involved in the Asian crisis. Generally, these countries have adopted a managed exchange rate system in which the local

**Table 5.6  Asian exchange rate regimes**

| Country | Date | Event |
| --- | --- | --- |
| Hong Kong | November 1974 to<br>October 1983<br>Mid-October 1983 to present | Free float<br>Fixed peg to US dollar @<br>HK$7.80: US$1.00 |
| Indonesia | November 1978 to present | Managed float against basket<br>of currencies |
|  | 15/11/78 | 51% devaluation relative to<br>US dollar |
|  | 30/03/83 | 39% devaluation relative to<br>US dollar |
|  | 12/09/86 | 45% devaluation relative to<br>US dollar |
| Malaysia | 21/06/73 to present | Free float |
| Philippines | February 1970 to present<br>12/10/83<br>13/06/84 | Managed float<br>devaluation<br>devaluation |
| Singapore | June 1973 to present | Managed float against trade<br>weighted basket of currencies |
| Thailand | 1970 to November 1984<br>7/11/84<br>22/07/81 | Rate fixed against US dollar<br>Pegged to basket of currencies<br>10% devaluation relative to<br>US dollar |
|  | 7/11/84 | 17% devaluation relative to<br>US dollar |

currency was allowed to trade within some band relative to the US dollar. This may have been appropriate in the past, when these countries tended to conduct more of their trade in commodities, services and financial assets with the USA and Europe. However, the increasing trend towards regional economic integration, together with greater proportions of intra-regional trade, has made such policies less appropriate.

The point to understand here is that when the dominant trading partner was the USA and foreign borrowing was denominated mainly in US dollars, it was rational for these countries to maintain a relatively stable US dollar value for their currencies. It also allowed the region's corporate sectors to form a natural hedge in their overseas transactions. The effectiveness of this hedge has declined over time, and the strong US dollar throughout 1997 led to sharp increases in the debt servicing costs of these countries. This put pressure on the sustainability of their current account deficits. Investors eventually realised this and sold the Asian currencies in order to force the exchange rates vis-à-vis the US dollar down to more appropriate equilibrium values.

Apart from giving insights into the well-documented problems inherent in fixed exchange rate systems, an important lesson that can be learned from the Asian currency crisis is that the countries should cooperate in the search for a more appropriate exchange rate management policy. Specifically, it seems sensible that they should investigate the adoption of an Asian Monetary System. This might involve the construction of an Asian Currency Unit (ACU) similar to the ECU which was used in Europe during the process of unification prior to the emergence of the Euro. The ACU could be some weighted average of the region's currencies, perhaps with the Yen occupying a central role (like the Deutschemark in Europe), in order to minimise the volatility of the region's exchange rates vis-à-vis the US dollar.

### The optimal sequencing of reforms

One of the key issues in economic and financial reform is the sequencing of the reforms—that is, which should come first. This is a very complex issue. Reform of financial markets is easier and quicker to implement than reform in the real economy. This does not imply, however, that such reforms as foreign exchange market deregulation should precede real sector reform. The sequencing of the reforms can be almost as important as their content, particularly in the initial stages of implementation as the economy adjusts to new conditions.

An example of the problems that incorrect sequencing of reforms can create is the Australian government's program of financial deregulation in the early 1980s. This reform program included freeing up interest rate setting, allowing foreign banks to enter the onshore retail market, and floating the Australian dollar. This financial deregulation preceded and outpaced real sector reform. The effects of this sequencing led to a burgeoning current account deficit and a build-up in the country's net foreign indebtedness. This came to a head in the late 1980s when the government was forced to slow down the pace of economic activity to control the current account deficit. The tight fiscal and monetary policy that was required contributed to the worst recession since the 1930s, accompanied by very high unemployment rates. It is important to understand that although this reform sequencing was not the only cause of Australia's recession, which was worldwide in nature, it did contribute to its depth. It is also important to note that Australia now enjoys the benefits of its sweeping financial and economic reforms.

The International Monetary Fund (IMF) is aware of these issues. It has acknowledged that real sector reform takes time, and that sequencing is important. In his address to the Annual Meeting of the Bretton Woods Committee on 13 February 1998 in Washington, the IMF Managing Director, Mr Camdessus, described the measures which will be needed to alleviate the current economic downturn in Asia. He said: 'Taken together, these reforms will require a vast change in domestic business practices, corporate culture and government behaviour. Of course, all of this will take time.' Later on in this speech, he also recognised the desirability of implementing 'a prudent and properly sequenced liberalisation'.

While the IMF has recognised the importance of the sequencing issue, this has not always been evident in its adjustment packages. The IMF should consider paying more attention to the sequencing issue when it designs rescue packages for financially troubled countries.

### There is no place to hide in the global financial system

The Asian financial crisis began almost ten years after the October 1987 stock market crash, which spread to virtually all world stock markets within a couple of days, and on the same day in many cases. The Asian crisis constitutes another example of how disturbances in one country or region are transmitted throughout the world within a very short time frame. Economic and financial analysts now agree that the concept of a closed economy or a closed financial system is outdated. The potential for widespread contagion, and the speed of that contagion, is a fundamental aspect of the modern global financial system.

The Asian crisis has demonstrated that there is no place to hide in today's internationally integrated economic and financial system. The crisis has also demonstrated that this is the case even in countries where the government has attempted to shield the economy from external disturbances through a web of trade and financial controls. This did not succeed in insulating them from the repercussions of the crisis. The message is clear. We are all connected in the world economy and we can't isolate ourselves from events occurring elsewhere in the world.

### Conclusions

The purpose of this chapter has been to outline recent developments in Australia's balance of payments and international indebtedness, and to describe the evolution of the Asian financial crisis, together with some lessons that can be learned. The chapter first described Australia as being a capital importing country which tends to run current account deficits accompanied by financial account surpluses. The implications of this for international indebtedness were shown to be a tendency for the level of net foreign debt to rise. While

Australia's net international indebtedness has risen sharply in the past decade and a half, most of this debt has been incurred by the private sector rather than by the government. The chapter then proceeded to describe the unfolding of the Asian financial crisis.

Amongst the major lessons which can be learned from the Asian crisis are, first, Malaysian Prime Minister Mahathir Mohammed is wrong when he blames speculators for causing the Asian crisis. He confuses the symptom with the cause. The speculative attacks on a number of Asian currencies reflected underlying structural weaknesses in these economies. Second, there is a need for improved bank lending practice in Asia, including better diversification of loan portfolios, more rigorous risk management, and less government involvement. Third, many Asian countries need assistance to develop their legal and regulatory infrastructure in order to better allow them to participate in the global financial system. Fourth, the exchange rate regime which operates in Asia has outlived its usefulness, and the region's governments should initiate serious dialogue to put in place a more appropriate system. Fifth, the sequencing of reforms is an important issue, particularly in the former 'tiger' economies of Asia. The IMF should pay more attention to this issue it its design of rescue packages. Finally, there is no place to hide in today's integrated global financial system. We need to recognise this and work together to achieve a greater degree of economic and financial policy coordination.

## Suggested reading

Readers who are interested in further analysis of issues presented here should visit the web sites of the International Monetary Fund and Reuters. These sites provide up-to-date developments of the Asian crisis and its aftermaths. Statistics and analysis on Australia's balance of payments are regularly published in the Reserve Bank of Australia *Bulletin*.

# 6 Fiscal policy 60 years after Keynes
## *J. W. Nevile*

Fiscal policy is concerned with the effects of government expenditure and revenue on the economy at an economy-wide level. It is not concerned with effects on individual industries or on particular groups of people such as old age pensioners, but with effects on variables such as the output of the economy as a whole, employment and unemployment, the rate of inflation, the exchange rate and the balance of payments. Keynesian discussions of fiscal policy concentrate on aggregate demand, or total demand in the economy. Government expenditure adds to aggregate demand and taxation revenue reduces aggregate demand. Since recessions are caused by too little aggregate demand, fiscal policy can be very important in determining the health of our economy, at least if the theory about how a capitalist economy works, that Keynes set out 60 years ago, still has validity.

The next section sets out the elementary Keynesian theory of fiscal policy, which suggests that fiscal policy is a powerful weapon to kickstart an economy in a recession or to rein it back when it is growing too quickly. It was very widely accepted in the so-called 'golden age', the first 25 years after the Second World War, when all Western economies grew faster than they have before or since. However, in the last 25 years, in Australia, as elsewhere, various arguments have been put forward pointing to factors which may reduce or nullify the effectiveness of fiscal policy. This has led to vigorous debate—the issues in that debate which are important in the Australian case are discussed in succeeding sections.[1] In the last decade neo-classical economists have focussed attention on the effects of fiscal policy on aggregate supply and productivity—these arguments are also discussed. The chapter finishes with a review of fiscal policy in Australia. For this purpose estimates of the structural deficit are presented.

## How fiscal policy affects aggregate demand

We will start by examining the simplest of all possible worlds, with an economy with no transactions with foreigners, no corporate sector and with investment autonomous so that it is not affected by what happens in the economy. In this world total output (Y) is equal to government expenditure (G) plus investment in the private section (I) plus personal consumption expenditure (C). Or, in symbols:

$$Y = G + I + C \qquad (1)$$

Since there are no transactions with foreigners all the proceeds of selling output remain within the economy and total income equals total output.

Before we can say anything about fiscal policy we have to know how government expenditure is financed. Assume, first, that all taxation is lump sum taxation like a poll tax. Income in the private sector equals total output less taxation revenue and, making the further assumption that consumption is proportional to income, we can write:

$$C = c\,(Y - T) \qquad (2)$$

Combining equations (1) and (2) gives the following equation for income and output.

$$Y = \frac{I + G - cT}{1 - c} \qquad (3)$$

Despite the extreme simplicity of the economic structure in the world we have assumed, the analysis has already produced a result that is of considerable importance and which carries over to the real world. Not only does an increase in government expenditure increase output and an increase in taxation revenue reduce output but, since c is less than 1, a change in government expenditure has a bigger effect on output than does an equal change in taxation revenue. Indeed, if government expenditure and taxation revenue are both increased by the same amount, output also increases by this amount. This result is known as the balanced budget multiplier theorem and is summed up in the statement that the balanced budget multiplier is equal to 1 (since the increase in output is equal to the increase in the size of the government sector multiplied by 1). In the real world, with foreign trade, taxes varying with income and other complications, the balanced budget multiplier rarely is exactly equal to 1; but it is almost always true that changing government expenditure has a proportionally bigger effect on output than changing taxation revenue. As the Americans say, with expenditure you get a bigger bang for your buck.

Now consider the case where taxation revenue varies with income, so that

$$T = tY \qquad\qquad\qquad (4)$$

Combining equations (3) and (4) gives:

$$Y = \frac{I + G}{1 - (1 - t)c} \qquad\qquad\qquad (5)$$

Suppose that in this world investment increases for some reason—output will also increase. So too will taxation revenue, but government expenditure will remain the same. If the government budget was previously balanced with G = T, there now will be a surplus. This result is extremely important, and also holds in the real world. It shows that the size of the government deficit or surplus reflects not only the size of government expenditure and taxation rates, but also the level of economic activity. In the real world both taxation revenue and government expenditure vary as output changes. For example, when an economy moves out of a recession, taxation revenue rises as income increases and some types of government expenditure, notably unemployment benefits, tend to fall. The stance of fiscal policy, i.e. whether it is expansionary or exerting a downward pressure on output, depends on the levels at which the various taxation rates and government benefits are set and the size of those government expenditures which do not change with the level of output. These things certainly have a big influence on the size of the government budget deficit or surplus, but so too does the level of output. The size of the budget deficit is a very poor indicator of the stance of fiscal policy.

Reading any newspaper in Australia the day after the budget has been introduced into the Federal Parliament, one finds great attention paid to the budget deficit. As far as the economy-wide effects of the budget are concerned, journalists seem to be interested in only one number: the size of the budget deficit. Yet both the results obtained in this section suggest that this is very misleading. It is not just the size of the budget deficit that is important but also the factors that contribute to this final figure. If the deficit declines, is this because of cuts in government expenditure or increases in taxation rates? In the real world one should go even further than this question. Different types of expenditure have different effects on output. For example, the purchase in America of aircraft for the RAAF will have little effect on output in Australia. Similarly, different types of taxation have different effects on output. To get an indication of the stance of fiscal policy it is desirable to look at both the size and composition of expenditure and revenue, not just the size of the deficit or surplus.

In addition, it is as important to take into account the effect of the economy on the budget as it is to take into account the effect of the budget on the economy. In the boom year of 1989/90 Commonwealth budget outlays and revenues showed a surplus of $8 billion. In only two years this changed to a deficit of $9 billion. The change was large, equal to 4.5 per cent of gross domestic product in 1991/92—but almost half of this large change was due to the change from boom to recession.

Of the two types of errors introduced by using the budget deficit as an indicator of the stance of fiscal policy, neglecting the effect of the economy on the budget is usually the more important. Unless there are major changes, such as the proposed introduction of a GST, the composition of total taxation revenue or of government expenditure does not change greatly from year to year, and the relative size of the government sector does not usually change rapidly either. But the economy can change very quickly from boom to recession, often in only one year. To allow for the effect of such changes on the size of the deficit it is helpful to use the structural deficit as an indicator of the stance of fiscal policy. This measures the size the deficit would be if income and output were not at their actual levels but at the normal levels which are the middle- to long-run goals of economic policy. If one has to use a single number to measure the stance of fiscal policy the structural deficit is probably the best. It is discussed more fully in a later section of this chapter, where estimates of the size of the structural deficit for Australia over the last twenty years are given. It should be emphasised that even the structural deficit has substantial limitations as a measure of the stance of fiscal policy. For example, in Australia the relative size of the government section, as measured by the ratio of government expenditure to gross national product, dropped by 3 percentage points in 1987/88. After allowing for the high level of economic activity in 1987/88 compared with the previous year, the drop was 2.3 percentage points. Even if taxation revenue had fallen by a similar amount, this is large enough to exert a significant downward pressure on gross domestic product through the balanced budget multiplier.

## Crowding out

The simple theory in the preceding section assumes that investment in the private sector is not affected by fiscal policy. The first attack on Keynesian fiscal policy argued that this is not a useful assumption and that increasing government expenditure reduces or crowds out private investment so that there is little or no effect in terms of increased output and income. The argument is that, if an increase in government expenditure is matched by increases in taxation, the increased taxation will reduce private expenditure by a similar amount; but, if the increased expenditure increases the size of the deficit, this will increase interest rates enough to reduce private investment by an amount as large or nearly as large as the increase in government expenditure.

The first case ignores the balanced budget multiplier theorem, but it is the second case that people usually have in mind when they argue that an increase in government expenditure reduces private expenditure. For example, in his column of 17 June 1993 in the *Sydney Morning Herald*, Max Walsh talks of the capacity of the public sector 'to undermine the private sector by confronting it with a high interest rate regime as a consequence of large structural deficits' and concludes that, despite the depressed state of the economy, expansionary fiscal policy will not be effective because 'further expansion of the public sector deficit will simply create higher hurdles for private sector investment'.

It is true that the analysis in the previous section implicitly assumed no change in monetary policy, in the sense that the monetary authorities maintain a constant rate of interest. If, instead, the monetary authorities maintained a constant stock of money, an increase in government expenditure would cause some rise in interest rates, though only in extreme circumstances would interest rates rise enough to crowd out an equal amount of private expenditure. It is not clear, however, why the monetary authorities would want to reduce the effects of expansionary fiscal policy in a recession by allowing interest rates to rise. Moreover, the analysis that shows increased government expenditure leading to higher interest rates if the stock of money is held constant, also shows that any increase in private expenditure, for example, on investment or even foreign expenditure on Australian exports, will also lead to a rise in interest rates in Australia if the monetary authorities are successful in preventing changes in the stock of money. In this respect expansionary fiscal policy is no different from any sort of stimulus that might lift the economy out of recession.

In any case the monetary authorities in Australia do not maintain a constant volume of money. Short-run interest rates, not the volume of money, are the monetary policy instrument, and changes in the volume of money are only one of many things taken into consideration when setting interest rates.[2] Long-term, not short-term, interest rates may be more relevant to investment decisions in the private sector. It is perhaps possible that large budget deficits might increase the spread between short-term and long-term interest rates, so that even if short-term interest rates were held constant long-term rates could rise, crowding out private investment. However, there is no evidence of this happening in Australia. There is virtually no correlation between the budget deficit for all levels of government in Australia combined, as a percentage of GDP, and the spread (or gap) between long-term and short-term interest rates.[3] In theory the spread should be bigger when short-term interest rates are expected to rise in the future (because of increased inflation or because they are unusually low as a result of easy monetary policy, or other factors). Larger deficits leading to expectations of greater inflation in Australia could lead to a rise in long-term interest rates, but there is no evidence that large deficits have affected expectations in this way.

Thus, if a bigger deficit leads to higher interest rates, it must cause Australia's monetary authorities to increase short-term interest rates, since the deficit does not affect the gap between long-term and short-term interest rates. There is one plausible reason why larger deficits might induce the monetary authorities to raise short-term interest rates: a larger budget deficit will, other things being equal, provide more stimulus to the economy; hence income, and also imports, will be at higher levels than if the budget deficit were smaller. If the monetary authorities think that the higher level of imports will cause the exchange rate to fall, and if they believe it important to prevent this happening, they may raise interest rates to 'protect' the existing value of the Australian dollar on the foreign exchange. This is a long chain of conditions. On some occasions something like this may have happened, but Figure 6.1 shows no obvious relationship between the size of the deficit and short-term interest rates. If anything there is an inverse relationship with interest rates.[4] It is flying in the face of the facts to argue that in Australia larger deficits cause higher interest rates.

## The size of the public debt, national savings and the current account deficit

If the public debt is very large, an undue proportion of government expenditure may have to be devoted to interest payments, reducing the freedom of action of the government and reducing the amount

**Figure 6.1 Budget deficits as a percentage of GDP and short-term interest rates**

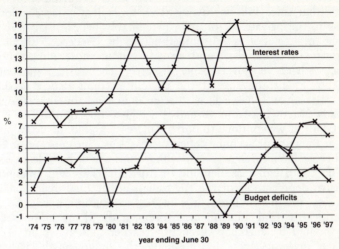

year ending June 30

available to spend on things highly valued by the community. In some countries there are concerns that the public debt is already too high, or that it is growing too rapidly compared to the rate of growth of GDP (so that if it is not too high now it soon will be). Some Australian media commentators have raised fears that our public debt is too large, but few if any economists have. There are simply no grounds for such concerns in Australia. At the end of June 1997 the total net debt of the whole of the Australian public sector (Federal, State and local) was 36 per cent of GDP. This includes debts incurred by publicly owned business enterprises which are not relevant in this context. Excluding debt of such businesses reduces the net debt to 24 per cent of GDP. The average ratio in OECD countries is nearly twice this and some of the countries with which we usually compare ourselves have even higher ratios, e.g. in Canada it is around 60 per cent. Moreover, there is no upward trend in the ratio in Australia. Except for a couple of years in the first half of the 1980s, the ratio of net debt of the general government sector to GDP has been in the range 24 to 30 per cent for two decades. Before that it was higher.

Another reason for concern about budget deficits is sometimes put forward in Australia: the low level of national savings and the implications of this for the current account deficit. For many years now, whenever the Australian economy has grown fast enough to significantly reduce unemployment this has led to large current account deficits on the balance of payments. These measure the amount we borrow from foreigners. Some academic economists argue that since this borrowing from foreigners is largely done by firms in the private sector, who presumably believe that it is profitable to do so, it is not something to be concerned about. The majority of economists, and virtually all of those responsible for policy advice to government, disagree. The basic argument for concern about the size of the current account deficit is simple. Australia already has a large foreign debt, and the amount we are already borrowing from abroad is a high proportion of our output (or GDP). If we continue to borrow increasing amounts from abroad (i.e. if the current account deficit increases as a proportion of GDP), sooner or later foreigners will wonder if we will be able to service the debt and will cease lending to Australia. This will precipitate a massive depreciation of the Australian dollar on foreign exchange markets and hence large falls in real consumption and a rapid, painful structural adjustment. Moreover, the depreciation may be precipitated by currency speculators earlier than it would occur if foreign investors were left to make the judgment themselves. If currency speculators have reason to think that signs of weakness will cause investors to stop lending, a speculative attack is likely to be successful. Although the circumstances are different, the East Asian crisis of 1997/98 is an outstanding example of what can happen. It is better to take now the measures necessary to improve the balance of payments and have a slower adjustment which will be less painful.

The current account deficit is equal to the difference between imports and exports (the trade gap) plus the net amount that Australians pay to foreigners in dividends, interest and gifts. It is also equal to the difference between investment and savings (the savings gap) plus again the net amount paid to foreigners in dividends, interest and gifts. This follows from the definitions of the various items in the national accounts so that when the statistician measures what has happened in the economy the savings gap is the same as the trade gap, and must be so by definition. But what if the trade gap which would result from the plans of participants in the economy does not equal the savings gap which would result from those plans? Will the trade gap change or will the savings gap adjust? The savings gap represents a net supply of foreign currencies and results in an inflow of foreign exchange on the capital account, as foreigners lend us money which helps finance our investment. On the other hand the trade gap is an excess of imports over exports which represents a net demand for foreign currencies to pay for the extra imports. Hence, if the planned trade gap is greater than the planned savings gap this will increase the demand for foreign currency, causing its value to rise or the Australian dollar to depreciate, which in turn will tend to make imports more expensive to Australians and our exports cheaper to foreign buyers. This can be expected to reduce the planned trade gap until it is equal to the savings gap. Conversely, if the planned savings gap is greater than the planned trade gap one would expect the exchange rate to appreciate, which would tend to increase imports and discourage exports, until the planned trade gap increased to equal the savings gap. Thus, in a country like Australia, which has a floating exchange rate, one would expect the savings gap to be the dominant one. No doubt both gaps may change, but there is a market mechanism in existence to ensure that it is mainly the trade gap that changes to bring about the equality between the trade gap and the savings gap.[5]

It follows that, if it is desired to reduce the current account deficit, the size of the savings gap must be reduced. This could be done by decreasing investment, but if this happens output, income and employment will also be depressed. This is why the current account deficit was reduced during the recession at the beginning of the 1990s. If there is to be a rate of economic growth large enough to reduce unemployment at a satisfactory rate, the level of investment will have to be increased not decreased. Hence, a necessary condition of reducing the current account deficit without increasing unemployment is to increase the rate of savings in Australia.

Fiscal policy can be important in achieving this. Not only can particular taxes encourage (or discourage) savings, but savings in the public sector are determined by the size and composition of government expenditure and by the size of government revenues. It is important not to fall into the trap of equating the deficit with public sector dissavings. Savings is the difference between income and consumption, not the difference between revenue and expenditure. Public savings is the difference between public investment and the deficit. Reducing the deficit can increase public savings, but not if it is done by reducing investment expenditure. Investment is necessary in the public sector just as much as in the private sector. (While it is true that there is sometimes wasteful public investment, it is equally true that there is sometimes wasteful private investment.) Fiscal policy can increase national savings by reducing current government expenditure or by increasing taxation. It cannot increase public savings by reducing public investment.

Australian governments have been looking for ways to reduce expenditure for ten years. It is now impossible substantially to reduce government current expenditure without cutting expenditure on things that the majority of Australians think important. If fiscal policy is to make a contribution to increasing savings in Australia,

**Figure 6.2  General government current revenue as a percentage of GDP: various countries 1996**

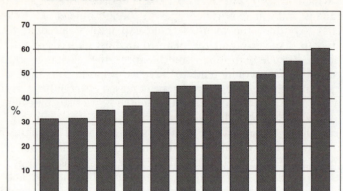

*Source:* OECD Economic Outlook, Dec. 1997

it should come through increasing taxation. Australia has a very low rate of taxation compared to most OECD countries. Figure 6.2 shows that government revenue as a proportion of GDP is only around 35 per cent, which is one of the lowest ratios in the OECD. It is important to increase the savings rate in Australia and fiscal policy can make a major contribution to this, but it will require an increase in taxation rates.

## Fiscal policy, productivity and the supply side

Over the last decade a new strand of thought on fiscal policy has grown up under the label of 'equilibrium fiscal policy'. Neo-classical economists writing on this topic have sidestepped the question of whether fiscal policy can affect aggregate demand, employment and unemployment by assuming that the economy is always in an equilibrium in which all unemployment is voluntary. Anyone who wants a job can always find one and the supply of labour always matches the demand for labour. In such an economy, policy to change aggregate demand through changes in government expenditure and tax rates will have no direct effect on output and employment such as it may have in an economy where there are unemployed unsuccessfully seeking jobs. Even casual empiricism will show that involuntary unemployment does actually exist, thus the theory of equilibrium fiscal policy is not likely to be useful in any analysis of the extent to which fiscal policy can affect aggregate demand. However, its focus on the supply side is a useful corrective to Keynesian fiscal policy and its emphasis on aggregate demand. Starting with the very large rise in oil prices in 1973, a number of events have underlined that supply is important as well as demand. One way of looking at equilibrium fiscal policy is to consider it a broad brush analysis of how fiscal policy affects supply in the longer run when fluctuations in unemployment can be thought to have averaged out.

Although government expenditure on things like education and health is akin to investment expenditure, the focus is on government expenditure in fixed capital equipment. This normally has an immediate effect in increasing the productive potential of the economy. In some cases the increase in production made possible (and assumed to happen in equilibrium fiscal policy writing) can be large. However, this immediate increase in production is not the end of the story. Government expenditure on economic infrastructure, e.g. roads or telecommunications, will raise the productivity of capital in the private sector, increasing the incentive for private investment. This is sometimes called 'crowding' in private investment. The assumption that the economy is always at an equilibrium where there is no involuntary unemployment (or is always at potential output) implies that each unit of public expenditure on fixed capital crowds out a unit of private expenditure. However, the private expenditure that is crowded out does not have to be all investment expenditure. Some may be consumption. Moreover, because total output is increased consumption may not decline in absolute terms even if it declines as a proportion of output because some is crowded out.

Even if private investment expenditure falls by as much as public investment expenditure increases, output will still increase if public capital is more productive, at least at the margin, than private capital. Empirical studies in Australia and the United States suggest that this is the case. In countries where government expenditure on fixed capital has been very large relative to private expenditure, e.g. Japan, private fixed capital is likely to have a higher marginal productivity than public capital, and an increase in public expenditure or fixed capital may not increase potential output. Australia, however, is not Japan. The obvious conclusion from Australian studies is that increasing public expenditure or fixed capital would both increase potential output and increase productivity in the private sector.

Another way in which fiscal policy may affect supply is through taxation rates changing work incentives. Some economists, and many more commentators in the media, argue that high taxation rates and especially high income tax rates, reduce incentives to work, leading to people working less, reducing total output or at least the rate of growth of output.

How much truth is there in this claim? Economic theory gives no answer one way or the other. Higher tax rates will make leisure look more attractive (since it is not taxed), but higher tax rates will reduce disposable incomes, giving an incentive to work longer to maintain a given standard of living. Economic theory can give no indication of which effect is bigger. One has to turn to empirical studies. Not enough empirical work has been done in Australia to enable one to give a confident answer, but a great deal has been done in the USA, and one can give a confident answer about what happens in that country. Things are probably not all that different in Australia. In the USA increasing or decreasing income tax rates have virtually no effect one way or the other on how much primary income earners work. (By 'primary income earner' is meant the main income earner in a family.) These workers are the most skilled and the most productive, the ones most likely to be contributing more to the production of the economy as a whole as well as to the family income. Increasing income tax rates does have a small but noticeable effect on how much secondary income earners work. With increases in tax rates, secondary income earners are likely to work less hours per week or even to drop out of the labour market. This will not have a big effect on the total amount produced. Moreover, some of the work that secondary income earners stop doing when tax rates rise may then be done by some of those currently unemployed. Thus, increasing (or reducing) income tax rates is likely to have little effect on the amount produced.

## Structural deficits

Before reviewing fiscal policy in Australia it is helpful to produce a measure of the stance of fiscal policy: whether it is expansionary, neutral or contractive. Earlier in the chapter it was argued that the most frequently used measure, the size of the budget deficit, can be very misleading. No one measure of the stance of fiscal policy is completely adequate, but probably the structural deficit is the best measure, giving a single number (for each year) by which to measure how much stimulus fiscal policy is giving to the economy.

The structural deficit measures what the size of the deficit would be if the economy were at the normal or desirable level of output which it is the goal of policy to achieve. This, of course, leaves open the question of how high a level of economic activity corresponds to the normal level that is the middle-run to long-run goal of policy. The traditional method is to estimate a trend through years that are judged to be years in which economic activity is at the desirable level. The judgment about what is a desirable level of economic activity may be coloured by the relative weights one gives to the evils of unemployment and inflation. In a commodity-exporting country like Australia, where the constraint on increasing economic activity is often the balance of payments, a judgment about the appropriate level of economic activity to be selected as a longer-run goal of policy also involves a judgment about long-run trends in export prices and other factors influencing the balance of payments.

The estimates of the structural deficit for Australia made in this section assume that in 1987/88 output and income were at the normal or desirable level. If 1973/74 is considered a year in which output was also at the normal level, or even slightly above it, this implies that, since the changes to the world economy following the first oil shock, the Australian economy has had the potential to grow at only 3 per cent p.a. in the long run. Certainly balance of payments figures in recent years suggest that it is not possible to maintain indefinitely a higher level of economic activity than that which occurred in 1987/88 until substantial structural change has taken place in the Australian economy. In 1987/88 unemployment averaged 7.6 per cent. If Australia is to reduce unemployment below this level and to reduce substantially the large number of long-term unemployed, there will have to be a trend rate of growth much greater than 3 per cent p.a. There is some evidence that the structural change necessary to make this possible is occurring, but in a backward looking exercise such as this, it is appropriate to stick to the 3 per cent figure.

In moving from the actual deficit to a structural deficit, adjusting for changes in the level of economic activity (the cyclical adjustment) is not all that is necessary. One also has to make an adjustment for inflation. A small but significant proportion of government expenditure in Australia is interest payments on the public debt. Inflation reduces the real value of government bonds held by the public, as it does the real value of all assets whose value is fixed in nominal terms. When the rate of inflation rises significantly, nominal interest rates also normally rise, though often with a lag. Part of the higher interest rate is a payment for the decline in the real value of the bond or debt. However, the whole of the interest payment on government debt is included in the outlay side of the government budget. The part corresponding to the decline in the real value of government debt held by the public should be excluded; paying this leaves the government no worse off, since it is balanced by the decline in the real value of government debt. Another way of looking at this, which produces the same conclusion, is to argue that the decline in the real value of government bonds held by the public is

a hidden tax caused by inflation and that this 'inflation tax' should
be included in the receipts side of the budget.

The argument that the decline in the real value of government
bonds held by the public should be treated as a tax when calculating
the structural deficit is generally correct, but does depend on the
purpose for which the structural deficit is being used. If, as is
generally the case, it is being used as an indicator of the stance of
fiscal policy with respect to effects on output and hence employment
and other macro variables, the argument is correct as long as people
realise that inflation reduces the real value of government bonds
that they hold. There is econometric evidence that in times of
inflation consumers regard much of their interest receipts as compensation for the effects of inflation on the value of capital lent
(see, for example, Nevile 1983, p.357). Thus, ignoring for the
moment the fact that the whole of interest receipts is taxable income,
that part of interest corresponding to the decline in value of government bonds is not regarded as current income and does not affect
consumption. Since the value of financial capital is maintained
through this part of interest payment, one does not have to consider
further effects on spending of any inflation-caused decline in the
real value of government bonds.

How is the situation changed by the fact that all of interest
receipts are potentially taxable? It is not changed at all, except that
the effective rate of tax on the remainder of income is higher, or
more correctly there is a tax on financial assets with a rate equal
to the product of the marginal tax rate and the rate of inflation.
For this reason disposable income is lowered by inflation, but the
tax that does this is included in receipts as normally measured. In
addition, the inflation tax should still be subtracted from the deficit
since the real value of bonds has declined and the compensating
interest payment is still included in government outlays.

If the structural deficit is being used as a measure of the size
of the call, in normal times, of the government sector on private
sector (or overseas) savings, the situation is a little different. Strictly
speaking the inflation tax still should be treated like a tax, but it
must also be subtracted from private savings when considering the
total amount of savings in the economy. For simplicity and convenience many prefer to ignore the inflation tax in calculating both
the government deficit and private savings; since it is included in
both places it cancels out. The size of the inflation tax is also shown
in Table 6.1, which gives the structural deficit, so the reader can
include it or exclude it as is felt appropriate.

The inflation tax is not just a tax on bonds. While in everyday
life people do not think of currency as part of the government debt,
notes and coins held by the public are actually government liabilities.

**Table 6.1  The structural deficit and its components**
**Australia 1973/74 to 1997/98 (percentages of GDP)**

| | Actual deficit | Cyclical correction | Inflation tax | Structural deficit(a) |
|---|---|---|---|---|
| 1973/74 | 1.4 | –0.3 | 4.7 | –3.0 |
| 1974/75 | 4.1 | 0.4 | 6.8 | –3.1 |
| 1975/76 | 4.2 | 0.4 | 5.1 | –1.3 |
| 1976/77 | 3.5 | 0.5 | 3.7 | –0.7 |
| 1977/78 | 4.9 | 1.4 | 3.2 | 0.3 |
| 1978/79 | 4.8 | 0.7 | 2.8 | 1.4 |
| 1979/80 | 3.6 | 1.0 | 3.6 | –1.0 |
| 1980/81 | 3.1 | 1.0 | 3.6 | –1.5 |
| 1981/82 | 3.4 | 1.2 | 3.4 | –1.2 |
| 1982/83 | 5.7 | 3.1 | 3.9 | –1.3 |
| 1983/84 | 7.0 | 2.0 | 2.6 | 2.5 |
| 1984/85 | 5.3 | 1.0 | 2.6 | 1.7 |
| 1985/86 | 4.9 | 0.4 | 3.8 | 0.7 |
| 1986/87 | 3.8 | 0.6 | 4.1 | –0.9 |
| 1987/88 | 0.6 | –0.1 | 2.9 | –2.2 |
| 1988/89 | –0.9 | –0.6 | 2.8 | –3.0 |
| 1989/90 | 1.0 | –0.6 | 2.2 | –0.7 |
| 1990/91 | 2.3 | 1.3 | 1.6 | –0.6 |
| 1991/92 | 4.4 | 2.4 | 1.0 | 0.9 |
| 1992/93 | 5.5 | 2.5 | 0.9 | 2.1 |
| 1993/94 | 4.5 | 1.9 | 0.8 | 2.0 |
| 1994/95 | 2.8 | 0.9 | 0.5 | 1.3 |
| 1995/96 | 3.4 | 0.5 | 0.8 | 2.1 |
| 1996/97(b) | 2.2 | 0.6 | 0.4 | 1.2 |
| 1997/98(c) | 2.1 | 0.5 | 0.3 | 1.2 |

(a)  Rows may not add to total due to rounding.
(b)  Based in part on preliminary data.
(c)  Based on forward estimates and estimates by the author.
*Sources:* Calculated from figures in various issues of the following: Reserve Bank of Australia, *Bulletin*; Reserve Bank of Australia, Occasional Paper No. 8A Commonwealth of Australia, Budget Statements and Budget Related Paper No. 1; ABS, *Government Financial Estimates, Australia*, Cat. No. 5501.0; ABS, *Public Sector Debt, Australia*, Cat. No. 5513.0; ABS, *State and Local Government Finance, Australia*, Cat. No. 5504.0

Hence the size of the deficit should also be adjusted for the inflation tax on currency. However, the amount involved is not large. In 1996/97 the inflation tax on currency was of the order of 150 million dollars, or less than $\frac{1}{20}$ of 1 per cent of GDP. 1996/97 was a year in which inflation was particularly low, but in the last twenty years the inflation tax on currency has always been well below $\frac{1}{2}$ of 1 per cent of GDP, and usually much smaller than that.

There is one final issue in calculating the structural deficit: what should be done with asset sales? There are good arguments for and against excluding the receipts from asset sales from government revenue. To a large extent the decision whether to do so depends on the purpose for which the estimates of the structural deficit are to be used. There is, however, one very strong argument for excluding the receipts from asset sales when these are large. The use of a figure for the structural deficit usually has the strong implication that, if the economy is at the 'normal' level of output and the deficit is at an appropriate level, the budget deficit can continue indefinitely without any problems. Since a large volume of asset sales cannot continue indefinitely, it is usually not appropriate to include the returns from asset sales when calculating the structural deficit.

This is particularly the case when one is concerned about the deficit as a measure of the public sector call on private sector savings. The sale of assets to Australians does not change the call of the public sector on private sector savings. The sale of assets to foreigners is not so straightforward but, except in the short run, it too has no effect on the appropriate level of savings in the private sector. Changing an asset from one form (e.g. business) to another form (e.g. cash) has no direct effect on savings. Nor does selling assets to foreigners have any immediate effect on the current account deficit of the balance of payments. Unless the proceeds of asset sales to foreigners are used in ways that increase exports or reduce imports, such sales will have a detrimental effect on the balance of payments in the longer run. However, selling assets to foreigners may help support the exchange rate in the short run.

The sale of assets is excluded from the figures for the structural deficit shown in Table 6.1. In this table both the cyclical adjustment and the inflation tax are subtracted from the actual deficit to get the structural deficit. The table is for the consolidated accounts of all three levels of government: Federal, State and local.

## Fiscal policy in Australia

Table 6.1 documents a very remarkable aspect of Australian fiscal policy—there has been a structural surplus in the large majority of years since 1973/74. Despite this there are constant calls by influential groups for tighter fiscal policy, even in recessions. For example, in 1992, in the midst of the worst slump in the twentieth century after the Great Depression of the 1930s the Business Council of Australia argued that: 'it is essential that the broad fiscal objective for the Commonwealth in 1992/93 should be to exercise prudent management and to reduce Government outlays. This would bring the Commonwealth budget deficit to about 2 per cent of GDP'.

This raises two questions. First, has there been a bias towards tight fiscal policy in Australia over the last two decades? Second, why do so many business organisations and media commentators call so often for tighter fiscal policy?

Even before 1973/74 Australia had relatively tight fiscal policy

**Figure 6.3  Structural deficits as a percentage of GDP and unemployment**

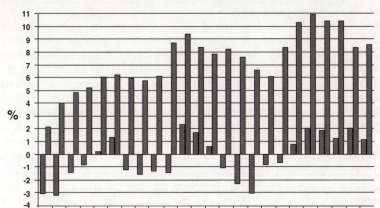

year ending 30 June

though it was relaxed during recessions. Tight fiscal policy was appropriate in most years before then because of the low level of unemployment, but after that date fiscal policy should have been used to reduce unemployment when it rose sharply. Did this happen?

Figure 6.3 shows the structural deficit and unemployment for the years 1973/74 to 1994/95. Before 1983 fiscal policy responded only mildly to changes in unemployment. In 1983/84, in response to the severe recession that developed in 1982/83, there was a substantial structural deficit which was gradually eliminated over the next three years. In response to the even worse slump that developed over 1990/91, there was again a structural deficit in 1991/92, but it was only 0.9 per cent of GDP compared with a 2.5 per cent structural deficit in 1983/84. In 1992/93 the structural deficit rose to 2.1 per cent. It was nearly three years after the recession started before there was an adequate response in the fiscal policy area.

Why was fiscal policy so slow to respond adequately to the recession and what were the reasons that some argued that it should be tighter in 1992/93 than it was in 1991/92?

Some commentators argue that expansionary fiscal policy is ineffective because it crowds out so much private sector expenditure that there is likely to be no net effect on output. To argue this in the 1990s is to allow ideology to blind one to the facts. The arguments and supporting statistics against crowding out, set out earlier in the chapter, were well known at the time. Moreover, international responses to the last major world recession, that of 1982, have shown that expansionary fiscal policy was effective. A number of countries, notably the United States and Australia, adopted expansionary fiscal policy with large budget deficits. These were precisely the countries in which employment expanded strongly and the unemployment rate fell substantially. By contrast, in countries with less expansionary fiscal policy unemployment fell only very slowly. For example, in the United States the unemployment rate was 9.5 per cent in 1983 and 5.4 per cent in 1988, whereas in Germany the unemployment rate was 8.2 per cent in 1983 and it was still 7.6 per cent in 1988. The crowding out argument is no longer credible.

Others argued in 1992, and still argue, that one must be very cautious about any stimulus to the economy through fiscal policy in case it increases inflationary pressure. It is true that unemployment is a very powerful weapon against inflation. Anything, including expansionary fiscal policy, which reduces unemployment thereby increases, however slightly, the chance of a rise in the inflation rate. It seems odd, however, to worry about this at a time when the rate of inflation is at a very low level by the standards of the last 25 years and the rate of unemployment is still far too high. Nevertheless, it is true that there are some people who always argue that greater priority should be given to controlling inflation than to reducing unemployment. Some may be motivated by knowledge of the effects of very high inflation rates in other countries, but one cannot help noting that generally people who argue thus are neither unemployed nor likely to become unemployed.

The final argument against expansionary fiscal policy flows from concern with the balance of payments and the current account deficit. Increasing taxation and/or cutting government current outlays will reduce the savings gap and reduce the current account deficit. This does not mean that expansionary fiscal policy is never appropriate. In a recession it is usually more important to reduce unemployment than to reduce the current account deficit, which has probably already fallen as the result of the recession. If despite high unemployment the balance of payments situation is very bad, which it was not in 1992 and 1993, some stimulus can be given to the economy by increasing both government expenditure and taxation without increasing the savings gap. The balance of payments constraint does not provide a valid argument against using expansionary fiscal policy in a severe recession.

Nevertheless, the balance of payments argument against expansionary fiscal policy does reflect a major problem facing the Australian economy. In the earlier section on national savings and the current account deficit, theoretical arguments led to the conclusion that fiscal policy did have a role to play in increasing national savings when this was necessary, and that in Australia the appropriate

**Figure 6.4 Savings by sector as a percentage of GDP**

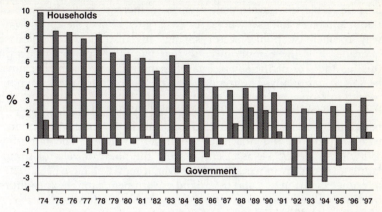

way to do this involved increasing taxation. The following paragraphs will look at the actual situation in the second half of the 1990s to assess how important it is for fiscal policy to be used to increase national savings.

The Australian Bureau of Statistics gives figures for savings in Australia by three sectors: the corporate sector (including public trading enterprises), the household sector and the general government sector. Apart from increases in the provisions it makes for income tax, the corporate sector rarely saves much. Similarly, the amount it dissaves is usually small and the sector is not of great consequence as far as savings is concerned. Figure 6.4 shows savings by the household sector and general government. It is noticeable that, for reasons already set out in the section on national savings and the current account deficit, the figures for general government dissavings are quite different from those for the budget deficit.

Both household and government savings show a definite cyclical pattern with savings being smaller (or dissavings greater) during recessions. However, there is a strong downward trend in household savings. Government savings show increasing fluctuations but no clear trend. In each succeeding recession dissavings are greater, but in the boom at the end of the 1980s positive savings were much greater than in previous booms.

Given the downward trend in household savings, it is not surprising that, except in recessions, when investment is low, there has been a large savings gap and large current account deficits. Household savings has always been larger than government savings and the important thing is to reverse the downward trend in household savings. The introduction of compulsory superannuation will achieve this, but only in the long run. At least for the next five to ten years it is desirable for government savings to increase over the cycle of boom and recession as a whole. As was argued above, the appropriate way to increase public sector savings in Australia is to increase taxation. It is the Commonwealth that has the responsibility to do this, as the size of the savings gap is a national problem that must be solved nationally. The trend, however, has been for the Commonwealth to reduce taxation, not increase it. In 1986/87 Commonwealth budget revenue was 27.8 per cent of GDP. This had declined to 25.9 per cent by 1989/90, and to 23.5 per cent in 1992/93. After that it rose slightly but did not reach the 1989/90 figure. The fall from 1989/90 to 1992/93 was desirable from the point of view of stimulating an economy in recession. However, it may well have been better to reduce taxation less and to expand government capital expenditure over these three years. (In fact public capital expenditure fell between 1989/90 and 1992/93.) In any case, whenever the Australian economy is growing rapidly the first priority of fiscal policy should be to increase taxation and public sector savings.

The fall in government expenditure on fixed capital between 1989/90 and 1992/93 is part of a pronounced downward trend in the ratio of this variable to GDP over the last twenty years. In the five years to 1976/77 government expenditure on fixed capital averaged 8.6 per cent of GDP. In the five years to 1996/97 it averaged only 4.2 per cent of GDP. Some of the decline is due to privatisation of public enterprises—but this is less than half. One of the biggest failures of fiscal policy in recent years has been the large reduction in public capital expenditure which resulted from the desire to reduce budget deficits in the least politically painful way. The longer this goes on the worse the prospects for future living standards in Australia. The need to raise public sector capital expenditure adds to the pressing need to increase taxation revenue in Australia.

## Recommended reading

Chand, Sheetal K. (1977) 'Summary measures of fiscal influence', *International Monetary Fund Staff Papers*, July.

Eisner, Robert (1994–95), 'Keynes is not dead, just drugged and dormant', *Journal of Post Keynesian Economics*, Winter.

Indecs (1995) *State of Play 8*, Chapter 9, Allen and Unwin, Sydney.

Nevile, J.W. (1987) 'Can expansionary fiscal policy increase employment' in Philip Maxwell (ed.), *Macroeconomics: Contemporary Australian Readings*, Harper & Row, Sydney.

Perkins, J.O.N. (1995) 'On the dangers of targeting the budget deficit', *The Economic and Labour Relations Review*, June.

Pressman, Steven (1995) 'Deficits, full employment and the use of fiscal policy', *Review of Political Economy*.

# 7 Money and monetary policy
## Mark Crosby and Ross Milbourne[1]

> Proof begins with the people who manage money. If anything is
> evident from this history, it is that the task attracts a very low level
> of talent, one that is protected in its highly imperfect profession by
> the mystery that is thought to enfold the subject of economics in
> general and of money in particular. (*Money: Whence it Came,
> Where it Went*, J.K.Galbraith, 1975, p.302)

In this chapter we will attempt to unravel the mysteries of monetary
economics. In particular, we examine the role played by money and
credit in the Australian economy. The Australian economy would
be very difficult to imagine without money or credit, and here we
focus on a small number of questions about the role that money
plays. These questions are: How important are the levels of the
money supply and the level of interest rates in the economy? What
is the role played by the Reserve Bank of Australia (RBA) in the
setting of the money supply and interest rates in Australia? How
important is monetary policy in determining output growth, unemployment, and inflation in Australia? What is the role played by
other financial institutions (such as banks) in the Australian
economy?

The financial sector in Australia, which includes institutions
such as banks, credit unions, building societies, mutual funds and
finance and insurance companies, performs two major roles. First,
it channels funds from lenders to borrowers. To do this an institution must assess the credit risks of those to whom it lends, and
charge appropriate interest rates on the basis of the risk of the loan

and its maturity (length of time). Second, some of these institutions, mainly banks, form a central part of the payments mechanism. Banks accept deposits from clients which are accessed through cheques for payment purposes, and transfers of funds are accomplished by transfers between the banks.

The role of monetary policy is to oversee the operation of the financial sector, and to ensure that the levels of credit and of interest rates maximise the welfare of the people of Australia. Intervention in financial markets by governments, through their central banks, is undertaken in almost all countries. A key question facing economists is whether governments should intervene in financial markets or leave the markets to themselves (a policy of *laissez-faire*). The two main arguments for intervention are (i) that the payments system is too important to let suffer from potential failure through imprudent banking practices by institutions; and (ii) that unregulated credit expansions or contractions could lead to more severe episodes of inflation and deeper recessions, thus worsening the business cycle.

In Australia, the RBA oversees monetary policy. The RBA, in its charter (1987, p.8), is entrusted

> to ensure that the monetary and banking policy of the Bank is directed to the greatest advantage of the people of Australia . . . [and] best contributes to:
>
> (a) the stability of the economy;
> (b) the maintenance of full employment in Australia; and
> (c) the economic prosperity and welfare of the people of Australia.

The RBA attempts to meet its charter through two main types of policies: prudential regulations on banks to protect them from insolvency and maintain confidence in the financial system;[2] and monetary policy that is designed to influence the level of credit in the economy via its price (the rate of interest). It is monetary policy which receives the most attention, and financial markets keenly await announcements of Reserve Bank policy.

## Goals of monetary policy

The RBA must decide what are its primary goals. The charter has been interpreted to imply that the RBA should have three main concerns: the rate of inflation, the rate of unemployment, and the level and growth of national income. The RBA charter was established at a time when full employment was the norm, with unemployment rates of 1 per cent or less. Over the past decade the rate of unemployment has generally hovered between 6 per cent and

10 per cent.[3] The rate of unemployment is related to the rate of economic growth because a higher rate of income growth usually creates higher employment growth. However, if the RBA overly stimulates economic growth, the likely outcome will be too high a rate of inflation. Thus, crudely put, central banks must try a balancing act in the short run between inflation and economic growth. If the RBA causes interest rates to be set consistently too low (loose monetary policy) inflation will eventually rise, while if interest rates are set too high (tight monetary policy) economic growth will be stifled.

If the RBA decides on an expansionary monetary policy, it lowers interest rates, which encourages borrowing for housing and business investment. This increases spending and income. However, the increased demand for goods and services is likely to lead to price rises, so that an expansionary monetary policy is also likely to increase the rate of inflation. Thus, at any time, the monetary policy choice of the RBA will depend on the state of the economy and on whether reducing inflation or stimulating income growth is the short-term goal.

There is some debate about which goal of monetary policy is most important. Those who are concerned mostly with inflation argue that monetary policy should be directed only towards inflation and not towards stabilising income and employment over the business cycle. Those who are concerned with income and employment generally argue that the stance of monetary policy should be expansionary in recessions and contractionary in booms. Such a policy, if successful, would reduce the amplitude of business cycles. This policy is called fine-tuning, so an alternative way to classify monetary policy is in the extent to which fine-tuning occurs over the course of a business cycle. Like many other central banks, the RBA has in recent times been focussing more on maintaining low inflation, and less on fine-tuning. This reflects a belief that fine-tuning is difficult, and also that low inflation should hopefully create an environment which encourages growth and reduces unemployment. If this is the case then low inflation should of itself reduce the amplitude of the business cycle.

## Indicators of monetary policy

How do we know whether monetary policy is currently expansionary or contractionary? It turns out that what matters is not just the level of interest rates and of credit, but also the relationship between interest rates and the inflation rate. The two main indicators that have been used to describe the stance of monetary policy are monetary aggregates and interest rates. There are a number of different measures of both.

*Monetary aggregates*

During the 1970s and early 1980s many central banks, including the RBA, at some stage tried to target the supply of money. The hope was that if money growth could be kept low and relatively constant, inflation would fall and a stable macroeconomic policy environment would be created. One difficulty in implementation of money targets is that there are a number of potential definitions of the money supply which could be targeted. One definition of the money stock is the monetary base, which is directly under the control of the RBA. Another definition is the total amount of funds easily available to be spent (or liquidity), in this case currency plus demand deposits. Thus M1 = C + D is one standard definition of the money stock, and is often referred to as *narrow money*. A broader definition of the money stock is M3 = C + D + T (that is, currency plus total bank deposits).[4]

Because non-bank financial intermediaries (NBFIs) also accept deposits from the public, a further definition of the money stock is *broad money*, defined as M3 plus the deposit holdings by NBFIs of the non-bank private sector. (In February 1998 these NBFI deposit holdings were $65 185 million.) The different money stock estimates, as at February 1998, were (in seasonally adjusted $million):

| | | | |
|---|---|---|---|
| Currency | 20 889 | Currency | 20 889 |
| + | | + | |
| Bank reserves at RBA | 8 817 | Demand deposits | 84 795 |
| **M0** | **= 29 706** | **M1** | **= 105 684** |
| | | + | |
| | | Time deposits | 227 470 |
| | | **M3** | **= 333 155** |
| | | + | |
| | | Deposits at NBFIs | 65 185 |
| | | **Broad money** | **= 398 340** |

M0 is under the direct control of the RBA. Note, however, that M0 is only a small proportion of M3 (less than 10 per cent); the difference between M3 and M1 (roughly $290 billion) is generated through the credit-creating activities of the banks. It is this level of credit creation that the RBA attempts to influence.

The RBA can potentially control the level of credit and broad money in the economy through the appropriate provision of the money base to the banking system. If the RBA were to reduce the amount of currency available to the banking system, some banks would find their reserves lower, and these banks would tend to

**Figure 7.1a  The relationship between selected interest rates**

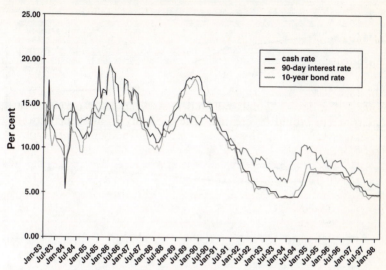

reduce the amount of new loans provided. Hence the RBA can control credit, though only indirectly, through control of bank reserves. If banks allowed their reserves to fall when the RBA reduced the money base, then the supply of credit in the economy would not change as a result of the reduction in base money. For this reason the RBA now attempts to influence credit by setting its price, in other words the rate of interest.

*Interest rates*

The RBA sets an operating target for the overnight cash rate, which is the interest rate on overnight loans made between institutions in the money market. The RBA Board specifies the required target for the cash rate, which then influences other interest rates in the economy. Figure 7.1a shows that there is a strong relationship between most interest rates, especially among interest rates of shorter maturity after 1990. Changes in the cash rate indicate changes in the stance of monetary policy, with rises in the cash rate being tightenings of monetary policy, and falls in the cash rate being easings.

There is a difficulty in inferring the stance of monetary policy from the level of the cash rate. This is because a cash rate of 10 per cent in a time of low inflation is much less expansionary than a cash rate of 10 per cent when inflation is high (say also 10 per cent). The interest rate that is relevant to borrowers and

**Figure 7.1b  The yield curve for three different periods**

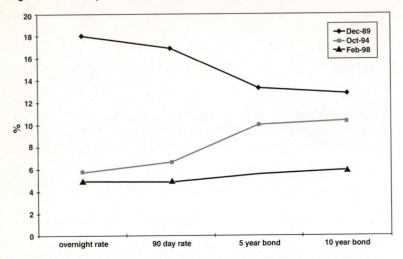

lenders is the *real interest rate*, defined as the nominal interest rate minus the (expected) rate of inflation.[5] High real interest rates reflect tight monetary policy, while low real interest rates indicate that monetary policy is loose. Figure 7.1a shows that the real interest rate (defined here as the cash rate minus the inflation rate) was very high in the late 1980s, but has declined since.

Another indicator of the stance of monetary policy is the slope of the *yield curve*. The yield curve is the graph of interest rates of different maturities. When short-term interest rates (such as the cash rate) are below long-term interest rates (such as ten-year bonds), the yield curve is upward sloping. A downward sloping yield curve, on the other hand, reflects the belief that interest rates and inflation will fall in the future, and is an indicator that monetary policy is tight. Figure 7.1b shows the graph of the yield curve in three different months. In late 1989 the yield curve was downward sloping, indicating that monetary policy was tight, while in 1994 and 1998 the yield curve was upward sloping.

## The operation of monetary policy

Once each month the Reserve Bank Board meets and decides on any changes in *monetary policy*. It considers a variety of data, including the current rates of unemployment, inflation and output

**Table 7.1  The transmission mechanism of monetary policy**

| | | aggregate → demand | output, labour market | → | prices |
|---|---|---|---|---|---|
| cash rate → | other interest → rates → | exchange rate intermediaries' balance sheets | | → → | output, prices monetary aggregates |

(target variables), as well as economic variables which help to provide some information on future trends in the target variables. Because changes in monetary policy are thought to affect the economy only with a lag, the RBA Board must guess what is likely to happen in the economy 12–18 months ahead. Variables useful in this prediction include the economic prospects of our major trading partners, overseas interest rates (which may affect the exchange rate), leading indicators of economic activity (such as housing starts), and leading indicators of inflation (e.g. wages growth and import prices).

Since January 1990 the RBA has followed such meetings with an announcement about the target cash rate. Thus, not only is the RBA Board affecting the overnight interest rate but it is also sending a signal to the market; the market would then fully expect other short-term interest rates to fall into line with this cash rate. As a consequence longer-term interest rates change insofar as they are determined by current short-term rates and the future expectation of short-term rates.

## The transmission mechanism of monetary policy

Table 7.1 (used in Milbourne 1990) gives a schematic view of the general transmission mechanism of monetary policy (i.e. the way in which RBA policy affects the economy) inherent in most theories. The cash rate and announcements of the RBA's intentions are used to influence other market interest rates. These affect aggregate demand, and thus output, employment and prices.

The main effect on aggregate demand is through investment, which is regarded as being sensitive to interest rates. A higher interest rate depresses aggregate demand, which leads to a reduction in output and thus to a reduction in the demand for labour by firms. This is then expected to have a moderating effect on price increases and thus to slow the rate of inflation.

A loosening of monetary policy involves a reduction in the cash rate, which should feed through to other interest rates. This should result, other things being equal, in an outflow of capital from Australia to countries where interest rates are higher, resulting in a reduction in the demand for Australian dollars on foreign exchange markets. The result is a depreciation of the currency; this makes imports more expensive in Australian dollars, and makes Australian exports more competitive in world markets. In addition, as much of Australia's exports are in agriculture and minerals, the prices of which are denominated in foreign currency (mostly $US), the income of exporters will rise. These factors lead to a rise in Australian spending and production and, eventually, to a rise in the price level. These theories have become more important since foreign exchange markets have been deregulated. Under fixed exchange rates, capital flows did not lead to changes in the exchange rate, and the influence of monetary policy on the economy was small.

## Theories of monetary policy

There are differing views among economists on the appropriate conduct of monetary policy. Keynesian theories were born out of the idea that governments should pursue active income stabilisation policies. In this way it was hoped to reduce the volatility of output over the business cycle. This is often referred to as *activist monetary policy*, or fine-tuning, with a general view that policy should be at the discretion of the government which should try and minimise the impact of different shocks which hit the economy.

The Keynesian theory was the popular view on the role of monetary policy until challenged by Milton Friedman (1968) in his presidential address to the American Economics Association. Friedman argued that governments or central banks should keep the money supply to a constant rate of growth, irrespective of the state of the business cycle. This approach was termed *monetarist*, but was the continuation of an argument advocated prior to Keynes by classical economists (whose views Keynes attacked).

The monetarist argument against an activist approach is that the lags involved in monetary policy are so great, and in Friedman's view so variable, that activist policy might be counterproductive. Expansionary monetary policies implemented now might raise economic activity in the economy in 18 months' or two years' time, when the economy might be going into a boom and the business cycle would be exacerbated rather than improved. In addition, many classical economists argue that even the best-intentioned governments get it wrong. Classical economists assume that a certain amount of unemployment (called the natural rate) is a feature of any economy with flows into and out of the workforce, and that attempts to reduce unemployment below this natural rate will simply involve inflation rather than any positive effects on economic activity. In this scenario, classical economists argue that it is more likely that monetary authorities will lead us towards excessive rates of inflation.[6]

Another view was put forward by Robert Lucas (1972), who argued that people would come to anticipate the increased inflation from a monetary expansion, so that the monetary expansion would have no effect on real income or employment. This is termed the *rational expectations* hypothesis, and yields the same policy conclusion as that of Friedman: attempts to use monetary policy in a counter-cyclical fashion will be to no avail.

More recently both academic economists (for example, see Goodhart 1994) and central banks have come to the view that the monetarist and the Keynesian views are both overly optimistic about the role that monetary policy can play in the economy. The Keynesian view that the economy can be stabilised by pre-emptive monetary policy relies on the central bank accurately forecasting the course of the economy in the medium term. Despite advances in the econometric modelling of the economy, this has proved very difficult. The monetarist view that money growth should be kept constant relies on a constant relationship between money base and the broader money aggregates. Experience with money targeting found that this relationship was unstable, so that it was very difficult to control the growth of broad money aggregates. For these reasons many central banks, including the RBA, now rely on an inflation target as the key to monetary policy. Interest rates are targeted in such a way that inflation is kept low.

In Australia the RBA argues that its principal contribution in the achievement of long-term output growth is to keep inflation low—the inflation target is currently 2–3 per cent on average. Over the course of the 1990s the RBA has been very successful in meeting this target. Inflation has averaged 2.25 per cent in the five years to 1997, while average growth in real output has averaged 3.5 per cent. This suggests that the level of talent in the RBA is perhaps high enough to cast doubt on the claim made by Galbraith in the quotation.

## Australian empirical evidence

What is the evidence on the effects of monetary policy? The first thing to note (Figure 7.1a) is the relatively close correlation between the cash rate and other interest rates, especially short-term interest rates. Longer-term rates tend to be 'smooth' relative to short-term rates but are affected by changes in policy. Thus it would appear that the RBA does influence interest rates, especially in the short term.

Figures 7.2 and 7.3a, b plot the growth rate of real income (gross national expenditure, or GNE) against the rate of growth M3

**Figure 7.2  The growth rate of M3 versus the rate of growth of real GDP**

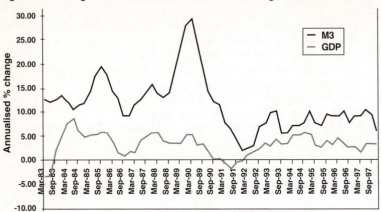

(Figure 7.2) and the nominal (Figure 7.3a) and real cash rate (Figure 7.3b). Figure 7.2 shows that there is some sort of relationship between M3 growth and income growth, but the relationship is not one that is useful for policy. To be a useful predictor, M3 has to *lead* real income (i.e. variations in income). The evidence since 1983 is that income leads M3, certainly at the turning points. This is supported by statistical evidence from research conducted at the Reserve Bank,[7] which finds that both M3 and broader monetary aggregates (which include deposits at NBFIs) lag behind both nominal and real income. Thus, changes in income seem to generate changes in money holdings and/or credit creation but not *vice versa*.

Figures 7.3a and 7.3b show a generally *positive* relationship between the growth rate of real income and the cash rate and real cash rate respectively. This almost certainly reflects the RBA response to the business cycle, in which the RBA raises interest rates to counteract booms and lowers interest rates to counteract recessions. Because of the lags in monetary policy, one way of seeing whether there is any effect of monetary policy on income is to compare the nominal cash rate with the income growth rate six quarters later.[8] This is done in Figure 7.4, which shows a generally negative relationship between the cash rate and the rate of income growth six quarters later. Of special note is the strong relationship between the cash rate rise starting in early 1988 and peaking in early 1990 (which is put 'ahead' six quarters to appear in mid-1989 to mid-1991 in Figure 7.4) and the following recession ('the recession we had to have'), beginning in the second half of 1989.

How are monetary variables related to the rate of inflation?

**Figure 7.3a  The growth rate of real income versus the nominal cash rate**

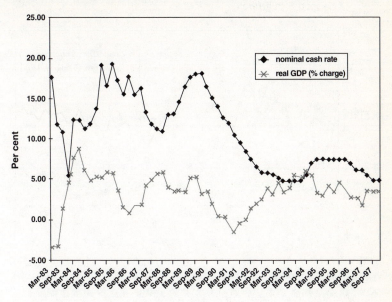

**Figure 7.3b  The growth rate of real income versus the real cash rate**

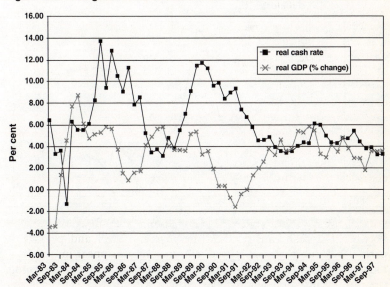

**Figure 7.4   The growth rate of real income versus the nominal cash rate lagged 6 quarters**

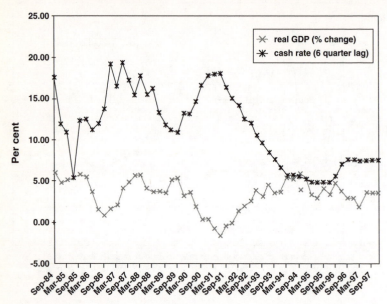

**Figure 7.5   The growth rate M3 versus the rate of inflation (change in the GDP deflator)**

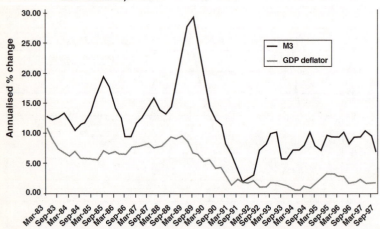

This is an important part of the monetarist story. Figure 7.5 plots the rate of inflation against the growth rate of M3. There is not much connection between the two. Of course, monetary policy might affect inflation with a lag—although, if so, the transmission would not appear to be through economic activity. This lack of correlation is reflected in more sophisticated statistical tests which allow for lagged relationships. Carmichael (1990) finds that wages growth, changes in the terms of trade and other cost factors have been more responsible for inflation than has monetary growth. This is not a definite conclusion: it could be that expectations of continuing and/or high rates of monetary growth conditioned wages growth, and thus a deeper explanation of the inflation of the 1980s in Australia may go back to monetary growth. This money–wages–inflation story is somewhat harder to accept from the mid-1980s, when the Accord played a role in the significant reductions in both real and nominal wage growth.

On the evidence presented above, there is some empirical support for a connection between interest rates and subsequent economic growth (roughly six quarters later). However, money growth does not appear to be closely related to output growth or inflation over any horizon which might be useful for the conduct of monetary policy.

## The evolution of RBA policy

The lack of consensus about the appropriate role of money and its effect on the economy, and the lack of solid empirical support for one or other theory, has made framing policy difficult. At the risk of oversimplification, the philosophy behind the conduct of monetary policy has gone through three distinct phases since 1975 (prior to which the Reserve Bank followed a somewhat Keynesian stabilisation approach).

In 1977 the RBA announced that it was moving towards monetary targeting by setting upper and lower bounds for the growth rate of the money supply (M3). This approach followed the *new classical theory* whereby it was hoped that announcements of the future rate of monetary growth would condition expectations of inflation and allow inflation to be reduced without causing a recession. However, the actual rates of monetary growth did not stay within the target range, in part for the reasons noted above, creating a credibility problem for the RBA. It was hoped that deregulation in 1983, which would put banks on a more competitive footing with the NBFIs, would bring stability to bank deposits and monetary aggregates and allow for less variability in these monetary aggregates. This did not occur, and the RBA formally abolished monetary targeting in 1985.

Following the abolition of monetary targeting, the RBA announced that its philosophy was to establish a check list of variables, which would be used to determine the stance of monetary policy. The list was never published, and commentators on Reserve Bank policy have argued that over various periods of time more weight has been given to some variables than others. This philosophy is a more Keynesian stabilisation approach, but with variables other than income as part of the objective. In the 1985/86 period the variable that the RBA was most interested in stabilising was believed to be the exchange rate; subsequent emphasis passed to the level of income, and finally to the rate of inflation. Concern with bringing down the rate of inflation and the rising level of foreign debt finally prompted the RBA to raise nominal interest rates in the period 1988/89.[9]

As discussed in Chapter 4, the great output growth decline began in 1989, and Australia went into a long recession. A number of factors contributed to this decline, most notably the adverse terms of trade situation in those years, but controversy remains on what role the sustained high interest rates had in dampening economic activity. Until further econometric evidence is assembled on this it would be difficult to assign the relative contributions. Needless to say, many economists believe that the high interest rates did contribute to the subsequent decline of output. This recession has been bad for income and employment, but it may have resurrected a belief in the importance and potency of monetary policy at a time when its role and importance were being questioned.

## Current Reserve Bank policy

Since 1990 the Reserve Bank has moved to a newly defined philosophy on monetary policy and a new operating procedure. The philosophy is that the RBA is now officially concerned with the rate of inflation, and in particular with protecting the current low rate of inflation over a medium-term perspective. However, it has maintained that it will continue to monitor developments in the Australian economy and operate on the cash rate if it feels conditions warrant this. Important here is the philosophical move more in the direction of the classical view of the economy—stabilisation policy would now involve changes in the cash rate only when there were major fluctuations in the economy, rather than continuous attempts to fine-tune.

RBA policy on inflation was given more precision in April 1993, when the Governor[10] indicated a desire to keep the underlying rate of inflation between 2 per cent and 3 per cent over the cycle. (The underlying rate of inflation is the consumer price index stripped of one-off factors such as temporary agricultural price variations or government price changes.) The interpretation of this was that the

RBA would raise interest rates if the rate of inflation rose above 3 per cent and lower them when inflation fell below 2 per cent.

There are two points to note here. First, it might seem odd to choose 2 per cent as a minimum. (Why not 0 per cent?) The reason is that most measures of the rate of inflation contain an upward bias because they generally do not take full account of improvements in the quality of goods.[11] Also, with a wages system which makes nominal wages rigid in a downwards direction, a moderate rate of inflation is the only way to achieve relative movements in real wages between occupations. As a former RBA governor put it, 'a little inflation greases the wheels'.

The second point is: why would the RBA publicly tie itself to such a rule? The answer is that in doing so the RBA is seeking credibility with both unions and the financial markets. Financial market participants generally like low and stable inflation because they believe that the greater certainty in planning by businesses is a key to stronger economic growth. Thus the RBA is trying to convince the community of its commitment to low inflation. The hope is that if unions and workers can be convinced of low and stable inflation, they might moderate their wage demands and thus produce a lower actual rate of inflation.

Are commitments to both low inflation and stabilisation policy necessarily compatible? Provided the RBA 'gets it right' and knows the natural level of employment or output around which it wishes to stabilise those variables, the two are not necessarily incompatible. When the economy is in recession, or above the average or natural level of unemployment, the RBA can usually afford some stimulation of the economy without threatening the inflation target. The risk to this strategy is that if the RBA does not have good information on the appropriate level of unemployment or output, or if market participants believe that it does not, this could prolong high inflation or high unemployment.

## Prudential regulation

In addition to setting the cash rate the RBA currently plays a role of regulator of the banking system. This role is about to be taken over by the Australian Prudential Regulatory Authority which will in the main have the same aims as the RBA regarding prudential regulation.[12] Banks play a special role in the economy because they are the only set of institutions whose actions can be directly influenced by monetary policy. Historically, this arrangement developed because banks play a key role in the payments-clearing mechanism. A failure to honour payments by one of the banks would not only severely endanger the payments mechanism, but might precipitate a bank run (a withdrawal of deposits from other banks), causing severe financial distress on other banks as well. This externality or spillover effect is what most central banks attempt to avoid through prudential regulation. A loss of confidence in the banking system can have severe effects on the real economy: the best examples of this occurred in Australia in 1891/93, and in the USA in 1931/33, where major bank failures were associated with severe economic depressions.

In order to monitor the financial health of banks, the RBA currently requires adequate disclosure by banks of their activities, especially their risk-management strategies. In addition, the RBA has imposed capital adequacy ratios on banks. This follows trends in other OECD countries, and is related to the belief that sufficient bank capital (i.e. equity of its shareholders) can be used in the last resort as a means to finance substantial bank losses. The capital adequacy ratio is defined on a risk-weighted basis, with more risky bank assets receiving a higher weighting (i.e. requiring more capital to be held). Currently, banks are required to hold a minimum level of bank capital which is 8 per cent of risk-weighted assets.[13]

## Conclusions

Monetary policy is conducted in Australia by the RBA. Over the twenty-plus years since Galbraith rebuked central bankers, monetary policy has undergone a number of changes. Galbraith was concerned that central banks were not doing enough to reduce fluctuations in the economy. Many central banks now are of the view that the best way for monetary policy to reduce business cycle fluctuations is to create a stable financial environment, the key to which is low and stable inflation. The 1990s have so far been a period of low inflation and satisfactory economic growth. The question now becomes whether this growth will continue so that unemployment will continue to fall. Certainly the hope is that this is the case.

# 8 Public expenditure: Taming Leviathan for the next millennium?

*Peter Groenewegen*

Public expenditure is often in the news, generally in a controversial manner. Threats of expenditure cuts, say in an area of health, or law and order, or education, invariably lead to an outcry in the community. It is not only the consumers (clients) of the reduced, or discontinued, service who are affected. The producers, whether in the medical profession, the police, corrective services staff or teachers' federation, will also volubly object. Increases in public expenditure tend to receive an equally negative airing in the media. Although beneficiaries drawn from producers and consumers will generally welcome the change, particularly if there are increased jobs attached, critics will also abound. They will point to the dangers of expenditure growth returning the government to deficit, affecting the national debt, the savings ratio and the foreign trade balance, bemoaning the event as yet a further sign of the resilience of 'big government' and the difficulties of containing 'Leviathan'. Yet few would argue that public expenditure is unnecessary. Some argue that it is a force for civilisation. Most voters, if asked, support increases to public expenditures on things they regard as useful (education, health, transport) even if, perish the thought, it means more taxation.

The media attention on public expenditure changes suggests both its importance and its controversial nature. Its importance can be indicated by a simple statistic—its share in Gross Domestic Product (GDP) or national output. In 1994/95, outlays for general government, or spending by governments on goods and services and on 'transfer payments' such as pensions, unemployment benefits and subsidies, were estimated to take 36.1 per cent of GDP. If outlays from public trading enterprises (such as government owned public transport, State owned financial institutions and public utilities) are added, the outlays from the public sector total 35.7 per cent of GDP for 1995/96. Although this ratio had fallen from a peak of 42.6 per cent in 1985/86, many still consider this demand on the nation's resources to be excessive. They seek to further curtail it by cutting public expenditure and by privatising government enterprises, the main way in which the Australian public sector has been reduced over the last decade relative to GDP. Others see the public sector as too small. They point to poor government supplied infrastructure and inadequate service provision. The last is reflected in long waiting lists for elective surgery and long queues for public housing, and in the substantial prevalence of poverty in an otherwise wealthy society, which can only be countered by better social welfare provision. The long-term outlook of the 1998/99 Budget strategy indicates a continuing trend in declining public sector size relative to GDP.

It is possible to say that these extreme opinions are more wrong than right. Both paint the public expenditure problem in far too simplistic a way. The appropriate size of public expenditure is never a simple black and white problem; there are a variety of satisfactory possibilities in this aspect of social choice. To be able to assess these issues more fairly and more comprehensively, complex political economy principles of public expenditure have to be grasped. An outline of the major elements required for such understanding is given in what follows. This in turn looks at some definitional issues, measurement problems, as well as some of the basic economic theories which have been developed to explain public expenditure determination and the nature and necessity of public ownership of particular types of enterprises. Towards the end of the chapter, a statistical overview of the last five years in Australian public expenditure illustrates the complexities of the argument outlined in what has gone before.

## Definitional issues

The public sector as a whole in Australia comprises two segments: the general government sector and the public trading enterprises sector. The former is defined as consisting of government departments and agencies which provide public services, largely non-market in nature, often for collective community consumption. The sector is also engaged in the transfer or redistribution of income by means of various welfare payments and subsidies. These activities are generally financed from taxes and compulsory levies (current revenue sources), an excess of expenditure (current revenue) over current revenue (expenditure) producing a deficit (surplus) and a positive (negative) financing requirement for government. The public trading enterprise sector was previously defined in terms of government owned enterprises. These produce goods and services financed from sales to consumers. An excess/deficiency of sales revenue over outlays lowers/increases the net financing requirement of the public sector as a whole.

As a federation, the Australian public sector can also be subdivided by level of government—Federal, State and local. Each of these in turn comprises a general government and a public trading enterprise sector. The Australian public sector is therefore a generic term, comprising as it does the national (Federal) government, six State and two Territory governments, as well as over 800 local governments. In Australia, the Federal Constitution roughly divides Federal from State expenditure responsibilities; State and Territory legislation governs the responsibilities assigned to local government units.

Public expenditure (or more appropriately, public outlays) can also be divided by economic type. Expenditure on goods and services needs to be distinguished from transfer payments. The former take real resources of labour and other inputs to transform them into public services either for free distribution to the community or for sale to the consuming public. Consumers of these services need not be confined to Australian residents. Tourists, for example, consume publicly provided goods and services, either free (road space, recreational amenities such as beaches) or at a price (train and bus fare, entry fees to national parks). Expenditure (outlays) on goods and services are also subdivided into current and capital, the last involving either the acquisition of assets (including stocks and intangible assets) or assistance to other sectors for the purpose of acquiring assets (capital transfers). Transfer payments more generally move resources between entities external to the public sector, thereby redistributing income (resources) between households and firms. This difference has implications for measuring the size of the public sector.

Expenditure can also be subdivided by purpose, useful for drawing comparisons in expenditure policy over time or between individual units of a particular level of government. These purposes, also used internationally for preparing public finance statistics, include general public services, defence, public order and safety, health, education, social security and welfare, housing and community amenities, recreation and culture and economic services including fuel and energy, agriculture, forestry and fishing, mining, manufacturing and construction, transport and communications.

## Measurement

Measurement of the size of the public sector is generally effected by
examining the share of public outlays in GDP, as done earlier in
this chapter. For this purpose, government expenditure on goods
and services tends to be valued at factor cost, that is, the cost of
the inputs required for the provision of services.[1] Market price
valuation only applies when public sector output is directly sold to
the community. Transfer payments are valued by the amount actually transferred. Unlike government expenditure on goods and
services, transfer payments do not reflect a shift of real resources
from the private to the public sector. They simply reallocate
resources within the private sector by channelling (redistributing)
them to those seen to be in special need, such as pensioners and
the unemployed, and, in the case of bounties or subsidies, industries
claimed to be deserving of assistance. It can therefore be argued
that transfer payments do not effectively enhance the public sector's
command over real resources: the aspect of public sector size captured in measuring it in terms of its share in GDP. In short, using
outlays which include government transfer payments in measuring
public sector size is somewhat problematic, because this measurement blends two different types of government control over
economic resources, even though both forms of outlay—expenditure
on goods and services, and transfers—embody a degree of public
coercion in the disposal of private income.[2]

There are other unsatisfactory implications of the input method
in measuring public sector size. With much government output
taking the form of fairly labour intensive services—for example,
education and health care services—room for productivity improvement tends to be rather limited, since it is generally difficult to
reduce the labour content of a unit of output without affecting the
quality of service. This implies a tendency for the value of government output to rise in line with the cost of labour services, a rate
of increase which generally outstrips the rise in market prices of
traded commodities. This imparts a bias towards growth in public
sector size from the manner in which it is conventionally measured,
accounting for a significant portion of the relative growth in public
sector size many OECD countries experienced in the post-war period
(see the evidence reported in Groenewegen 1990, pp.43–4). Substantial cuts in public sector employment, imposed by the Howard
government to cut Commonwealth outlays over the two years ending
1997/98, hence entail substantial reductions in the quality of service.

The input measure of government expenditure distorts in
another way. It rarely reflects the degree of satisfaction people derive
from government provided services. The available evidence suggests

that the majority of voter-citizens value essential public services (health care, education, law and order, transport, communications) greatly and are often willing to pay higher taxes in support of their preference. Politicians, however, have become so trapped in what they see as the vote winning strategy of tax cuts that they fail to act on such community preferences for more satisfactory public service levels. So-called productivity dividends from regular across-the-board pruning of departmental allocations to produce a leaner public service also produce leaner service quality unless there are genuine productivity gains to be reaped from improvements, such as from computer technology.

The above has concentrated on measuring public sector size in terms of its role as regulator, reallocator and, above all, as user of resources. Other ways of measuring the public sector which suggest themselves arise from different perceptions of government's role. Government as producer concentrates on measuring its share in national output, marketed and unmarketed. Government as employer is another avenue to measuring public sector size, by looking at the share of government employees (including those working in the public trading enterprise sector) in the total work force. Government as borrower, a role on which discussion in the 1990s has frequently focussed, can be captured by measuring the relative size of the public debt, particularly with respect to foreign indebtedess, though the trend in expenditure cutting and debt redemption from privatisation proceeds has permitted some governments in Australia to become debt free. Finally, government as redistributor can be measured in terms of the relative importance of government transfers or, more precisely, in terms of the difference the presence of government makes to the distribution of income before, and after, taking taxation and transfers into account.

## Theories of public expenditure and public sector size

Theories of pubic expenditure are very much predicated on views on the nature of public goods, that is, the characteristics which distinguish them from private goods. Pure private goods have two essential characteristics. First, the exclusion principle must apply, that is, consumers are able to obtain exclusive rights over the objects of their desires and, what is more important, the seller can exclude from their consumption those individuals not willing to pay for them. Second, private goods are rivals in consumption; individual consumption benefits are reduced if consumption is shared with someone else; that is, the more that one person consumes the less is available for others. Public goods are the polar opposite of pure private goods. Public good characteristics appear as soon as the exclusion principle cannot be efficiently applied, and as soon as consumption is non-rival. The exclusion principle is very technology dependent. This can be illustrated from the introduction of cable television and the developments in electronic card charging for road use, which allow exclusion of non-payers from services often non-rival in consumption and from which previously it had proved too difficult or too expensive to exclude non-paying customers. It should be noted that the public/private good distinction is not a black and white one. Most goods have both public and private good characteristics in different proportions. For example, education has both a private good dimension (it can be charged for on a service basis and its benefits can be privately appropriated, a feature partially captured in the use of HECS) and a public good dimension (inappropriable social benefits from a well educated population and work force reflected in the less than full cost recovery rate of HECS payments). These public benefits in goods supply with a strong private good content are often called externalities. Such externalities from goods and services need not always be beneficial. Pollution from smoke or aircraft and traffic noise are examples which raise important issues for public policy.

It should also be noted at the outset that the notion of public goods does not greatly help in defining the limits to public sector activity, as some economists had thought when the concept was first developed in the final decades of the nineteenth century. Public good characteristics are largely irrelevant to the issue of what goods are to be supplied by the public sector. Although this issue is settled by political decisions, there is a tendency for goods in which public good characteristics dominate to be provided by the public sector.

The importance of political choices in determining the range of public activity is most easily illustrated by examining changes in the provision of public utilities. In Australia, many of these were traditionally publicly provided. Increasingly, however, telecommunication services, gas, electricity and water supply are being privately provided. Postal and rail services are still largely publicly provided, though in New South Wales since 1996 privately owned rolling stock can use the State rail tracks for freight movement. Arguments for privately providing such services rest on efficiency derived from the profit motive, the benefits of competition and the dismantling of government monopolies in this area. The Hilmer Report's demands for greater competition in the Australian State sector stresses an appeal for privatisation, enhanced for many Australian governments by the debt reduction potential offered through the sale of assets to the private sector. The imminent Telstra sale by the Commonwealth is a good example. However, the real benefits from such privatisation policies are not nearly as clear cut as their supporters often imply, and the evidence for the efficiency gains from privatisation is at best ambiguous.

The political choice element in determining the extent of public service is also illustrated by Musgrave's (1969) concept of merit goods. Their extent is determined by government preferences, sometimes aided by a deliberate search for community preferences via opinion polls or social surveys. Social desirability is the criterion on which merit goods are based. This concept is so elastic that, once admitted, no limit in principle can be placed on the size of the public sector apart from that provided through the political process. Examples of merit goods range from full employment, the elimination of poverty and homelessness, to the accessibility of all to adequate health care and education. Other merit goods include support for the arts and sport, including financial assistance for a national team to participate in the Olympic Games or other international competitions, the training of athletes and other potential sport stars at government funded sports institutes; the creation of national parks, preservation of wilderness areas, heritage and endangered species protection, and so on.

The size of the public sector is also influenced by political and economic choices about the nature of service provision. Corrective services provision may be seen as part and parcel of the public good of law and order, but it may be provided through either publicly or privately provided prisons. For substantial parts of this century, Australian defence (the prime example of a public good) was supplied through publicly owned factories producing ammunition, weapons, uniforms and many of the other requirements of modern defence forces. Such equipment is now all privately produced. Many former in-house provided services to government (cleaning, catering and printing) are now contracted out to the private sector. At the local government level, garbage disposal, street cleaning and re-cycling services are now likewise contracted out. Government administration has acquired an entrepreneurial role in organising the production of services through hiring the cheapest resources to do so. Whether cheap is also efficient depends on the importance of quality maintenance, a more controversial issue. There is far too little evidence in Australia to support the widely held view that contracting-out to the private sector is invariably more efficient.

More generally, public sector activity is explained in terms of market failure. If the market cannot provide a service, and its provision is deemed desirable, a social organisation such as government needs to supply it. Several examples of market failure have already been mentioned. Critics of government intervention point to the high potential for government failure. With the growth of the public sector, cases of government failure have multiplied. More spectacular failures include the inability to achieve anywhere near full employment during the post-1970 decades, to eradicate poverty and homelessness, and to maintain a clean and unpolluted environment. Such government failures are uncontroversial. Other, more controversial, failures are increasingly raised, often by Opposition spokespersons, and concern maintenance of satisfactory educational standards, over-supply of many health services and chronic under-supply of others, ineffective corrective and rehabilitation programs, rising crime rates, and inadequate infrastructure for transport, especially motor transport.

## A sequential view of public expenditure decision-making

Theoretical issues involved in public expenditure analysis can be summarised by listing the four main aspects of the public expenditure decision-making process. Decisions need to be made about:

1  the total level of public expenditure;
2  the relative size of the major programs of public expenditure such as defence, social welfare, law and order and transport;
3  the set of specific projects which constitute a program such as child care provision, aged persons services, within social welfare provisions (and the necessary counterpart of either rejecting or postponing other projects);
4  the design of accepted projects (and the alternative designs which need to be rejected or postponed) such as whether to assist care of the aged in the home or in government institutions or through subsidies to private institutions.

Although earlier discussion has indicated that many of these choices are political, the economic element in this decision-making process should not be ignored. The various theoretical explanations offered with respect to each of these stages are briefly summarised in what follows.

Three types of theoretical explanations have been favoured by economists for determining the total level of public expenditure. These are: the voluntary exchange models, the maximum welfare models and analyses which seek to determine the optimum size of the budget through voting, of which the public choice theories are a variant. Although all of these theories have roots going back to the nineteenth century, most of the major theoretical developments in this area have taken place in the post–World War II era.

The *voluntary exchange models* use the tools and concepts of the microeconomics of the private market in seeking a solution to the problem of optimum budget determination. This problem can be posed as follows. The private, competitive market promises efficiency in production and exchange. Hence, if market criteria can be applied to the public sector, efficiency, in the Pareto sense, may be achieved in the sphere of government produced goods and services through the budget. The supply and demand apparatus is applied to the budget process in the following way. The demand for public goods comes from individual members of the community, either directly or, more generally, through their elected representatives. It is expressed by a willingness to pay a price for public goods provision in the form of taxation. Total supply offered will then be determined by the public demand and measured by the contribution to the cost of providing that supply the public is willing to bear. A pure public good, available equally to all once it has been provided, may make individuals hide their preferences by placing inaccurate tax bids, since as soon as the good is supplied, they will benefit irrespective of any tax contribution they have offered, or would be prepared to make. The determination of the budget in this way is therefore a special case of the theory of exchange. It implies the voluntary exchange of resources given up by individuals through tax offers in return for a supply of goods and services offered by the state. Given the supply function of the public good based on the technical conditions of production, together with the demand schedules, suitably aggregated from individual preferences, an equilibrium budget can be determined by the interaction of supply and demand. However, demand functions for pure public goods cannot easily be deduced from tax preferences given the likelihood of the free rider problem. Hence, a grand optimum solution in the nature of private market general equilibrium solutions is not readily applicable to the public sector, as Samuelson (1954, pp.184–5), a key theorist in this area, readily admitted. (For a simpler, more general discussion, see Groenewegen 1990, pp.58–63.)

The *maximum welfare approach* is based on two simple propositions derived from the efficiency rules of modern microeconomics. Firstly, resources available to the public sector should be distributed among different public uses so as to equalise the return of satisfaction for the last unit of each type of outlay. Secondly, public expenditure should extend up to the point where the satisfaction obtained from the last dollar spent is equal to the satisfaction lost from the last dollar taken in taxes, thereby equalising the marginal satisfaction derived from resource use in the public and private sectors. This is a simple application of the equi-marginal rules so widely used in microeconomic decision theory. Although these rules of budget determination efficiency remind us of the crucial interdependence between taxation and public expenditure decisions, and of the fact that allocative efficiency is important in budgetary planning, their underlying complexity, arising largely from problems in aggregation, makes it difficult to transform these general rules into operational guidelines of practical use to budget makers. It should also be noted that the first equi-marginal rule, seeking to equalise the marginal degree of satisfaction for each type of outlay, concerns the second stage of the public expenditure decision-making framework because it theoretically determines the relative size of the various public expenditure programs. This follows from the fact that its application assumes a particular distribution of budgetary resources among broad programs of government activity such as health, welfare or law and order.

Given the problems inherent in the more economic theoretical approaches just outlined, those interested in theorising about budget determination have increasingly turned to solving the problem from a political perspective by *seeking to analyse aspects of social and public choice* or, as the second is sometimes also known, the calculus of consent. This also is not very straightforward. For example, it can be shown that even revealed preferences through an individual voting process do not invariably produce optimum outcomes in social choice, while as long as interpersonal comparisons of utility are ruled out, the only satisfactory translation of individual into social preferences is either imposed or dictatorial. The last proposition derives from what is known as Arrow's impossibility theorem (briefly discussed in Groenewegen 1990, pp.69–70). The political process in Australia, as in most other democratic countries, relies on majority voting, so that budget decisions in practice tend to be made by the government formed through a majority party, or coalition of parties, in the lower house. However, with the increasing importance of small parties in the upper house holding the balance of power (as the Democrats have often done in the Senate in the 1990s), bargaining over some specific budget provisions may occur. (The Keating Labor government haggled over the 1993/94 Budget with the Green senators from Western Australia, subsequently the Howard government has had to do so with the Democrat and Independent senators.)

Preferences for public goods in practice therefore involve more than the individual citizens on whom attention is focussed in the voluntary exchange model. When politicians' preferences are admitted, there is immediate potential for conflicts of interest and indeterminate outcomes in the budget process. Public service bureaucrats may also have preferences for public goods, influenced perhaps by the effects they may have on their opportunities for promotion, or enhanced personal power through increased service provision under their control. Moreover, private producers of public goods and services have an interest in greater public expenditure if this implies additional contracts and greater profits.

This wider perspective makes simple public expenditure theories deficient. This should be recalled when studying public expenditure incidence analysis which attempts to assign the benefits of public expenditure to households of varying composition and income size (more details in Groenewegen 1990, pp.85–8). The previous paragraph indicates that benefits from public expenditure go well beyond their consumers, hence their measurement needs to go further than assigning monetary values of the benefits to consuming households. Cost cutting in Canberra during 1996 and 1997 had repercussions far wider than lost employment opportunities for current and potential public servants. There were important effects on the Canberra private sector, and in other regions affected by program curtailment from the subsequent reduction in effective demand.

Majority voting solutions have other drawbacks. More than likely such outcomes are non-Pareto efficient. This can be grasped intuitively. Only unanimity in voting for particular public goods or services always yields Pareto efficient results since it enables those who are likely to lose from a particular proposal to veto it by voting against it. Simple majority voting on the budget allows oppression of the minority or their effective fiscal exploitation. In short, there appear to be no simple solutions to the theoretical problem of overall budget determination.

Fortunately the third and fourth stages of the budget process are more practical. Mechanisms need to exist to ensure that the substantial resources appropriated by government are effectively and efficiently used. Financial analysts therefore stress the need for cost-benefit analysis of all major government capital projects. They also demand publication of the results, together with explicit government explanations of its actions when it proceeds with projects which economic analysis has rejected. One limitation of such public investment analysis is that all too often it is ignored by government for political reasons, a further indication of how important political considerations are in the expenditure decision-making process. Another, and more important, shortcoming is that techniques like cost-benefit analysis and program budgeting have inherent limitations arising from difficulties in specifying and measuring some of the crucial variables they use. These limitations must be understood if the value of these techniques for public expenditure decision-making is to be satisfactorily grasped.

Some terminology needs to be clarified first. In explaining these techniques, reference is invariably made to programs, projects, inputs and outputs involved in the public expenditure decision. Programs can be defined in terms of broad government functions, as done at the second stage of the expenditure decision framework. In the case of social welfare, this can be subdivided into general programs such as day care services for children and into specific activities within that program such as licensing of day care centres, their funding, and advising on their organisation and operation. Detailed specification of the activities in these programs (for example, the various methods of licensing which can be used) enables more precise identification of the nature of the alternatives, hence more precision in identifying the necessary inputs and clarifying the objectives or benefits these inputs are designed to yield.

At this stage, efficiency needs to be distinguished from effectiveness with respect to program or activity evaluation. *Efficiency* is now allocational efficiency, involving a relationship between inputs and outputs (costs and benefits) evaluated in terms of cost minimisation in achieving a specified objective or gaining maximum effects from a specific appropriation of resources. Once again, this is a specific application to the public domain of microeconomic resource allocation rules originally developed for private sector market activity. *Effectiveness* of a program refers to the degree of success with which a program meets the government objectives for which it was designed. For example, a particular program of cash benefits designed to cater for a particular type of need may in fact go largely to persons or households outside that specific need category. More accurate targeting of social welfare benefits is an effectiveness issue in government spending which occupies all sides of the political spectrum, as illustrated by the promises to eliminate welfare frauds regularly reiterated during election campaigns. Reviews to test the effectiveness of programs require the completion of several steps. Identification of the program's desired objectives is required first of all. This has to be followed by a detailed review of how program delivery meets these desired objectives.

Greater concern with efficiency and effectiveness of government spending programs has meant pressure to change the conventional government accounting framework in budget presentation to a program budgeting format. This attempts to define program outputs and attempts to identify the resources (inputs) required to achieve them. After all, efficiency in the sense in which it was defined above draws on the relationship between the inputs and outputs of a program, which therefore need to be clearly identified.

This is less simple than it sounds. For example, what is the objective of the education program? If defined as the achievement of equal opportunity for all Australians, it is exceedingly difficult to quantify, thereby reducing its usefulness for analysis. If defined in terms of enhancing general skill levels for all Australians entering the work force, both the skills and the performance tests for their achievement need to be specified. Those who have followed the education debate will be aware of the effort that has gone into clarifying these types of objectives to enhance their measurability as

performance indicators. Although program budgets have been prepared by Australian governments as part of their budget material,
and efficiency auditing has been called an additional responsibility
for government auditors, gains from such innovations in terms of
enhanced efficiency and effectiveness of government expenditure
decision-making probably remain disappointingly small. Cost and
expenditure cutting engaged in by Australian governments during
the 1990s reflect more the political and administrative ease of
cutting the item in question than detailed analysis of the long-term
efficiency consequences of the cut. This is illustrated in the Federal
cost cutting of the Howard government, particularly in its first two
budgets, which reflected its political imperatives rather than the
precise conclusions of effectiveness and efficiency analysis.

Cost-benefit analysis may be used to choose the most appropriate
design of accepted projects in terms of resource allocation efficiency
criteria. It may thereby assist the fourth stage of the expenditure
decision-making process. Cost-benefit analysis allows comparisons
and ranking of projects in terms of their relative benefit, either
expressed as a benefit-cost ratio or calculated as the internal rate of
return of the project from its discounted expected costs and benefit
flows over time. Both types of measure reflect the private sector
criterion of the necessity for an adequate return on the investment
of scarce capital resources. Problems arise from difficulties in identifying, and measuring, the relevant cost and benefit flows over time,
choosing the appropriate discount rate by which to reduce future cost
and benefit flows to their present value, and in taking account of the
relevant constraints under which the project needs to operate.

Despite their imperfections, techniques in public expenditure analysis are valuable for improving the quality of information on which
decisions have to be made. Likewise, economic theories of public
expenditure remind us of crucial aspects of the problem: the important
nexus between taxation and expenditure which is all too often ignored,
and the presence of interest groups in the process. More generally,
they emphasise the need to always aim at satisfactory outcomes in
terms of efficiency and effectiveness. In these respects, public expenditure theory provides the tool box through which the right questions
can be asked about public expenditure decision-making.

## Public expenditure in Australia (1990/91, 1995/96)

In order to give some examples of appropriate issues in public
expenditure analysis, some aspects of Australia's public expenditure
experience for the nineties can be explored on the basis of the data
in Table 8.1. This provides details of the relative importance of
outlays by broad economic function among the various levels of

Table 8.1 Outlay by purpose, relative importance (% of total) by level of government 1990/91, 1995/96 (actual)

| | Total public sector | | Commonwealth | | NSW | | Vic | | Qld | | SA | |
|---|---|---|---|---|---|---|---|---|---|---|---|---|
| | 1990/91 | 1995/96 | 1990/91 | 1995/96 | 1990/91 | 1995/96 | 1990/91 | 1995/96 | 1990/91 | 1995/96 | 1990/91 | 1995/96 |
| General public services | 7.6 | 7.9 | 6.0 | 5.8 | 4.3 | 6.9 | 6.1 | 8.8 | 4.4 | 3.1 | 11.5 | 10.8 |
| Defence | 5.5 | 5.6 | 7.9 | 7.2 | — | — | — | — | — | — | — | — |
| Public order and safety | 3.6 | 3.7 | 0.7 | 0.7 | 7.2 | 8.8 | 5.9 | 7.3 | 7.8 | 8.3 | 6.8 | 7.7 |
| Education | 12.5 | 12.6 | 7.2 | 7.4 | 24.5 | 26.2 | 25.4 | 23.5 | 27.0 | 26.2 | 24.2 | 21.2 |
| Health | 13.5 | 15.7 | 12.2 | 14.3 | 15.9 | 21.2 | 17.5 | 19.6 | 14.7 | 20.5 | 16.9 | 18.3 |
| Social security and welfare | 21.7 | 29.1 | 29.2 | 35.8 | 4.4 | 6.5 | 3.4 | 5.9 | 2.4 | 3.9 | 3.6 | 4.9 |
| Housing and community amenities | 2.9 | 1.3 | 1.0 | 0.1 | 4.9 | 2.2 | 5.6 | 1.7 | 1.6 | 0.6 | 5.5 | 2.1 |
| Recreation and culture | 2.4 | 2.2 | 1.1 | 0.9 | 1.9 | 2.2 | 2.2 | 1.3 | 2.0 | 2.9 | 3.0 | 2.8 |
| Fuel and energy | 2.1 | 0.9 | 0.6 | 0.7 | 2.3 | 0.3 | 3.6 | 1.3 | 4.7 | 3.5 | 2.4 | 0.2 |
| Agriculture, forestry and fishing | 3.4 | 1.7 | 3.7 | 1.4 | 2.1 | 1.9 | 1.3 | 1.4 | 2.8 | 3.0 | 0.6 | 1.1 |
| Mining, manufacturing and construction | 0.6 | 0.5 | 0.5 | 0.3 | 0.3 | 0.3 | 0.2 | 0.4 | 0.5 | 0.7 | 0.7 | 0.5 |
| Transport and communications | 9.2 | 3.4 | 6.7 | 1.2 | 11.4 | 6.1 | 9.3 | 6.0 | 11.2 | 11.5 | 6.8 | 5.7 |
| Other economic affairs | 2.0 | 3.1 | 1.9 | 3.1 | 1.5 | 2.3 | 0.7 | 0.9 | 1.0 | 2.4 | 1.3 | 1.6 |
| Other purposes | 12.8 | 12.1 | 21.4 | 21.2 | 19.3 | 15.2 | 18.9 | 21.9 | 19.8 | 13.3 | 16.6 | 23.3 |

**Table 8.1 (cont'd)**

| | WA | | Tas | | NT | | ACT | | Local | |
|---|---|---|---|---|---|---|---|---|---|---|
| | 1990/91 | 1995/96 | 1990/91 | 1995/96 | 1990/91 | 1995/96 | 1990/91 | 1995/96 | 1990/91 | 1995/96 |
| General public services | 7.0 | 7.5 | 6.2 | 8.1 | 9.6 | 9.6 | 8.7 | 8.8 | 20.7 | 23.7 |
| Defence | — | — | — | — | — | — | — | — | — | — |
| Public order and safety | 6.9 | 9.1 | 5.3 | 6.0 | 8.2 | 10.1 | 7.5 | 10.1 | 0.6 | 3.3 |
| Education | 22.4 | 24.2 | 20.8 | 22.1 | 18.9 | 19.5 | 26.1 | 30.7 | 0.2 | 0.2 |
| Health | 16.6 | 21.3 | 15.2 | 18.2 | 13.8 | 20.1 | 22.1 | 22.4 | 2.4 | 3.5 |
| Social security and welfare | 4.2 | 5.1 | 2.3 | 8.7 | 1.8 | 2.8 | 4.1 | 5.1 | 3.2 | 9.3 |
| Housing and community amenities | 4.3 | 1.6 | 2.6 | 1.6 | 6.6 | 2.1 | 2.6 | 5.3 | 17.3 | 21.9 |
| Recreation and culture | 1.7 | 2.4 | 2.4 | 2.7 | 4.3 | 5.2 | 5.0 | 6.3 | 16.2 | 25.0 |
| Fuel and energy | 4.3 | 0.4 | 6.0 | — | 4.1 | 1.0 | 2.7 | — | 6.1 | -0.2 |
| Agriculture, forestry and fishing | 2.4 | 1.7 | 2.7 | 3.3 | 3.8 | 3.0 | — | — | -0.1 | -0.1 |
| Mining, manufacturing and construction | 0.7 | 0.8 | 0.4 | 0.4 | 1.3 | 1.0 | 1.8 | — | 1.8 | 2.2 |
| Transport and communications | 8.2 | 6.5 | 7.3 | 4.8 | 7.9 | 5.2 | 13.4 | 5.6 | 25.9 | 15.2 |
| Other economic affairs | 2.4 | 2.2 | 2.1 | 2.7 | 5.8 | 3.6 | 0.8 | 1.1 | 0.9 | -0.5 |
| Other purposes | 18.7 | 17.3 | 26.8 | 24.4 | 14.0 | 16.7 | 5.2 | 4.5 | 4.9 | -3.3 |

*Source:* ABS *Government Financial Estimates, Australia 1997–98* (Cat. No. 5501.0), Canberra, November 1997

government in Australia, allowing comparisons not only between Commonwealth, State and local government but also between individual States and Territories.

A first point illustrated by Table 8.1 is the exclusive power over defence by the Commonwealth government. During the 1990s this function has taken a substantial but declining proportion of national as well as Commonwealth resources, a position partly reversed by the Howard Coalition government. As captured by the data in Table 8.1, no other functions are exclusive to any particular level of government, though some functions such as spending on agriculture, forestry and fishing are absent from the pattern for the ACT because of the nature of its jurisdiction.

Table 8.1 also gives visibility to the relative unimportance of some functions for particular levels of government. Public order and safety is of relatively small significance for the Commonwealth and for local government as compared with the States; local governments have few responsibilities with respect to education and, to a smaller degree, health. On the other hand, local government spending on recreation and culture, transport, and housing and community services, is relatively large.

A second point to be gleaned from Table 8.1 is the overwhelming significance of social welfare, health and housing spending in Australian public expenditure. Social welfare takes over half of public resources nationally, at the Federal level and at the State level, though there are differences in the specific direction of spending as between Commonwealth and States, and as between individual States and Territories. Social security and welfare, largely composed of social security cash benefits to welfare recipients, is by far the major Commonwealth welfare spending area and one in which it has gained exclusive constitutional responsibilities to a significant extent. Education spending is the biggest user of resources for all State governments, in many cases taking over a quarter of their budgetary resources. The last remark draws attention to the potential for differences in relative spending between State and Territory governments, of which Table 8.1 gives various examples. A few of these can be singled out. Spending on transport and communication is particularly high in Queensland; spending on health is high in the ACT, spending on public order and safety is rather low in Tasmania, South Australia devotes a relatively large proportion of its resources to general public services.

Such relative differences can arise from several factors. They can arise from specific regional preferences, as suggested by the theory of public expenditure. They can also flow from demographical and geographical characteristics. A young population suggests greater relative spending on education, an ageing population greater spending on health. Population density characteristics influence spending on transport and communication. Individual citizens' preferences, so important in theories like the voluntary exchange models, tell therefore only part of the story. Changes of government can induce alterations in functional preferences but the two years of Table 8.1 are not very suitable for testing this proposition. Whether the preferences revealed by the functional relativity differences among the States comes from citizens, politicians, bureaucrats or producers is likewise not easy to argue without a great deal of additional data and analysis.

A few other silences from this particular anatomy of Australian public expenditure can be mentioned. Table 8.1 indicates nothing about whether spending levels are deficient or excessive; it says nothing about whether the resources devoted to a particular function are efficiently or effectively used. For these sort of questions, more and different information is required, and the analysis is much more complex. Nor does the data of Table 8.1 permit conclusions about the more recent expenditure cutting exercises of 1996/97 and 1997/98. More generally, it can be said that since the Australian public sector is already quite small by international standards, this expenditure cutting has seriously affected service levels. Business lobby groups, the social welfare lobby and the arts community, including the ABC, joined higher education in protests at 1996/97 Budget cuts. The 1996/97 Budget wished to lower Commonwealth outlays relative to GDP from 27.2 per cent in 1995/96 to 25.4 per cent in 1997/98, the type of proportion which prevailed in the mid-1970s. The 1998/99 Budget has projected a steady decline in the proportion of Commonwealth outlays relative to GDP to 22.8 per cent by 2001/02.

The discussion in the previous sections provides an introduction to the nature of the required data and, perhaps more importantly, the warning that in seeking solutions to such problems, completely satisfactory answers are often difficult to find. Despite this short-coming, public expenditure analysis has to be seen as both an important and an exciting part of economic study of the Australian economy and society. After all, not only the incomes of a significant proportion of Australians, but also the civilisation of our country, depends to a significant degree on the spending decisions made by its several governments.

### Further reading

Peter Groenewegen, (1990) *Public Finance in Australia. Theory and Practice,* Third edition, Prentice Hall, Sydney, Chapters 2–5, 20.

Commonwealth Budget Paper No. 1, *Budget Statements,* Canberra; Australian Government Publishing Service (issued annually as part of the Budget).

# 9 Taxation and tax policy in Australia

## *Neil Warren*

### What are taxes?

Two things are certain in life: death and taxes. In part compensation, it has been said that taxes are the price we pay for a civilised society. For government the challenge has been to design a tax system which 'plucks the goose with the minimum of hissing', despite the community's demand that certain goods and services be provided by the public sector and that the government ensures there is a fair and equitable distribution of income and wealth.

Taxes are compulsory levies imposed by government. They find implementation in many different ways and with varying objectives. Not only do they provide government with substantial sources of general revenue, they are also used to correct for market failure, to influence international trade and as the price for public provision of private goods.

Any study of taxation must therefore begin by recognising that tax systems are complicated by having a multitude of objectives. In this chapter the focus is on the taxes that are designed to fund government general revenue. Taxes whose objective is to correct for market failure, such as those on petrol, tobacco and alcohol, will not be closely examined nor will the tariffs imposed on imports which result in customs duty collections. Similarly, we shall not examine the merits of the current Australian Petroleum Resource Rent Tax which is designed to tax above-normal profits earned by those businesses extracting petroleum.

General revenue taxes are those which have as their basic

objective the raising of needed government revenue in a way which is economically efficient, equitable, simple to administer and does not adversely affect economic growth.

This chapter aims to provide the reader with a good understanding of the current Australian tax system and to outline those issues which are the focus of the current and ongoing tax policy debate. However, none of this analysis can proceed unless we first develop criteria against which we can evaluate the current tax system and possible reforms.

## What is a good tax system?

Adam Smith in his *Wealth of Nations* (1776, Book 5, Ch. 2) proposed four desirable criteria for a good tax system: equality, economy of collection, certainty, and convenience of payment.

The last two have been the focus of considerably less attention from economists than from accountants, businesses and tax administrators. For economists, the first two requirements have been considered in terms of three desirable criteria for a tax system:

1 the tax burden should be fairly distributed (*equity*)
2 disincentive effects should be minimised (*economic efficiency*)
3 administrative burdens for tax collector and taxpayer should be minimal (*simplicity*)

A good tax system is therefore one which is equitable, efficient and simple. The difficulty is giving these criteria practical meaning. Economic efficiency has been interpreted as ensuring taxes do not distort the allocation of resources and result in a level of economic welfare below what could otherwise be achieved. In practice the most efficient tax is a lump sum tax. Such a tax does not distort a person's decision to consume or to save, to work or take leisure or to consume one good as against another. However, lump sum taxes such as a poll tax are not equitable.

An equitable tax system is one which taxes equals equally (horizontal equity) and different individuals differently (vertical equity). However, the difficulty is that what is equitable to one person might be inequitable to another. Should society's goal be to make the worst-off person as well off as possible, to maximise the sum of the individual's welfare, or some other objective? What is seen as vertically equitable is therefore totally dependent on how we weigh the utility of different individuals when measuring social welfare. This still leaves the question of how to define horizontal equity. After all, how do we define like circumstances for individuals? Should this be through the adoption of a broad income definition or through taxing the family unit? These are complicated issues that are not easily resolved.

Even if a concept of equity could be agreed to by society, the problem is that the equity and efficiency objectives are more often than not in conflict. What is equitable may not be efficient and what is efficient may also not be administratively simple. The task for the economist is to resolve these conflicts. While the optimal tax literature[1] has focussed primarily on finding a compromise between equity and efficiency when designing an optimal tax system, it has done so while ignoring administrative issues.

It could be argued for example that the preoccupation in Australia over the past fifteen years with moving ever closer to a comprehensive income tax is due to our uncompromising stance on efficiency and equity issues while overlooking the importance of administrative and compliance costs.

As later sections will highlight, many of the problems with taxation in Australia can be attributed to a failure of the Australian tax system to meet the criteria for a good tax system. It is in this context that the debate over the future direction of tax policy will be examined in the later sections of this chapter.

## Tax taxonomy

To the average taxpayer, the tax system probably appears to be one designed to tax whatever can be taxed. Nevertheless, there is a clear purpose to the structure of the current tax system. This is best illustrated by developing a taxonomy of taxes. The traditional taxonomy of general revenue taxes has taxes defined into three basic categories: income taxes, expenditure taxes, and wealth taxes.

This taxonomy has its origins in a literature which argued that in theory at least, the only tax which needs to be implemented is a comprehensive income tax. The origins of this thinking can be traced back to the Haig-Simons accretions principle. Their argument can be shown simply in (1):

$$Y = C + \Delta W \tag{1}$$

where Y is all accretions to economic spending power such as through income earned, C is consumption and W is additions to net capital wealth.

A comprehensive income tax (CIT) would tax all accretions including windfalls, gifts and inheritances received and any asset revaluation (e.g. capital gains). In this case, a wealth tax is probably unnecessary since wealth is merely an accumulation of unspent after-tax income. Wealth is therefore future consumption. A case might arise for a wealth tax if intergenerational equity issues were considered important enough to warrant a net wealth tax. In reality, no income tax is comprehensive and some forms of income are taxed at concessionary rates. As a result, a case for a net wealth tax arises as an indirect method of taxing lowly taxed income streams. A prime example in Australia is the special tax status of the owner-occupied family home where imputed rents are not taxed as income, nor are capital gains. It is here that State property taxes find justification.

A major criticism of a comprehensive income tax is that such a tax works against national savings by double-taxing savings, firstly by taxing income from which individuals do their savings, and secondly by taxing the income earned on those savings before they are spent. In response, an argument is mounted for the taxation of expenditure (C in (1)) and not income. There is a considerable literature on the case for a direct expenditure tax.[2] Such a tax has a major advantage over a CIT in that it does not distort the decision on when to consume (and therefore the savings decision). In fact, it would be relatively easy to convert the personal income tax to an expenditure tax by allowing a deduction for savings over the period the income is measured. However, an expenditure tax would only work if gifts and bequests were deemed as consumption. Without such an assumption, the expenditure tax could be avoided.

While there is a considerable and persuasive literature on the merits of an expenditure tax, such a tax has not found implementation anywhere. The fundamental problem is how to make the transition from a system that has an income tax to one that has an expenditure tax. It is generally accepted that such a transition would take at least ten to fifteen years and that over this period the two systems would probably operate in parallel. The basic problem is that people must be permitted to consume their past savings without being taxed under the new expenditure tax. In reality the transition is so problematic that no country has been prepared to make the journey. A further complication is that the method of taxing companies would also have to change, to one that taxed the cashflow, and this has major ramifications for how capital is taxed. Since no country has wanted to step outside accepted international practices for taxing companies, this has provided another argument against a personal expenditure tax.

While no country has adopted a direct expenditure tax, all countries have indirect expenditure taxes. In a world with a CIT, it could be argued that such a tax is not necessary (Brooks 1993) but such a tax does not exist, and even if it did, avoidance and evasion might exist. Furthermore, the optimal tax literature highlights the fact that an income tax distorts the work–leisure choice and that one solution to this might be to tax the goods and services that are complements of leisure. In the case of CIT avoidance and evasion, an expenditure tax may prove an effective method of taxing expenditure from these income sources. In the latter case such a response is inferior to improving the enforcement of the income tax.

Another major reason for expenditure taxes is their use in correcting for market failure. This lies behind the levies on petrol, tobacco and alcohol. Revenue from tariffs on imported goods might also fit into this category if those imposts are designed to enable an infant industry to mature and compete on world markets.

In practice, tax systems comprise a range of different taxes. Income, expenditure and net wealth taxes exist in various forms in all systems. Where those systems differ is in the contribution provided by each of these taxes and just how rigorously they are implemented and enforced. Tax systems structure is also heavily influenced by the method of governing in a country and the expenditure responsibilities of each tier of government. In the next two sections, we shall examine the Australian tax system and how it differs from those in other countries.

## Australian tax system

Australia is a federation of States, brought together in 1901 to form a customs union. The rights and responsibilities of each level of government are enshrined in the Constitution. Although the Constitution only asserts that States cannot levy duties of customs and excise (Section 90) or taxes on interstate trade (Section 92), this has not stopped the progressive accumulation of almost all significant taxing powers in the hands of the central government.

The loss of franchise taxes by States in 1997 was just part of an ongoing trend towards States slowly losing more and more of their taxing powers. The most significant loss was in 1942 when the Federal Government introduced the Uniform Income Tax Act. This effectively prevented the States from levying their own income taxes, not because the States had somehow lost the right to this tax, but because the Commonwealth threatened to cut grants to any State that imposed such a tax. The resulting structure of the Commonwealth tax system is evident from Table 9.1.

Income taxes contribute around 72 per cent of all Commonwealth taxes, the contribution from personal income taxes being 53 per cent. Taxes on the provision of goods and services makes up around 25 per cent of Commonwealth revenue but the wholesale sales tax contributes less than half of this revenue. In fact, the wholesale sales tax contributes around the same as excise duties on petrol, tobacco and alcohol,[3] and the remainder is made up by customs duties.

**Table 9.1 Commonwealth, State and local tax revenue: 1996/97[c]**

| Type of tax | Commonwealth | | State | |
|---|---|---|---|---|
| | $m | % | $m | % |
| **1 Taxes on income** | | | | |
| *11 Income taxes levied on individuals* | | | | |
| 111–113 Personal income tax | 64 185 | 51.5% | | |
| 115 Prescribed payments by individuals | 1 671 | 1.3% | | |
| 119 Other income tax levied on individuals | 421 | 0.3% | | |
| Total | 66 278 | 53.2% | | |
| *12 Income taxes levied on enterprises* | | | | |
| 121 Company income tax[a] | 18 966 | 15.2% | | |
| 122 Income tax paid by superannuation funds | 2 595 | 2.1% | | |
| 124 Prescribed payments by enterprises | 145 | 0.1% | | |
| Total | 21 706 | 17.4% | | |
| *13 Income taxes levied on non-residents* | | | | |
| 131 Dividend withholding tax | 163 | 0.1% | | |
| 132 Interest withholding tax | 519 | 0.4% | | |
| 133 Other income tax levied on non-residents | 556 | 0.4% | | |
| Total | 1 238 | 1.0% | | |
| Total | 89 222 | 71.6% | | |
| **2 Employers' payroll taxes** | | | | |
| *21 Employers' payroll taxes* | | | 7 632 | 23.4% |
| *23 Other employers' labour force taxes* | | | | |
| 231 Fringe benefits tax | 3 062 | 2.5% | | |
| 232 Superannuation guarantee charge | 42 | 0.0% | | |
| Total | 3 105 | 2.5% | | |
| Total | 3 104 | 2.5% | | |
| **3 Taxes on Property** | | | | |
| *31 Taxes on immovable property* | | | | |
| 311 Land taxes | | | 1 614 | 4.9% |
| 312 Municipal rates | | | 95 | 0.3% |
| 313–319 Other | | | 279 | 0.9% |
| Total | | | 1 987 | 6.1% |
| *33 Taxes on financial and capital transactions* | | | | |
| 332 Financial institutions' transactions taxes | | | 1 983 | 6.1% |
| 333 Government borrowing guarantee levies | | | 85 | 0.3% |
| 334 Stamp duties on conveyances | | | 2 711 | 8.3% |
| 335–336 Other stamp duties | | | 2 275 | 7.0% |
| Total | | | 7 054 | 21.6% |
| Total | | | 9 042 | 27.7% |

**Table 9.1 (cont.)**

| Type of tax | Commonwealth | | State | |
|---|---|---|---|---|
| | $m | % | $m | % |
| **4 Taxes on provision of goods and services** | | | | |
| 41 *General taxes* | 13 293 | 10.7% | | |
| 42 *Excises and levies* | | | | |
| 421 Petrol excise | 10 570 | 8.5% | | |
| 422 Tobacco excise | 1637 | 1.3% | | |
| 423 Beer excise | 875 | 0.7% | | |
| 424 Other alcohol | 208 | 0.2% | | |
| 421–425 Excises | 13 291 | 10.7% | | |
| 426 Agricultural production taxes | 603 | 0.5% | 13 | 0.0% |
| 427 Levies on statutory corporations | | | 427 | 1.3% |
| Total | 13 893 | 11.1% | 440 | 1.3% |
| 43 *Taxes on international trade* | 3 296 | 2.6% | | |
| 44 *Taxes on gambling* | | | | |
| 441 Taxes on government lotteries | | | 594 | 1.8% |
| 442 Taxes on private lotteries | | | 316 | 1.0% |
| 443 Taxes on gambling machines | | | 1 506 | 4.6% |
| 444 Casino taxes | | | 419 | 1.3% |
| 445 Race betting taxes | | | 651 | 2.0% |
| 449 Taxes on gambling nec | | | 11 | 0.0% |
| Total | | | 3 497 | 10.7% |
| 45 *Taxes on insurance* | | | | |
| 451 Insurance companies' contributions to fire brigades | | | 499 | 1.5% |
| 452 Third party insurance taxes | | | 242 | 0.7% |
| 459 Taxes on insurance nec | | | 1 043 | 3.2% |
| Total | | | 1 784 | 5.5% |
| Total | 30 486 | 24.5% | 5 722 | 17.5% |
| **5 Taxes on use of goods and performance activities** | | | | 0.0% |
| 51 *Motor vehicle taxes* | | | | 0.0% |
| 512 Stamp duty on vehicle registration | | | 1 148 | 3.5% |
| 513 Drivers' licences | | | 212 | 0.6% |
| 514–516 Other | | | 2 232 | 6.8% |
| Total | 26 | 0.0% | 3 590 | 11.0% |
| 52 *Franchise taxes* | | | | |
| 521 Gas franchise taxes | | | 22 | 0.1% |
| 522 Petroleum products franchise taxes | | | 1 570 | 4.8% |
| 523 Tobacco franchise taxes | | | 2 855 | 8.8% |
| 524 Liquor franchise taxes | | | 774 | 2.4% |
| Total | | | 5 221 | 16.0% |
| 53 *Other* | 398 | 0.3% | 256 | 0.8% |
| Total | 424 | 0.3% | 9 069 | 27.8% |
| **9 Fees and fines** | | | | |
| 91–93 *Compulsory fees* | | | 640 | 2.0% |
| 912 Aviation en route charges | 317 | 0.3% | | |

**Table 9.1  (cont.)**

| Type of tax | Commonwealth | | State | |
|---|---|---|---|---|
| | $m | % | $m | % |
| 914 Light dues and Navigation Act charges | 47 | 0.0% | | |
| 918–939 Other fees | 1 002 | 0.8% | | |
| Total | 1 365 | 1.1% | | |
| 94 *Fines* | 27 | 0.0% | 515 | 1.6% |
| Total | 1 392 | 1.1% | 1 155 | 3.5% |
| Taxes, fees and fines[b] | 124 638 | 100.0% | 32 618 | 100.0% |
| Taxes, fees and fines as a percentage of GDP | 24.60% | | 6.50% | |

(a)  Amounts collected under petroleum resource rent taxes are included in TFFC 121 (Company income tax).

(b)  Excludes income taxes paid by public trading enterprises amounting to 1,202 for 1996–97

(c)  Local Taxes on Property were $5310 million and Local Fees and Fines were $394 million. As a percentage of GDP Local Taxes, Fees and Fines were 1.13%

*Source:*  ABS Taxation Revenue Cat. No. 5506.0

When States are brought into the picture, the results are very different, as Table 9.1 also shows. For the States, nearly a quarter of all tax revenue is collected from the payroll tax. Franchise taxes, which the States lost as a result of a challenge to their validity in the High Court in 1997, contributed around 16 per cent of their revenue in 1996/97. Not surprisingly, their loss was a major blow to State governments, despite the fact that comparable levies are now imposed and collected by the Commonwealth on behalf of the States.

The reliance of the States on financial taxes and capital transfer type taxes is also abundantly clear. Nearly 30 per cent of State revenue comes from these sources. The vulnerability of these taxes (such as FID) and the growth tax of recent years, gambling taxes, to new technology is a cause of real concern to the State governments.

These threats to State tax revenue come at a time when, as Table 9.2 illustrates, the State governments are responsible for some 43 per cent of all government outlays but raise only 19 per cent of total tax revenue. This is the much-talked about problem of vertical fiscal imbalance (VFI). Just how important this problem is can be disputed, but what is uncontroversial is that States are dependent on substantial revenue transfers from the Commonwealth. This inevitably means there is always scope for States to deflect criticism for their tax design or their expenditure program onto the Commonwealth, whether this is justified or not.

**Table 9.2  Outlays and tax revenue by level of government: 1995/96**

| Level of government | Outlays | | Taxes | |
|---|---|---|---|---|
|  | $m | % | $m | % |
| Commonwealth | 96 150 | 53.1% | 118 442 | 77.3% |
| State | 78 229 | 43.2% | 29 328 | 19.1% |
| Local | 6 683 | 3.7% | 5 401 | 3.6% |
| Total | 181 062 | 100.0% | 153 151 | 100.0% |

*Source:* ABS Taxation Revenue Cat. No. 5506.0

## An overview of global and domestic tax trends

No discussion of domestic tax reform is complete without a brief overview of trends and developments in other countries. After all, much of the stimulus for tax reform in Australia comes from the need to remain internationally competitive. This has meant that close monitoring of international tax trends and developments is important in any evaluation of the performance of the current tax system.

### OECD trends in taxation

Australia operates in a global trading environment and changes in the tax regimes in other countries have important implications for the Australian economy and its competitiveness. While there are many ways of undertaking international comparisons, one of the more general but most informative is an examination of the tax trends in other OECD countries. Table 9.3 provides such information, highlighting just how restrained the growth of government in Australia has been over the past twenty years compared to the trends evident in European countries.

There are several quite important lessons to be learned from the OECD experience:

- conceptually complex taxes have stabilised or declined in importance; e.g. income taxes and the globalisation of business;
- taxes on difficult-to-tax income sources such as income from capital have stabilised or declined;
- taxes which were once not administratively simple have now become simple to administer due to technological changes, and these taxes have subsequently grown in importance, e.g. VAT;
- as a result of the above factors, there has been a reduced role for income taxes and an increased role for consumption taxes in funding increased expenditure;
- hypothecated (or earmarked) taxes have grown in importance, being attractive to politicians (but not to economists). These hypothecated taxes have been used to directly fund health,

Table 9.3 Growth of taxes in OECD countries (unweighted averages)

| % Share of total taxes (using OECD tax codes) | OECD | | | Australia | | | | New Zealand | | |
|---|---|---|---|---|---|---|---|---|---|---|
| | 1965 % | 1995 % | Ratio 1995/1965 | 1965 % | 1995 % | 1995 incl SGC* % | Ratio 1995/1965 | 1965 % | 1995 % | Ratio 1994/1965 |
| Personal income including FBT | 25.9 | 27.0 | 4% | 34.4 | 42.1 | 40.1 | 22% | 39.4 | 45.1 | 14% |
| Company income | 8.9 | 8.0 | –10% | 16.3 | 14.7 | 14.0 | –10% | 20.7 | 12.0 | –42% |
| Social security on employees | 5.8 | 8.0 | 38% | – | – | – | – | – | – | – |
| Social security on employers | 10.0 | 14.1 | 41% | – | – | 4.8 | – | – | – | – |
| Other social security contributions(c) | 2.2 | 3.0 | 36% | – | – | – | – | – | – | – |
| Payroll tax excluding FBT | 1.0 | 0.8 | –20% | 3.1 | 5.2 | (b)5.0 | 68% | – | – | (b)– |
| Broad based consumption taxes | 11.9 | 17.6 | 48% | 7.4 | 8.7 | 8.3 | 18% | 7.7 | 22.7 | 195% |
| Specific consumption taxes | 24.1 | 13.1 | –46% | 22.7 | 14.5 | 13.8 | –36% | 18.5 | 8.5 | –54% |
| Property | 7.8 | 5.4 | –31% | 11.4 | 8.7 | 8.3 | –24% | 11.5 | 5.2 | –55% |
| Other | 2.4 | 3.0 | 25% | 4.7 | 6.1 | 5.8 | 30% | 2.2 | 6.5 | 195% |
| All taxes | 100.0 | 100.0 | | 100.0 | 100.0 | 100.0 | | 100.0 | 100.0 | 100.0 |

| All tax/GDP | % 1965 | % 1995 | Ratio 1995/1965 |
|---|---|---|---|
| OECD—Total | 26.3% | 37.4% | 42% |
| OECD—America | 25.1% | 27.0% | 8% |
| OECD—Europe | 27.2% | 40.1% | 47% |
| OECD—Pacific | 22.1% | 30.0% | 36% |
| New Zealand | 24.7% | 38.2% | 55% |
| Australia (excluding SGC) | 23.2% | 30.9% | 33% |
| Australia (including SGC) | 23.2% | 34.2% | 47% |

Notes:  Percentage growth in per capita GDP in US$ illustrates the change in the nominal value of a bundle of goods which individuals in the different countries could buy in the USA.

(a)  The superannuation guarantee charge (SGC) is compulsory for employers.

(b)  Payroll tax includes FBT equal to 1.5% for Australia and 0.9% for NZ in 1994. This amount has been reallocated to personal income tax.

(c)  Refers mostly to contributions by the self-employed and non-employed.

Source:  OECD Revenue Statistics: 1965–1996

welfare and unemployment programs. They are liked by politicians because of their direct relationship to benefits received and are therefore easy to sell to the electorate. Economists do not like hypothecated taxes as they result in the revenue raised being tied (or earmarked) to certain expenditures, which amongst other things can result in overspending in the area of government financed by such taxes;

- there has also been a discernible trend towards schedular income taxes and away from global income taxes. Global income taxes are those which add all income sources together and tax them under one schedule. Schedular income taxes tax different sources of income at different rates under different schedules. Examples of schedular income taxes include interest withholding taxes and payroll based taxes (which tax only wage and salary income).

When we compare the OECD trends with those evident in the Australian data over the same period, an interesting picture emerges. Most striking is the impact on Australia of not having a broadly based consumption tax.

Another difference is Australia's increased reliance on global income taxes and the minimal attention given to the possible introduction of schedular income taxes or hypothecated taxes. While Australia has rigorously sought to apply its global income tax, other countries such as Sweden have moved in the direction of taxing different income sources at different rates under different tax rates schedules. In particular, Sweden has a 25 per cent tax on capital income and the UK has an interest withholding tax.

In the case of hypothecated taxes, Australia does have the Medicare levy and, in the recent past, a training levy and a guns levy; from time to time there is talk of a jobs levy. While many OECD countries determine their citizens' entitlements to health, unemployment benefits and aged pensions by contributions through hypothecated taxes, Australia has no dedicated social security levies. However, it does have the Medicare levy and has effectively contracted out the future provision of aged pensions through the introduction of the superannuation guarantee levy (SGC) in 1992. This levy is currently 7 per cent, will rise to 9 per cent in 2002, and is compulsorily paid by employers into their employees' superannuation fund.

Adding the SGC into Table 9.3 does change the picture for Australia but great care should be taken in interpreting this information. For example, some countries such as the UK allow citizens to contract out of the government superannuation scheme and compulsorily contribute to private schemes. Rightly, if we are to include SGC in the Australian data, we should also include all other

**Table 9.4 Real effective tax rates by country for domestic investments**

| | Institutional investors | Average personal tax rate payer | Top personal tax rate payer |
|---|---|---|---|
| **Australia** | **10.5** | **52.4** | **84.6** |
| France | –13.3 | 9.5 | 33.0 |
| Germany | –9.3 | 29.8 | 93.5 |
| Japan | na | 48.4 | 48.4 |
| Netherlands | 6.7 | 57.8 | 144.7 |
| UK | 24.2 | 43.6 | 60.6 |
| USA | 9.3 | 47.2 | 61.2 |
| *OECD Average* | *7.3* | *41.2* | *75.2* |
| Indonesia | 1.0 | 16.7 | 51.6 |
| Korea | 1.9 | 3.5 | 23.3 |
| Malaysia | –19.5 | –8.3 | 40.9 |
| Singapore | –19.7 | .8 | 34.1 |
| Taiwan | 1.4 | 1.4 | 1.4 |
| Thailand | –20.7 | –20.7 | 45.2 |
| *Asia Average* | *–9.9* | *1.1* | *32.8* |

*Note:* Inflation of 4.5% and real interest rates of 5%. Financing weights are country specific.
*Source:* Pender and Ross (1995), p.14

compulsory superannuation contributions imposed in all other countries. Such a task cannot easily be undertaken, particularly since many superannuation schemes are unfunded and entitlements are not directly related to contributions.

Suffice to say that while Australia has moved more into hypothecated taxes than the table shows, it is still far from the level in other OECD countries. However, it is questionable whether such a move is good economics. If the benefits to the taxpayer equal the costs then these taxes are much like user-pays or a benefits principle tax and therefore are not a problem. However, in most cases, neither are the benefits and costs equal nor is the revenue raised equal to the related expenditure. In this case, such taxes do not make good economic sense.

While examining trends in the OECD countries is interesting, we should also examine how our tax rates compare to those of our Asian trading partners, particularly in the taxation of income from capital.

## Income tax trends in Asia and the OECD

Table 9.4 presents data on the real effective tax rates on institutional and personal income tax payers for selected OECD and Asian countries. These results indicate the magnitude of the tax incentive given to domestic investments in Asian countries and the relatively high rates on Australian domestic investors. These findings are even

**Figure 9.1  Nominal company tax rates**

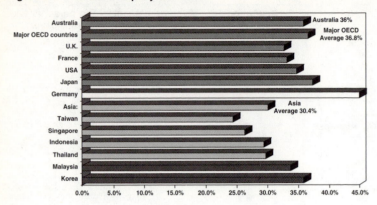

*Sources:* Preston (1990), p.29. Pender and Ross (1995), Appendix 1

more pronounced after including the special concessions often avail-able to Asian investors.[4]

Figure 9.1 presents data on the nominal (or official) company income tax rates in selected OECD and Asian countries. Again, we see that the OECD countries have higher rates on average than Asian countries and that Australia's rate of 36 per cent is amongst the highest across all countries.

Clearly, tax competition resulting from the special tax concessions offered by some Asian countries places other countries like Australia at a competitive disadvantage. The dilemma for Australia is that attempting to match such concessions would have a significant adverse fiscal impact at a time when the benefits are uncertain.

The evidence from the above analysis would indicate that tax competition in global capital markets is most evident amongst the Asian economies that are seeking to attract increased flows of global capital. Despite the recent Asian current currency crisis, it is reasonable to expect these countries will bounce back and to remain (if not become even more) aggressive competitors in the race to attract international capital.

## Tax trends in other federations

Another area which distinguishes Australia from its trading partners is through the way taxes are levied by the different tiers of government. While Table 9.5 indicates that while States in the Australian federation levy a comparable level of taxes to those in other federations, the Australian case is different because of the method in which State taxes are collected.

**Table 9.5 Tax revenue to level of government: 1994**

|  | Central | State | Local | Social security | Total |
|---|---|---|---|---|---|
| Australia | 76.9 | 19.5 | 3.6 |  | 100 |
| Austria | 49.7 | 10.5 | 11.0 | 28.8 | 100 |
| Belgium | 60.2 |  | 5.2 | 34.5 | 100 |
| Canada | 39.2 | 33.8 | 10.1 | 16.9 | 100 |
| Germany | 32.1 | 21.1 | 7.6 | 39.1 | 100 |
| Switzerland | 26.7 | 20.7 | 15.9 | 36.6 | 100 |
| USA | 41.1 | 19.9 | 13.6 | 25.5 | 100 |

*Source:* OECD Revenue Statistics 1996

**Table 9.6 State taxes as a percentage of GDP: 1994**

|  | Income and profits | Payroll | Property | General consumption taxes | Specific consumption taxes | Taxes on use | Other | Total |
|---|---|---|---|---|---|---|---|---|
| Australia |  | 1.4 | 1.7 |  | 1.0 | 1.7 |  | 5.8 |
| Austria | 2.1 |  |  | 1.7 | 0.3 | 0.2 | 0.2 | 4.5 |
| Canada | 6.2 |  | 0.9 | 2.8 | 1.6 | 0.7 |  | 12.2 |
| Germany | 4.5 |  | 0.5 |  | 0.2 | 0.4 |  | 5.6 |
| Switzerland | 5.4 |  | 1.2 |  | 0.1 | 0.4 |  | 7.1 |
| USA | 2.1 |  | 0.2 | 1.8 | 0.9 | 0.4 |  | 5.4 |

*Source:* OECD Revenue Statistics 1996

Table 9.6 indicates that Australian States do not have access to income and profit taxes nor to general consumption taxes. They are instead totally dependent on property, payroll and use taxes. In contrast, US States make significant use of general consumption taxes. These are typically in the form of 'sales and use' taxes, which are designed to tax not only the purchase of goods but also their regular use. Moreover, such taxes overcome the benefits that might accrue to citizens from cross-border shopping. A good example of a use tax is one on all motorised vehicles. The Australian States, in contrast, levy only narrow-based consumption taxes which in 1997 were declared unconstitutional and are now collected by the Commonwealth on behalf of the States.

The other distinguishing feature of the Australian federation is the taxation powers of local government. Table 9.7 indicates that local government in Australia is almost totally dependent on property taxes for its revenue (with some supplementation from fees and fines). In other federations, local governments also have access to income and consumption taxes.

## Tax expenditures

Earlier discussion defined a tax as a compulsory payment. However, there is a grey area of taxation which occupies the area between

Table 9.7  Local taxes as a percentage of GDP: 1994

| | Income and profits | Payroll | Property | General consumption taxes | Specific consumption taxes | Taxes on use | Other | Total |
|---|---|---|---|---|---|---|---|---|
| Australia | | | 1.1 | | | | | 1.1 |
| Austria | 1.6 | 0.8 | 0.5 | 1.0 | 0.4 | 0.1 | 0.3 | 4.7 |
| Canada | | | 3.1 | | | | 0.5 | 3.6 |
| Germany | 2.4 | | 0.6 | | | | | 3.0 |
| Switzerland | 4.6 | | 0.7 | | | | | 5.3 |
| USA | 0.2 | | 2.8 | 0.4 | 0.2 | 0.1 | | 3.7 |

Source: OECD Revenue Statistics 1996

taxation and government expenditure. These are so-called tax expenditures which are financial benefits that individuals and businesses derive from taxation concessions. Examples of such concessions include tax exemptions and deductions, tax rebates, and tax rates different from some benchmark. The effect of these tax expenditures is to make the tax burden different from what it would have been without the concession. These concessions are called tax expenditures because they could equally have been delivered through the expenditure or tax side of a government's budget.

Knowledge of the size and distribution of tax expenditures is important to good government, ensuring that tax breaks or concessions are made transparent. In an ideal world these tax expenditures would be brought on-budget. In Australia, the Commonwealth Treasury releases a detailed *Tax Expenditure Statement* each year, but this does not coincide with the release of the Commonwealth Budget. In fact, the Federal Budget is released on the second Tuesday of May each year and the tax expenditure statement is released in December. However, there is one tax expenditure which is explicitly identified in the Budget (since 1989/90), and that is the Diesel Fuel Rebate to the agricultural and mining sectors, worth some $1.4 billion.

Aggregate tax expenditure by the Commonwealth is detailed in Table 9.8. By far the biggest tax expenditures result from superannuation concessions, the tax-exempt status of some of the government transfer payments and the availability of a range of income tax rebates to pensioners, beneficiaries and low income earners.

No doubt, if imputed income from owner-occupied dwellings was included, the tax expenditures estimates would be considerably higher. In fact, in 1995/96, imputed rent to home owner-occupiers was around $41 billion. The tax expenditure attributed to this group alone, if estimated, could reasonably be expected to be $2 billion to $3 billion.

**Table 9.8 Tax expenditures classified by taxpayer affected**

| | 1992/93 $m | 1994/95 $m | 1996/97 $m | 1999/00 $m |
|---|---|---|---|---|
| Taxpayer | | | | |
| Businesses | 952 | 2 020 | 2 344 | 1 946 |
| Defence | 355 | 361 | 417 | 448 |
| Donors | 0 | 169 | 196 | 227 |
| Employees | 584 | 380 | 360 | 340 |
| Employers | 14 | 956 | 804 | 914 |
| Financial institutions | 111 | 86 | 55 | 11 |
| Government | 0 | 130 | 145 | 165 |
| Hospitals | 0 | 115 | 125 | 140 |
| Superannuation beneficiaries | 5 780 | 5 770 | 6 250 | 7 340 |
| Non-profit organisations | 73 | 339 | 335 | 385 |
| Personal income taxpayers | 4 006 | 4 987 | 4 737 | 5 819 |
| Property owners | 2 | 4 | 6 | 7 |
| Primary producers | 85 | 207 | 306 | 303 |
| Students | 19 | 28 | 29 | 31 |
| Miscellaneous | 548 | 609 | 632 | 861 |
| Total | 12 529 | 16 161 | 16 741 | 18 937 |

*Source:* Tax Expenditure Statement 1995–96, The Treasury, January 1997, AGPS, Table 9.7

The size of this imputed rent tax expenditure has attracted the interest of welfare groups who are concerned about the magnitude of the tax concession going to home owner-occupiers.

## Tax incidence

Informed discussion about taxation and tax policy cannot proceed without a clear appreciation of how the current tax system performs against the criteria of a good tax system. An important starting point in any such analysis is a recognition that ultimately, the burden of all taxes must be on households, regardless of where the taxes were initially imposed.

However, estimating the incidence of taxes is far from straightforward. This is because the burden of a tax, at its simplest, has four components, including:

- the tax revenue raised;
- the impact of tax induced economic distortion on the economy;
- the cost to taxpayers of complying with their obligations under the law when paying taxes; and
- the cost to the government of administering the tax laws.

It could be argued that even this coverage is not comprehensive since tax burdens fund government expenditure programs which themselves create benefits and potential distortions to consumer and

**Table 9.9  Estimated taxes paid and other characteristics of households, by quintile of gross household income, 1996/97**

|  | Quintiles Bottom | 2nd | 3rd | 4th | Top | All |
|---|---|---|---|---|---|---|
| *Amount per week ($)* |  |  |  |  |  |  |
| Private income | 34 | 242 | 629 | 1037 | 1966 | 782 |
| Government cash benefits | 200 | 204 | 100 | 55 | 24 | 117 |
| Gross income | 234 | 446 | 729 | 1092 | 1990 | 898 |
| Current expenditure | 266 | 466 | 648 | 838 | 1151 | 674 |
| *Percent of gross income* |  |  |  |  |  |  |
| Income tax | 0.9% | 6.3% | 15.6% | 20.4% | 27.6% | 20.4% |
| Indirect tax | 30.8% | 29.1% | 24.0% | 20.5% | 17.3% | 21.0% |
| Federal indirect tax | 13.2% | 13.7% | 11.5% | 10.0% | 8.7% | 10.2% |
| State indirect tax | 14.1% | 13.0% | 10.6% | 9.0% | 7.4% | 9.2% |
| Local indirect tax | 3.4% | 2.5% | 1.9% | 1.6% | 1.2% | 1.7% |
| Company tax | 4.3% | 5.2% | 4.0% | 3.4% | 5.7% | 4.7% |
| All taxes | 35.9% | 40.6% | 43.5% | 44.2% | 50.6% | 46.1% |

*Source:* Harding, Lambert and Warren (1998), Table 9.3

**Table 9.10  Estimated taxes paid and other characteristics of households, by family type, 1996/97**

|  | Couple, 1 dep. child | Couple, 2 dep. children | Couple, 3+ dep. children | Sole parent, 1 dep. child | Sole parent, 2+ dep. children | Single, non-aged | Couple, non-aged |
|---|---|---|---|---|---|---|---|
| *Amount per week ($)* |  |  |  |  |  |  |  |
| Private income | 1008 | 1036 | 1041 | 286 | 160 | 500 | 925 |
| Government cash benefits | 59 | 71 | 125 | 177 | 297 | 59 | 50 |
| Gross income | 1067 | 1106 | 1166 | 463 | 456 | 559 | 975 |
| Current expenditure | 805 | 850 | 920 | 409 | 464 | 418 | 708 |
| *Percent of gross income* |  |  |  |  |  |  |  |
| Income tax | 23.1% | 23.5% | 23.0% | 10.2% | 4.8% | 23.1% | 22.2% |
| Indirect tax | 20.0% | 18.7% | 20.2% | 21.4% | 24.3% | 21.8% | 21.4% |
| Federal indirect tax | 10.0% | 9.3% | 10.0% | 10.4% | 11.8% | 10.0% | 10.1% |
| State indirect tax | 8.4% | 7.7% | 8.4% | 9.5% | 11.0% | 10.2% | 9.7% |
| Local indirect tax | 1.6% | 1.7% | 1.6% | 1.5% | 1.8% | 1.6% | 1.6% |
| Company tax | 5.0% | 3.3% | 4.2% | 3.2% | 3.3% | 4.7% | 4.7% |
| All taxes | 48.0% | 45.5% | 47.3% | 34.8% | 32.7% | 49.6% | 48.3% |

*Source:* Harding, Lambert and Warren (1998), Table 9.9

producer behaviour. However, we shall overlook these expenditure side complications. Table 9.9 presents estimates of the incidence of all tax revenue raised in 1996/97 across all households. Undertaking such incidence estimates involves many difficult and controversial assumptions[5] about how taxes are shifted to households, the results in Tables 9.9 and 9.10 indicating some important trends in the impact of taxes on households. In particular, Table 9.9 shows that while the overall tax system is progressive,[6] this progressivity is due

**Table 9.11  Efficiency gains from consumption tax reforms: 1990/91**

| | Total welfare loss | | | Gain in welfare compared to current system | |
|---|---|---|---|---|---|
| | $m | % Total Taxes | %GDP | $m | %GDP |
| Current tax system | −9670 | −8.1% | −2.5 | | |
| Single rate GST on a broad base | | | | | |
| – replaces all indirect taxes | −8980 | 7.6% | −2.4 | 690 | 0.18 |
| – replaces wholesale sales tax, petrol excise and payroll tax | −8910 | 7.5% | −2.3 | 760 | 0.20 |
| Single rate GST on a narrow base | | | | | |
| – replaces all indirect taxes | −9100 | 7.6% | −2.4 | 570 | 0.15 |
| Optimal indirect tax system | −8680 | 7.3% | −2.3 | 990 | 0.26 |

*Source:* Chisholm (1993), Table 9.14

primarily to the progressivity of the personal income tax. Indirect taxes are generally regressive in their impact.

Table 9.10 shows that amongst the different family types, the tax burden does vary surprisingly little. When variation occurs, it is due mostly to changes in the income tax burden. Also, the most regressive of the indirect taxes appear not to be the Federal indirect taxes but the State taxes which impact most heavily on the low income households, particularly those with heads who are aged, or one earner families with young children.

While the above results would indicate that the overall tax system in Australia is progressive, these results overlook the deadweight loss and compliance costs associated with the taxes imposed.

Estimating the deadweight loss resulting from taxes is complicated by the need to obtain detailed information on the response of consumers and producers (including labour suppliers) to different tax regimes. Table 9.11 shows that such burdens are estimated to be quite significant. Moreover, these estimates by Chisholm (1993) are modest compared to those by researchers in other countries. Nonetheless, the deadweight loss of taxes in 1990/91 was estimated to be around 8.1 per cent of revenue raised or 2.5 per cent of GDP.

A third important cost associated with the operation of a tax system is the cost to the taxpayer of complying with the tax laws. Table 9.12 details estimates of the compliance costs associated with Commonwealth taxes in 1994/95. These costs are equivalent to some 7.0 per cent of the tax revenue raised.

A fourth and final cost of taxes is the cost to government of administering the tax laws. An indication of this cost can be obtained from the cost of funding government tax collection agencies. In the case of the Australian Tax Office (ATO), it raised

**Table 9.12  Compliance cost of Federal taxes, 1994/95**

|  | Personal taxpayers | Business taxpayers | All taxpayers |
|---|---|---|---|
| Social compliance cost | 1544 | 8874 | 10 417 |
| Value of deductible compliance costs | –211 | –2446 | –2657 |
| Cash flow benefit/cost | 201 | 1781 | 1580 |
| Taxpayer compliance cost | 1534 | 4647 | 6181 |
| TCC relative to tax revenue | 4.0% | 9.4% | 7.0% |
| TCC relative to GDP | 0.34% | 1.02% | 1.36% |

*Source:* A Report into Taxpayer Costs of Compliance (AGPS: Canberra) 1997, p.ix

**Table 9.13  The hidden costs of taxation**

|  | % of tax revenue |
|---|---|
| Deadweight loss | 8.1% |
| Compliance cost | 7.0% |
| Administration cost | 2.0% |
| **Total** | **17.1%** |

$105.6 billion in 1996/97 from personal and company income tax, the fringe benefits tax and the wholesale sales tax, but it cost the government $1.26 billion to operate. When it is recognised that total taxes collected in 1996/97 were $163 billion and the taxes raised by the ATO are the easiest to administer, then the cost to government of administering all taxes is probably closer to $3 billion or around nearly 2 per cent of revenue raised.

As Table 9.13 shows, while the tax incidence results in Tables 9.9 and 9.10 are interesting, they do not include the hidden burdens of taxation which will have an important impact on who bears the ultimate burden of taxes.

## Personal income tax[7]

Given that the personal income tax raises around 41 per cent of all tax revenue, it is not surprising that it attracts so much attention. Tax policy debates have given a considerable volume of attention to the design of personal income taxes. Much of this debate can be attributed to the choice of the tax base, tax rate schedule, tax unit and its interaction with the welfare system. Each of these issues will be examined in this section.

### Income definition

Income is relatively broadly defined, although it does not include fringe benefits which are taxed not at the individual level but when they are paid by employers.[8] Income from capital gains is also taxable but only when realised and then only real (after inflation)

**Table 9.14 Personal income tax schedule 1996/97**

| Bracket | MTR |
| --- | --- |
| $0—$5400 | 0% |
| $5401—$20700 | 20% |
| $20701—$38000 | 34% |
| $38001—$50000 | 43% |
| $50001 and above | 47% |
| Medicare levy[12] | 1.5% |

gains are taxable. In contrast, income from other sources such as interest and dividends is not adjusted for inflation prior to taxation. However, dividends are grossed up to include any company tax already paid on them.[9]

The base of the personal income tax is also not as broad as that adopted under the social security system where income is imputed to individuals whether it is received or not, as is the case with bank deposits that are deemed to receive at least some minimum rate of interest. This is designed to prevent welfare recipients lowering their income from investments in order to improve their welfare payments under the income tests used to determine welfare entitlements.

A second area where the welfare system deems receipt of income is from the ownership of the family home. This occurs through the application of different assets test for home owners and non-home owners when determining welfare entitlements.[10] In effect, benefits are being imputed to individuals from asset ownership, whether they occur or not. This does not occur under the personal income tax which only taxes realised income. When the Federal government first introduced its personal income tax in 1915,[11] income was defined as including imputed rent for home owner-occupiers—this element lasted only a short time because it proved unworkable.

*Rate schedule*

Australia operates a global income tax. Income from all sources is added together and taxed under one tax rate schedule. The schedule for 1996/97 is shown in Table 9.14.[12] This schedule is quite progressive and as we saw earlier, it is the personal income tax which is the primary source of progressivity in the Australian tax system, counteracting the regressive impact of Federal, State and local government indirect taxes.

The alternative to a global income tax is a schedular tax system in which different income sources are taxed separately under their own tax rate schedules. An example is an interest withholding tax. Under schedular regimes, tax on interest is withheld at source and forwarded direct to the government by financial institutions. The appeal of these taxes is their administrative simplicity and the scope they offer for taxing different income sources in a way which reflects their sensitivity to tax rates. It was this latter argument that was behind Sweden's recent introduction of a 25 per cent tax on capital income. Competition from other European countries for highly mobile capital saw Sweden respond by taxing capital at more competitive rates. Other income sources are still taxable under their traditional income tax but at rates up to and over twice that applying under the schedular tax on capital.

Another issue which pervades the debate over the tax rate structure is whether a tax-free threshold should be adopted and how progressive the rate structure should be. The debate over the merits of a tax-free threshold is largely spurious. None of the proponents of change are effectively arguing for no threshold, only that the threshold should be means tested. In New Zealand, the income tax does not have a threshold and is imposed at two rates (in January 1998) of 21.5 per cent up to $NZ34 200 and at 33 per cent above this level. A low income rebate (LIR) of $NZ617.60 for incomes below $NZ9500 is available. However, because the LIR is with-drawn at a rate of 2.5 per cent for income above $NZ9500, there are in effect three income bands under the New Zealand personal income tax, and a threshold. Even if the threshold is not delivered through the income tax, it will effectively be delivered through the social welfare system.

It is therefore not the threshold that is being debated but the rate schedule. Here the issue is whether a linear[13] or a progressive rate structure should be introduced. In the end, the decision is as much political as economic.[14] The political dimension relates to how high the marginal tax rates should be on middle and higher income groups and whether some linear tax might be preferable, with any progressivity in the overall tax and welfare system introduced through the welfare system.

The economic dimension centres on the marginal tax rates confronted by the average worker and the interaction of the personal income tax and social welfare system for those in receipt of welfare payments. The latter relates to the all-important issue of the effective marginal tax rates (EMTR). Ingles (1997) and Harding and Polette (1995) examined this issue at length and it was the focus of much discussion in the tax reform debate leading up to the 1998 Federal election. High EMTRs arise because not only are most benefits taxed under the income tax but because as a person's private (or market) income increases, their welfare entitlements are reduced because of the application of income tests. For example, if welfare entitlements were withdrawn at a rate of 50¢ for every dollar earned in the labour market, and a personal income tax rate of 20 per cent was imposed on total income earned, the welfare recipient would confront an EMTR of 60 per cent. In practice, for some groups, EMTRs are greater than 100 per cent as a result of the interaction of a number of welfare entitlements.

High EMTRs are hard to reduce when a categorical means tested welfare system is operated, as in Australia. Reducing income tax rates is one small way to address this issue but welfare withdrawal rates are the primary source of high EMTRs. One simple solution might be to reduce withdrawal rates but this would be at a significant cost and result in a much larger group of individuals becoming subject to higher EMTRs.

An issue more easily resolved is whether a tax schedule should be indexed for the effects of inflation. As incomes increase due to inflation under a progressive tax rate schedule, average tax rates increase. This problem is referred to as bracket creep and appeals to politicians because it results in increased personal income tax collections without any explicit government action to increase tax collections. This taxation by stealth can be eliminated by indexing the tax brackets to the inflation rate so that the average tax rate does not increase with increasing incomes. This will mean that the average tax rate on incomes remains stable (as long as the indexation factor is the income inflation rate).

Some governments have explicitly introduced indexation into their tax legislation. Australia did so in 1975/76 but it was short-lived—full indexation lasting only for one year. The reasons for its demise were largely political—politicians felt they were not being given credit for the tax adjustments each year (which is true) but credit was not due to them. Indexation is good economics but probably not great politics.

*Tax unit*

The unit to tax under the personal income tax has been a controversial issue and one which has its genesis in the income splitting debate. The argument here is that for families with the same composition (such as two adults and two children), where one family has one earner and the other has two earners, Australia's personal income tax is not horizontally equitable. The basis for this claim is the observation that one family is able to claim two thresholds but the other can claim only one. At first glance this argument has some appeal, but upon closer inspection real problems arise.

Firstly, it assumes that market incomes are the sole source of a family's welfare. In reality, home production results in benefits to the family that are not taxable. In contrast, if both partners are working, some of these benefits will have to be purchased in the market place or will not be supplied. Income earned in the market is therefore not a good indicator of the family's welfare and therefore is a poor basis of taxation. This argument has led some to argue for individual taxation (Apps 1996).

Secondly, moving to family unit taxation assumes that the tax system is the only domain for delivering benefits based on needs. If the government is intent on assisting families, there is always the option to assist them through the operation of the welfare system. After all, the unit used to determine entitlements in the welfare system is the family.

Thirdly, it overlooks the impact a family unit system of taxation can have on work incentive, particularly for the secondary earner. If income is jointly taxed and only one family member is in market employment, when a second person enters market activity they will have imposed on them the marginal tax rate currently facing the family. Since it is generally accepted that secondary earners are more sensitive to marginal tax rates than the primary earner, a family unit system of taxation provides an important disincentive to the secondary earner to enter the work force.

Despite this observation, family unit taxation is found in many countries (Sommerhalder 1996). The USA adopts the couple as the tax unit, as does Germany. France adopts a quotient system which taxes the whole family, not just the couple. Under the French system, a family's income is aggregated and then sliced into segments depending on the family's quotient, determined by the mix of adults and children in the family. For example, a married couple with two children has a quotient of three. Their family income is divided by three and applied to the tax schedule. To determine the family's tax liability, the tax estimate is then multiplied by three.

In Australia as in New Zealand, the UK, Sweden, Belgium and the Netherlands, the individual is the tax unit. The general trend over recent decades has been away from family unit taxation to individual taxation. This has been pushed both by a desire to simplify income taxation and as a reflection of the fact that female partners are not mere appendages of the male, as was so often the assumption in times gone by.

## Company income taxation

Companies are merely legal constructs designed to enable groups of individuals (shareholders) to come together to produce goods, raise funds and operate with limited liability. In contrast, partnerships or sole traders do not have limited liabilities. The taxation of companies can be seen as a form of withholding tax on personal income received from dividends. In this context it is reasonable to ask why company taxes are needed at all. The traditional argument is that companies confer on individuals certain privileges and that these warrant some level of taxation.

A more convincing argument is that in a capital importing country like Australia, a company tax is necessary to tax profits earned by non-resident shareholders in companies operating in Australia. Without such a tax, these non-resident shareholders would be taxed on their dividends in their home country, which would result in no net benefit to Australia or to the companies from not being taxed in Australia.

One issue which has been the focus of much debate is how companies should be taxed. In practice, there are three methods: the classical system, full imputation and partial imputation. The classical system first taxes company profits at the company level and then taxes the dividends paid out to shareholders as part of their personal income tax liability. The full imputation system differs from the classical system in that shareholders are given a credit for company tax on the dividends they receive. This is done by grossing up the dividend received to reflect the company tax already paid. Two classes of dividends are therefore paid to shareholders by companies, those which are fully franked and those which are unfranked.

A franked dividend is one which will be grossed up in a person's income tax by the rate of company tax (which is currently 36 per cent). As a result, a $74 fully franked dividend would be included in a person's income tax return as $100, for which the person would then claim a $36 tax credit for company tax already paid. An unfranked dividend is included in a person's tax return at face value. Unfranked dividends arise because taxable profits can differ from actual profits due to the availability of special concessions such as those for research and development and accelerated depreciation. Full imputation was introduced in Australia in 1987/88.

Under the partial imputation system only part of the credit for company tax is available as a credit against the personal income tax liability of shareholders. The USA adopts the classical system and the UK partial imputation. In recent years there has been some discussion in Australia (mostly in government circles) about moving to partial imputation. This would appear to be the result of increased claims for imputation credits under the personal income tax, now around 23 per cent of all company tax collections and rising with increased share ownership (Warren 1998).

The economics of imputation is sound. In fact, it is reasonable to argue that even full imputation does not go far enough. Dwyer and Larkin (1995) argue that companies should be treated like trusts. This is an issue which lies at the heart of an important debate about the direction of tax reform in Australia and deserves a brief elaboration.

## Taxing trusts

In the recent debate over the need for tax reform, the growth in the number of trusts and private companies has attracted much attention. The reason for concern is apparent from Table 9.15. The difficulty for governments is that much of this growth can be attributed to changes in the operation of the labour market, a trend positively supported and encouraged by government in both its rhetoric and actions, in particular through labour market reforms, the contracting out of service delivery and the privatisation of government corporations.

Trading trusts have been of particular concern to government. The appeal of such entities over companies is that they enable a full passing through of all income and the concessions that go with these income sources, which is not possible with companies. This issue becomes particularly important for businesses where significant capital gains are expected. When real capital gains are distributed to trust beneficiaries, their status as real capital gains is maintained and can be detailed by the beneficiary as real capital gains in their personal income tax return. In contrast, when real capital gains are paid to shareholders of companies, the benefits arising from the dividends being paid from real capital gains is lost and the shareholders are taxed on the nominal value of the capital gain.

While the economics of this argument are convincing for companies to be treated as trusts (Dwyer and Larkin 1995), the Australian government (and the ATO) have been reluctant to embrace this position because of its revenue implications. Moreover, the government has indicated that it wants to go in the other direction and both tax trusts like companies and reduce the availability of imputation credits to shareholders (Costello, 1998).

The difficulty for the government in clamping down on trusts, particularly discretionary trusts that allow the income of the trust to be distributed to trust beneficiaries at the discretion of the trustee, is they have a long and illustrious history. Trusts have been with us for around five centuries and as Table 9.15 shows, there are now nearly four hundred thousand such trusts in existence in Australia.

## Consumption taxation

The debate over the need for reform to consumption taxes is not new. In 1975 the Preliminary Report by the Asprey Committee[15] stated that 'Outside the area of motoring, drink and tobacco, Australian taxation of goods and services can be dismissed as a

**Table 9.15 Growth in companies, trusts, partnerships and employment: 1991/92 to 1995/96**

| | 1991/92 | 1992/93 | 1993/94 | 1994/95 | 1995/96 | % Change 1994/95 to 1995/96 |
|---|---|---|---|---|---|---|
| Number of companies | | | | | | |
| —Resident | 391 959 | 423 453 | 458 403 | 493 729 | 528 343 | 7.0% |
| —Non-resident | 2 488 | 3 347 | 1 394 | 1 238 | 1 287 | 4.0% |
| Number of companies | | | | | | |
| —Private | 364 540 | 394 003 | 426 570 | 461 624 | 479 587 | 3.9% |
| —Public | 22 266 | 22 603 | 24 023 | 25 066 | 19 028 | −24.1% |
| —Strata title | | | | | 20 183 | – |
| —Other | 7 641 | 10 194 | 9 204 | 8 277 | 10 832 | 30.9% |
| —Total | 394 447 | 426 800 | 459 797 | 494 967 | 529 630 | 7.0% |
| Total partnerships and trusts* | 866 302 | 848 722 | 898 405 | 946 403 | 971 991 | 2.7% |
| —Partnerships | | | | 573 741 | 573 981 | 0.0% |
| —Trusts | | | | 363 198 | 398 010 | 9.6% |
| Number of individual taxpayers | 9 288 826 | 9 272 971 | 9 391 090 | 9 619 010 | 9 851 521 | 2.5% |
| Total employment (million) | 7.637 | 7.634 | 7.781 | 8.093 | 8.389 | 3.7% |

*Sources:* ATO Taxation Statistics 1995–96, CDROM Tables T2, P4, C6

trivial relic' (p.131). At that time, the Federal Treasury stated that there was a unanimous view that 'the present narrowly-based goods and services tax system seems unlikely to be well adapted to producing substantial additional revenue'.[16] The general conclusion at the time was that if increased revenue was required from goods and services taxes, the wholesale sales tax was not the desired approach. Instead, a GST (or VAT)[17] was needed.

However, little interest was shown in consumption tax reform until 1985, when the then Labor government called a National Tax Summit at which it proposed the introduction of a broad based consumption tax (BBCT).[18] In fact, the government proposed three possible tax reform packages in the Draft White Paper (DWP)[19] it prepared for consideration at the National Tax Summit. Two of these options included BBCT and income tax reforms; the third proposed only income tax reforms. In the end, no clear consensus could be gained for any one option and so a minimalist approach was adopted, involving only income tax reforms.

It was not until 1991 that consumption tax reform was again the focus of public debate. With the launch in November 1991 of the Liberal–National Party *Fightback!* package of reforms came a commitment to the introduction of a 15 per cent GST and a significant tax mix change. Initially the *Fightback!* GST had a relatively comprehensive base but in December 1992 the base was revised and made food tax-free (or zero-rated). In the March 1993 election the Liberal–National Party coalition failed to get public support for its tax reform package.

In March 1996 the Liberal–National Party was elected to government and in 1997 again raised the issue of tax reform and sought to make a GST a major plank in their proposed tax reform package. One may well ask why it is that calls for consumption tax reform continue to occur despite the obvious political risks. The answer lies in the clear failure of the current consumption tax system to meet Australia's future tax needs. For the Federal government this means a reliance on excise duties on petrol, tobacco and alcohol, and a wholesale sales tax (WST) which is imposed on a selected range of goods covering only around 10 per cent of household consumption. The Federal government does not tax services. State governments can levy services taxes but do so only in relation to gambling and some tourist services such as accommodation. However, with the recent loss by States of the right to levy taxes on petrol, tobacco and alcohol, it can be expected that they will turn more to this potential revenue source in the future.

These problems with Australia's consumption taxes have been compounded by a decline in tariffs (and hence customs duties) and a decline in the consumption of alcohol (particularly beer) and tobacco. These trends are clear from Table 9.16. The increased contribution by the WST is the result of efforts to increase the base of the WST and increases in rates.

If governments want the contribution by indirect taxes to total revenue to remain constant, alternative methods of raising indirect taxes must be found. It is here that a GST finds a strong case. Another advantage of a GST which subsumed the current WST is that it would serve to reduce the level of input taxing evident under the WST. Currently, only around 50 per cent of the WST is borne directly by households. The remainder is on capital goods and other inputs into the production and distribution process.

While the need for a GST is generally accepted, what is not accepted is the form in which it should be introduced. In an ideal world, the GST would have a broad base and a single rate, with all goods taxed when consumed by households. In practice, however, goods and services can be taxed, exempt or zero-rated. When a good is taxed under a GST, the value of sales is taxable but a credit is given for any GST on inputs. When a good is exempt, inputs into its production are taxable but the output of the good is not taxable. As a result, intermediate inputs into the production of the good are taxable and therefore some tax is embedded in the price of the good.

**Table 9.16  Distribution of taxes by tax type: Australia 1969/70 to 1995/96**

| Year | All income taxes | Customs duties | Excise duties | Crude oil levy and PRRT | Wholesale sales tax | Total Common-wealth taxes | State franchise taxes | State payroll tax | All State taxes | All local taxes | All taxes | All taxes/ GDP |
|---|---|---|---|---|---|---|---|---|---|---|---|---|
| 1969/70 | 52.3% | 5.4% | 11.7% | 0.0% | 7.4% | 82.6% | 0.5% | 0.0% | 12.4% | 5.0% | 100.0% | 24.3% |
| 1974/75 | 57.2% | 4.7% | 9.4% | 0.0% | 6.5% | 80.1% | 0.6% | 5.6% | 15.7% | 4.1% | 100.0% | 27.4% |
| 1979/80 | 53.9% | 4.5% | 7.8% | 6.6% | 5.4% | 79.8% | 1.0% | 5.0% | 15.4% | 4.8% | 100.0% | 28.0% |
| 1984/85 | 53.4% | 4.4% | 6.6% | 6.4% | 7.5% | 80.3% | 1.7% | 4.6% | 15.8% | 3.9% | 100.0% | 30.6% |
| 1989/90 | 55.7% | 3.4% | 6.9% | 1.1% | 8.8% | 78.6% | 2.1% | 4.5% | 17.3% | 3.5% | 100.0% | 31.1% |
| 1990/91 | 56.3% | 2.9% | 6.9% | 1.4% | 7.9% | 78.4% | 2.2% | 4.9% | 17.9% | 3.8% | 100.0% | 31.2% |
| 1991/92 | 54.6% | 2.9% | 7.5% | 0.8% | 8.0% | 76.1% | 2.5% | 5.2% | 19.8% | 4.1% | 100.0% | 29.4% |
| 1992/93 | 54.2% | 2.9% | 7.4% | 1.3% | 7.9% | 75.2% | 2.9% | 5.0% | 20.6% | 4.2% | 100.0% | 28.9% |
| 1993/94 | 52.7% | 2.6% | 7.8% | 0.9% | 8.4% | 74.3% | 3.2% | 4.8% | 21.6% | 4.1% | 100.0% | 29.0% |
| 1994/95 | 53.2% | 2.5% | 7.9% | 0.6% | 8.5% | 75.7% | 3.1% | 4.8% | 20.5% | 3.8% | 100.0% | 30.1% |
| 1995/96 | 54.2% | 2.1% | 7.7% | 0.5% | 8.6% | 76.1% | 3.3% | 4.7% | 20.2% | 3.6% | 100.0% | 30.8% |

*Source:* ABS Taxation Statistics, Cat. No. 5506.0

Firms that purchase these inputs will not be able to claim a credit for this tax since it will not be identifiable.

In the case of a zero-rated good, no tax is payable on the outputs and any tax on inputs is refundable. As a result, the effective tax rate on outputs is zero—hence the term zero-rated.

In many countries with a GST (or VAT), food is either zero-rated or taxed at a rate lower than the standard rate. Financial services, insurance and residential rents are typically tax exempt. In some countries a multiple rate GST is imposed, but this adds greatly to tax compliance costs. The New Zealand GST is probably the best model, being broad based and levied at a single rate of 12.5 per cent.

Being a multiple stage tax, a GST also has the advantage of self-enforcement. Because the GST on inputs is a credit against GST on outputs, producers have an incentive to ensure the correct amount of GST is paid on inputs. However, such a tax does have the disadvantage of being paid by a large number of taxpayers. In 1996/97, the WST had 75 715 taxpayers. A GST can be expected to have around twenty times this number. Also, if a multiple rate GST is imposed (as with a zero-rate on food), compliance costs for these taxpayers could increase. For this reason a single rate broad base consumption tax is the preferred model.

Where a GST is particularly controversial is in its impact on tax equity. It is important when considering this issue to accept that equity is an issue which should relate to the overall design of the *tax and welfare systems*, not just to the GST. In this context, the apparent regressivity of a GST can be overcome through compensatory adjustments to other taxes (such as the personal income tax) and increases in welfare payments to lower income groups.

What is less controversial about the introduction of a GST is the claim that it will provide a tax design capable of providing a buoyant source of revenue with minimal distortion and of providing an avenue for funding the rationalisation of other indirect taxes.

In August 1998, the Howard Government released a report (Costello, 1998) proposing the introduction of a 10 per cent GST in July 2000 accompanied by a modest change in the tax mix towards a greater dependence on consumption taxes. The Howard Government was re-elected in October 1998 and the cooperation of the Australian Democrats saw the GST become a certainty. The proposed reforms will zero-rate (or make GST-free) exports, health and medical care, education, childcare, charitable activities, religious services, water and sewerage, and precious metals. Activities that are to be input taxed include financial services and residential rents. All other goods consumed by households are to be subject to GST. The tax is expected to have some 1.6 million taxpayers.

**Table 9.17 All Federal, State and local taxes on assets and asset transfers as a percentage of total taxes**

| | 1983/84 | 1986/87 | 1989/90 | 1992/93 | 1995/96 |
|---|---|---|---|---|---|
| Taxes on ownership of motor vehicles | | | | | |
| —Registration fees | 1.5% | 1.3% | 1.2% | 1.5% | 1.3% |
| —Stamp duties on new vehicles | 0.5% | 0.6% | 0.6% | 0.6% | 0.7% |
| —Licence fees | 0.2% | 0.2% | 0.2% | 0.2% | 0.2% |
| —Other fees | 0.0% | 0.0% | 0.0% | 0.1% | 0.1% |
| Financial institution duties | 0.4% | 0.4% | 0.5% | 1.2% | 1.3% |
| Taxes on insurance | | | | | |
| —Stamp duties | 0.4% | 0.3% | 0.3% | 0.3% | 0.3% |
| —3rd party | 0.0% | 0.0% | 0.0% | 0.1% | 0.1% |
| —Other | 0.8% | 0.6% | 0.5% | 0.7% | 0.7% |
| Other stamp duties | 2.2% | 2.7% | 3.2% | 2.8% | 2.8% |
| State property taxes | 0.8% | 0.9% | 1.3% | 1.6% | 1.2% |
| **Sub-total** | **6.9%** | **7.0%** | **7.8%** | **9.1%** | **8.7%** |
| All State taxes | 16.8% | 16.3% | 17.8% | 20.3% | 20.1% |
| All local taxes | 3.9% | 3.5% | 3.4% | 4.0% | 3.6% |
| All taxes | 100.0% | 100.0% | 100.0% | 100.0% | 100.0% |

*Source:* ABS Taxation Revenue, Cat. No. 5506.0

The revenue from the GST is to be used to fund personal income tax cuts, welfare increases, and the abolition of the WST and a number of State taxes including some Stamp Duties, FID and accommodation taxes. The revenue from the GST will be handed to the State governments in such a way that the Federal government is no worse off following the introduction of the tax reforms.

## Wealth stock and transfer taxes in Australia

Australia does not have an annual broadly based wealth tax nor estate and gift duties. The closest Australia comes to imposing such taxes are the property rates used to fund local government, and State property and asset transfer taxes. These taxes are briefly reviewed below along with information on wealth distribution and a brief review of the case for a broad based wealth tax.

### Asset and asset transfer taxes in Australia

As the OECD comparison earlier highlighted, property taxation in Australia is almost twice the OECD average, despite Australia not having broadly based wealth taxes. Table 9.17 shows that Australia also has a broad array of other taxes on assets and asset flows which account for nearly 8.7 per cent of all taxes raised. This is so even when excluding the revenue raised from the tax on real capital gains under the income tax. Local governments are almost totally dependent on taxes on property for their revenue needs.

State governments rely on direct and indirect taxes on wealth for over 40 per cent of their revenue. This fact is not recognised by those who argue for increased wealth taxation in Australia. More often than not, the proponents of a wealth tax are arguing for a better distribution of wealth and see a general wealth tax or at least an estate and gift duty as a minimum requirement.

While a raft of taxes is already levied by States on various forms of wealth and wealth transfers, they are not broad based wealth taxes. Rather, they are taxes on selected sources of wealth such as investment property, and even then are taxed using a schedule with a high tax exempt threshold or exclude politically sensitive assets such as the family home. This is the case with most State property taxes. Obviously State governments have considerable scope for increasing their revenue of asset based taxes, if only by reducing the thresholds and broadening the base of current property taxes.

The interesting question to ask though, is: What would be the revenue potential and distributional impact of a broad based net wealth tax in Australia?

## Distribution of private sector net wealth

Australia has a relative dearth of information on wealth distribution. No direct information is collected on this nor has there been a comprehensive survey for over 80 years. This leaves researchers with the task of gleaning information from ancillary sources such as income and expenditure surveys and from estate and death duty information (when such information was available).

Table 9.18 presents estimates of the distribution of various forms of wealth held by the household sector in 1993. Superannuation is the least unequally distributed asset held by households. This should not be surprising since there is now an element of compulsion associated with superannuation contributions.

The distribution of family home ownership is not too different from that of superannuation. This is also not surprising given the tax preferential treatment given to these two forms of savings and the long-held (tax subsidised) aspiration of all Australians to own their own home.

## Case for a death and gift duty or an annual net wealth tax

A question that is frequently asked is whether the unequal distribution of wealth in Australia evident in Table 9.18 merits the introduction of an annual net wealth tax or at least an estate and gift duty. The answer depends on economic as well as political considerations. As we saw earlier in this section, Australia already has substantial wealth based taxes, particularly its property taxes

Table 9.18 Estimated distribution of household assets by asset type: income units by wealth percentile, Australia 1993

| Wealth percentile | Housing gross % | Housing loans % | Housing net % | Interest bearing assets % | Dividend yielding assets % | Value of rental property % | Mortgage in rental property % | Net rental property % | Net business assets % | Sub-total fungibles % | Superannuation % | Total wealth % |
|---|---|---|---|---|---|---|---|---|---|---|---|---|
| 1 – 10 | 0.0 | 0.2 | 0.0 | 0.1 | 0.0 | 2.3 | 9.3 | -2.0 | 0.0 | -0.1 | 0.1 | -0.1 |
| 11 – 20 | 0.0 | 0.2 | 0.0 | 0.5 | 0.0 | 0.3 | 0.7 | 0.0 | 0.0 | 0.1 | 0.3 | 0.1 |
| 21 – 30 | 0.1 | 0.9 | 0.0 | 1.0 | 0.1 | 0.8 | 2.2 | 0.0 | 0.1 | 0.2 | 2.4 | 0.6 |
| 31 – 40 | 1.8 | 9.5 | 0.7 | 2.2 | 0.2 | 2.2 | 6.7 | -0.5 | 1.8 | 0.9 | 6.6 | 2.0 |
| 41 – 50 | 6.0 | 17.0 | 4.4 | 3.2 | 0.7 | 3.9 | 7.4 | 1.7 | 5.7 | 3.9 | 7.3 | 4.5 |
| 51 – 60 | 10.2 | 16.1 | 9.3 | 3.6 | 0.6 | 4.3 | 4.9 | 4.0 | 6.2 | 7.2 | 7.8 | 7.3 |
| 61 – 70 | 13.3 | 16.4 | 12.9 | 5.5 | 0.7 | 7.3 | 8.9 | 6.2 | 9.2 | 10.1 | 10.0 | 10.1 |
| 71 – 80 | 16.3 | 13.0 | 16.8 | 8.0 | 2.2 | 10.8 | 11.3 | 10.5 | 10.0 | 13.4 | 14.1 | 13.5 |
| 81 – 90 | 20.7 | 13.5 | 21.7 | 14.1 | 3.5 | 19.4 | 18.9 | 19.7 | 16.0 | 18.8 | 20.3 | 19.1 |
| 91 – 100 | 31.6 | 13.2 | 34.2 | 61.8 | 92.0 | 48.7 | 29.6 | 60.5 | 51.0 | 45.6 | 31.1 | 42.9 |
| Total | 100.0 | 100.0 | 100.0 | 100.0 | 100.0 | 100.0 | 100.0 | 100.0 | 100.0 | 100.0 | 100.0 | 100.0 |
| 91 – 95 | 12.7 | 7.4 | 13.5 | 11.1 | 6.1 | 19.3 | 14.3 | 22.4 | 17.0 | 13.7 | 13.9 | 13.8 |
| 96 – 99 | 12.8 | 4.1 | 14.1 | 24.0 | 19.8 | 24.0 | 12.3 | 31.2 | 19.8 | 18.0 | 13.7 | 17.2 |
| 100 | 6.0 | 1.6 | 6.6 | 26.6 | 66.0 | 5.5 | 3.1 | 6.9 | 14.2 | 13.9 | 3.5 | 12.0 |

*Source:* Baekgaard (1997), Table 9.8b

and the taxation of capital gains under the income tax. The main issue appears to be whether these taxes are sufficiently comprehensive. With the exclusion of the family home from most tax bases (except when property ownership is transferred), it could be argued that Australia's global income tax does not tax the returns from all major forms of wealth and that a separate wealth tax is necessary.

If imputed income from the family home was taxable or capital gains on the family home was taxable, and negative gearing on residential rental property not allowed, the case for a wealth or an estate and gift duty would be considerably weakened. This is not the case, however, thus it is reasonable to expect that the call for some form of wealth tax will continue—at a minimum. This will involve calls for reduced tax concessions to property investments.

An additional concern not alluded to above is the implication of not having a net wealth tax for the transfer of wealth between generations and consequent perpetuation of wealth inequality across generations. This is one of the more profound reasons for a wealth tax, especially for a death and gift duty, even if a comprehensive income tax were in place.

## International tax competition in a global trading environment

A potential danger for tax systems around the world is the increased mobility of international capital and the growth of new technologies like the Internet. Both these developments have important implications for international tax competition and consequently for tax design.

### International capital mobility

With highly mobile capital, capital importing countries such as Australia are vulnerable to any factor which is perceived by international investors as affecting the returns to capital in one jurisdiction over another. Taxation is one such factor and this means countries must be vigilant in monitoring the international competitiveness of their tax systems.

Earlier we examined how Australia's tax system is different from other OECD and Asian countries. In relation to taxing companies, Australia was amongst some of the highest taxing countries with its global tax on company income. In recent years, other countries have been examining the scope schedular income taxes provide for taxing income streams according to their responsiveness to tax rate differentials between countries.

Sweden, for example, introduced a 25 per cent tax on capital income in an effort to compete with other countries in Europe as the location of capital investment. Other countries have sought to encourage selected income sources through withholding taxes such as on interest and dividends. Through this mechanism the withholding tax is seen as a final tax and is typically levied at some concessionary rate.

In those areas where concessionary treatment is deemed unnecessary, income is taxed at higher rates. This is typically the case with wage and salary earners who are seen as largely insensitive to tax rates—after all, individuals cannot en masse relocate to another country. While this may be true in a physical sense, new technologies such as the Internet will enable workers to supply their labour resources in other jurisdictions, and possibly use the technology to avoid paying tax on this income source by depositing their earnings in a tax haven country.

## The challenge from new technologies

The past two years have seen major efforts by governments around the world to come to terms with the implications for their tax systems of the growth of the Internet. The US Treasury has released a number of reports on this issue, as has the US President. The European Union has also been discussing the introduction of a Bit Tax.[20] Why the flurry of interest?

The answer lies in the scope the technology provides for businesses and individuals to become internationally mobile as factor suppliers, producers and consumers. Furthermore, consumers and producers might be able to shop for the best tax jurisdiction to locate their activities. For example, the Internet could allow a company to relocate to a low tax jurisdiction while still using its previous work force through telecommuting work practices. Here we are not just considering tax haven countries but potentially our major trading partners, who might decide to lower their tax regimes to attract the relocation of global traders.

Countries such as Australia cannot go it alone in regulating or developing tax rules to apply to activities on the Internet. They will either have to follow the lead of other countries or suffer a loss of businesses and workers and hence an erosion of their tax bases. A multilateral approach to taxing Internet activities is therefore the only approach that will work—and then there will still remain the problem of errant states which set themselves up as havens for Internet website and tax evaders.

There is no doubt that a country could still attempt to tax Internet activity within its jurisdiction, but just how successfully would be determined by how sensitive local businesses were to the tax differentials between countries.

The greater the responsiveness of business to tax differentials, the greater and faster will be any response to tax competition from other countries (or States). The recent case in Australia, where Queensland cut in half the stamp duties on share transactions, is a good example of the tax competition likely in the future. Here was a highly mobile financial activity where changes in differential rates would prove irresistible to traders. In this context the other States were forced to adopt a comparable stamp duties regime for fear of losing all their tax revenue from this source to Queensland.

For the Federal government the Internet poses a long-term threat to all income taxes, particularly when high powered data encryption technologies become more readily available. In addition, taxes on consumption which can be digitised are vulnerable. At risk here are taxes on computer software and music and video services. The risks the State governments confront arise through the Internet challenge to their gambling tax revenues and to taxes on financial services. The Internet can already be used to evade State gambling taxes and the Financial Institutions Duty (FID).

The increased level of international cooperation on the challenge posed by the Internet comes from concerns about negative tax competition involving a downward spiral of tax rates. Obviously such tax competition will not be sustainable—hence the high level of international cooperation in addressing this issue.

## Other tax policy issues

This chapter cannot hope to cover all tax issues. Rather our goal has been to give the reader a taste of the nature of many of the controversies which are the focus of much of the tax policy debate in Australia and overseas. Other issues not considered include benefits principle taxation, which involves user-pays levies such as Higher Education Charges, airport landing fees, road user charges, and primary producer levies, and issues such as environmental levies designed to prevent public asset degradation and resource rent taxes.

Nonetheless, the reader should now have a reasonable foundation for going forth and engaging in a constructive debate over the nature and direction of tax reform in Australia.

# 10 The labour market since Howard

*John Burgess,*
*William F. Mitchell and*
*Martin J. Watts*

This chapter examines the developments in the Australian labour market and industrial relations over the two years following the election of the first Howard government in March 1996. According to analysis by the Brotherhood of St Laurence (1998), an estimated 12 per cent (at least 1.7 million people) of the Australian population were living in a household with an income below the poverty line in November 1995. Unemployment, living in a sole-parent family and disability were identified as the key factors associated with poverty. The developments in the labour market together with the policy changes that have occurred in the two years have not redressed the key source of poverty—unemployment. Rather, policy developments appear to be contributing to rising inequality and social exclusion and to the growth in number of the working poor. The single most important problem facing Australia is the persistently high unemployment level, which only fell by 0.2 per cent over the first two years of the Howard government.

Initially we provide an overview of the main labour market trends that have emerged or persisted since 1986, focussing mainly on employment and changes in the level and distribution of wages. The evolution of the industrial relations system under the Coalition government is then examined. The final section discusses the breakdown of labour market programs and the Work for the Dole Scheme. Our central theme is that the labour market policies of the Coalition government over its first two years, which were designed ostensibly to improve the functioning of the labour market, instead

**Table 10.1   Unemployed people by age and whether looking for full- or part-time work, November 1997**

| Age | Looking for full-time work | | Looking for part-time work | | Total | |
|---|---|---|---|---|---|---|
| | Unemployed (000s) | UR (%) | Unemployed (000s) | UR (%) | Unemployed (000s) | UR (%) |
| 15–19 | 77 800 | 27.4 | 65 200 | 14.7 | 143 000 | 19.6 |
| 20–24 | 110 700 | 13.5 | 23 100 | 8.1 | 133 800 | 12.1 |
| 25–34 | 146 600 | 7.7 | 20 600 | 4.9 | 167 200 | 7.2 |
| 35–44 | 120 400 | 6.8 | 22 400 | 4.1 | 142 700 | 6.1 |
| 45–54 | 85 500 | 5.7 | 23 000 | 3.5 | 99 200 | 5.2 |
| 55+ | 41 600 | 6.6 | | | | |
| 55–59 | | | | | 36 300 | 7.2 |
| 60–64 | | | | | 11 600 | 4.8 |

Source:   ABS, *The Labour Force Australia*, November 1997, Cat. No. 6203.0, Table 10.24
Note:      UR = unemployment rate

tended to intensify polarisation and disadvantage in the labour market.

## Unemployment

Figure 10.1 captures the history of unemployment and the average duration of unemployment in Australia since 1950. The average duration of unemployment has increased from three weeks in 1966 (the first available data) to 50 weeks in 1997. Long-term unemployment (one year or longer) is now entrenched. Mitchell (1996, 1998) and Mitchell and Watts (1997) show that the rise in unemployment is largely due to the failure of governments to maintain a sufficient growth in GDP. Thus, in the absence of programs to promote employment growth, the long-term unemployed have very little chance of regaining employment.

Table 10.1 breaks down unemployment into age groups and into work preference (full-time or part-time). Youth unemployment rates are very high and have never recovered from the large cuts in public sector apprenticeship schemes in the mid-1970s. Youth aged 15–19 face around a 19.6 per cent unemployment rate overall and they constitute about 7.8 per cent of the labour force. The problem has been somewhat attenuated by the large increases in school retention rates, the changing demographic distribution of the labour force and the decline in teenage labour force participation (Biddle and Burgess 1998). Nevertheless, full-time youth employment has successively declined over the past 30 years (Wooden 1996).

Recorded unemployment has doubled since 1978, but this alone grossly understates the severity of the decline in the labour market.

**Figure 10.1 Unemployment rate and average duration of unemployment in Australia**

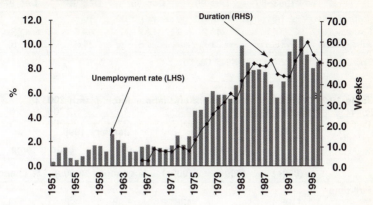

Source: Foster (1996) provided by Derek Sicklen

Mitchell and Watts (1997) estimate that hidden unemployment in 1997 was around 500 000 persons.

## Employment

Chapter 4 provides further analysis of the unemployment situation in Australia, so the focus of this chapter is employment. An analysis of the changes in employment in Australia since March 1996 mirrors the bleak picture contained in Figure 10.1. Employment is no longer a guaranteed means of avoiding the disadvantage usually associated with unemployment. Employment growth has been very moderate since March 1996 (2.69 per cent) relative to labour force growth (2.30 per cent), leading to a very modest decline in the unemployment rate. The demand side of the market has not been able to provide enough jobs to match the number of persons who desire them. For the unemployment rate to remain constant, real GDP growth must be equal to the sum of labour force and labour productivity growth. In the midst of ongoing debates about labour market deregulation, minimum wages and taxation reform, the most salient, empirically robust fact that has pervaded the last two decades is that the actual GDP growth rate has rarely been above this required rate, which is necessary to bring the unemployment rate down.

The already high gender segmentation in the labour force that became apparent during the 1980s continued to worsen over the two years. Two factors have contributed to this. First, almost half of the new jobs created were part-time. More workers than ever are now relying on part-time work for their incomes (see Table 10.2).

**Table 10.2  Part-time employment as a percentage of total employment**

|             | 1983–89 | Dec 90 | Dec 95 | Dec 96 | Dec 97 |
|-------------|---------|--------|--------|--------|--------|
| Males       | 5.7     | 8.5    | 11.0   | 12.0   | 12.2   |
| Females     | 37.7    | 40.2   | 42.7   | 42.6   | 43.0   |
| All persons | 18.8    | 21.7   | 24.5   | 24.9   | 25.5   |

Source: ABS, Labour Force, Cat. No. 6203.0

**Table 10.3  Changes in employment and labour force, March 1996 to January 1998**

|            | March 1996 | | January 1998 | | | |
|------------|------------|-------------|------------|----------|-------------|----------|
|            | Employment (000s) | Labour force (000s) | Employment (000s) | % change | Labour force (000s) | % change |
| **Full-time** | | | | | | |
| Male       | 4198.4 |        | 4281.8 | 1.98 |        |      |
| Female     | 2054   |        | 2084.1 | 1.47 |        |      |
| Persons    | 6252.4 |        | 6365.9 | 1.81 |        |      |
| **Part-time** | | | | | | |
| Male       | 523    |        | 566.3  | 8.30 |        |      |
| Female     | 1518.6 |        | 1585.5 | 4.40 |        |      |
| Persons    | 2041.6 |        | 2151.8 | 5.45 |        |      |
| **Total**  | | | | | | |
| Male       | 4721.3 | 5180.9 | 4848.1 | 2.68 | 5279.1 | 1.89 |
| Female     | 3572.6 | 3883.9 | 3669.5 | 2.71 | 3994.7 | 2.85 |
| Persons    | 8294   | 9064.8 | 8517.6 | 2.69 | 9273.8 | 2.30 |

Source: ABS, Labour Force, Cat. No. 6203.0 (seasonally adjusted). Minor rounding errors may occur

Second, women rely on part-time work much more than men (see Table 10.3). Many part-time jobs are casual and/or low-paid. The rise in importance of part-time work has often been interpreted as a reaction to the desire by workers for more flexible work arrangements. But the percentage of part-time workers who want to work more hours has more than doubled since 1978, which indicates that the demand constraint and structural changes towards casualisation have been forced upon the work force. In November 1997, 597 000 part-time workers (or 27.7 per cent) wanted to work more hours. There is also a high degree of underemployment in the labour market. This is reinforced by the steady percentage of unemployed workers who desire full-time work (78.5 per cent).

There has also been a fundamental shift in the composition of industry employment in the last decade which has been reinforced by the severe public sector budgetary cutbacks in 1996 and 1997. Figure 10.2 compares the average annual (compound) growth rates in employment over three periods: the expansionary period of 1984–89,

**Figure 10.2 Average annual percentage changes in industry employment, 1984–89, 1990–95 amd 1996–97, Australia**

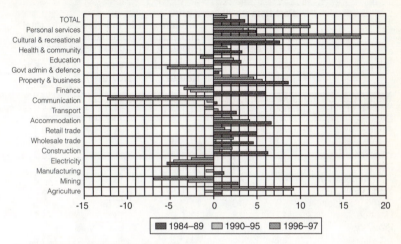

Source: ABS Cat. No. 6248.0 Wage and Salary Earners
   The changes are the average annual (compound) growth rates for each period.

the recession and recovery period of 1990–95, and the period since the Howard government was elected (1996–97).

The two years of Howard government produced total employment growth barely above the 1990–95 period which was plagued by deep recession. In contrast to the recovery period of 1984–89, the employment growth achieved by the economy under Howard was dismal. Employment levels in the production industries (mining, manufacturing, electricity, gas and water, agriculture, forestry and fishing, and construction) were flat or in decline over the Howard period. Manufacturing is the largest production industry and since March 1996 it *not only declined absolutely* but its share in total employment also declined, from 15 per cent to 13 per cent.

The service industries showed dichotomous behaviour. Personal services, culture and recreational services, health and community, property and business, exhibited employment growth, while communications and education declined. Retail and wholesale trade were stifled. The decline in education reflected the harsh public sector cutbacks. Government administration and defence (mostly the former) declined substantially.

The growth of the service industries intensified the segmentation mentioned earlier. Table 10.4 summarises the trends in industry employment over the first months of the Howard government. Many of the trends were already established prior to this period, but the sharp decline in public sector employment was directly attributable

**Table 10.4  Percentage changes in industry employment, May 1996 to November 1997**

| | Part-time as a percentage of total employment (per cent) | | Δ in part-time employment (000s) | Δ in full-time employment (000s) | Δ in total employment (000s) |
|---|---|---|---|---|---|
| | May 1996 | Nov 1997 | May 96 to Nov 97 | May 96 to Nov 97 | May 96 to Nov 97 |
| Agriculture | 24 | 22 | −1.8 | 35.7 | 33.9 |
| Mining | 3 | 3 | 0.3 | −4.6 | −4.3 |
| Manufacturing | 10 | 11 | 11.1 | 22.7 | 33.8 |
| Electricity | 5 | 4 | −1 | −8.1 | −9.1 |
| Construction | 13 | 14 | 2.1 | −1.7 | 0.4 |
| Wholesale trade | 13 | 14 | 2.3 | −11 | −8.7 |
| Retail trade | 42 | 44 | 40.9 | −20.2 | 20.7 |
| Accommodation | 47 | 47 | 12.2 | 13 | 25.2 |
| Transport | 13 | 13 | 0.8 | −7.4 | −6.6 |
| Communication | 12 | 13 | −1 | −16.5 | −17.5 |
| Finance | 17 | 18 | −0.3 | −13.8 | −14.1 |
| Property & business | 24 | 35 | 111.9 | −41.1 | 70.8 |
| Govt admin. & defence | 12 | 14 | 3.7 | −18.1 | −14.4 |
| Education | 32 | 33 | 7.8 | −17.2 | −9.4 |
| Health & community | 39 | 38 | 1.6 | 29.2 | 30.8 |
| Cultural & recreational | 38 | 40 | 17.4 | 14.9 | 32.3 |
| Personal services | 29 | 30 | 8.3 | 12.3 | 20.6 |
| **Total** | **25** | **27** | **216.3** | **−31.9** | **184.4** |

*Source:*  ABS AUSSTATS

to the policies of the current government. The other notable aspect of this period was the sharp shift in mix between full-time (down 31 900) and part-time (up 216 300). In the fastest growing industries (like property and business) part-time work has become the norm. This sharp change in mix is also evident in the retail industry.

Table 10.5 documents the movements in employment for wage and salary earners since 1983 by sector and level of government. After the election of the Howard government, the overall public sector lost around 102 000 wage and salary earner jobs (or 6.5 per cent of the public sector workforce). The losses were substantially due to harsh Federal budgetary policies under which some 67 000 jobs were shed, representing 18.9 per cent of the Commonwealth public sector work force inherited by the Howard government. The States cut around 28 000 jobs (2.6 per cent) and local government has cut 6000 jobs (3.9 per cent). This led to the public sector declining as an employer relative to the private sector, which gained

**Table 10.5  Wage and salary earners—employment, full-time, part-time by sector and level of government**

| Sector | Aug 1983 | Aug 1990 | Aug 1985 | Feb 1996 | May 1996 | Aug 1996 | Nov 1996 | Feb 1997 | May 1997 |
|---|---|---|---|---|---|---|---|---|---|
| **Private (000s)** | 3624 | 4763 | 5175 | 5149 | 5300 | 5295 | 5358 | 5308 | 5391 |
| % of total jobs | 68.8 | 73.2 | 76.7 | 77.0 | 77.0 | 77.7 | 78.0 | 78.5 | 78.4 |
| FT % of total full-time | 65.6 | 70.1 | 73.9 | 74.2 | 74.3 | 75.7 | 76.2 | 76.3 | 76.3 |
| PT % of total part-time | 82.3 | 82.6 | 82.9 | 83.6 | 82.8 | 82.4 | 82.1 | 83.6 | 83.2 |
| **Public (000s)** | 1642 | 1742 | 1573 | 1538 | 1586 | 1517 | 1515 | 1458 | 1484 |
| % of total jobs | 31.2 | 26.8 | 23.3 | 23.0 | 23.0 | 22.3 | 22.0 | 21.6 | 21.6 |
| FT % of total full-time | 34.4 | 29.9 | 26.1 | 25.8 | 25.7 | 24.3 | 23.8 | 23.7 | 23.7 |
| PT % of total part-time | 17.7 | 17.4 | 17.1 | 16.4 | 17.2 | 17.6 | 17.9 | 16.4 | 16.8 |
| **All sectors (000s)** | 5266 | 6504 | 6747 | 6686 | 6885 | 6813 | 6873 | 6766 | 6875 |
| FT % of total jobs | 80.8 | 75.1 | 69.4 | 70.3 | 68.8 | 70.1 | 69.9 | 70.0 | 69.3 |
| PT % of total jobs | 19.2 | 24.9 | 30.6 | 29.7 | 31.2 | 29.9 | 30.1 | 30.0 | 30.7 |
| **Federal (000s)** | | | 339 | 353 | 355 | 303 | 293 | 291 | 288 |
| FT % of all federal | | | 90.6 | 91.1 | 90.9 | 89.9 | 89.8 | 91.1 | 90.3 |
| **State (000s)** | | | 1078 | 1029 | 1076 | 1069 | 1076 | 1019 | 1048 |
| FT % of all State | | | 73.6 | 75.2 | 72.3 | 72.6 | 71.9 | 73.8 | 73.1 |
| **Local (000s)** | | | 156 | 155 | 155 | 146 | 147 | 148 | 149 |
| FT % of all local | | | 76.1 | 74.8 | 74.6 | 75.8 | 74.0 | 72.8 | 70.6 |

*Source:* ABS Wage and Salary earners, Sector and Level of Government, Australia, AUSSTAT, 6248.0

91 000 jobs over the period. Total wage and salary employment thus declined by some 11 000 jobs.

Finally, working time continues to be both polarised and deregulated. The growing bimodal distribution of working hours in Australia is highlighted (EPAC 1996, Ch.3). In particular, the increase in the share of part-time employment has meant that average working hours per week have declined, even though average weekly hours for full-time and part-time workers have increased (ABS, Catalogue 6203.0). There are now 'over-worked' full-timers. The ABS suggests that around 40 per cent of males, and 30 per cent of all workers, are working 45 hours plus per week, which constitutes around 60 per cent of all full-time workers.

A combination of factors has conspired to deregulate working time patterns in Australia. On the demand side the deregulation of product markets and the growing service sector share has meant

**Table 10.6  Average weekly earnings, November 1983 to August 1997**

| ANZSIC industry | Nov 83 | Aug 97 | AWE growth |
|---|---|---|---|
| Mining | 512.9 | 1204.3 | 134.8 |
| Manufacturing | 333.0 | 669.3 | 100.9 |
| Electricity | 398.3 | 837.1 | 110.2 |
| Construction | 344.1 | 699.2 | 103.2 |
| Wholesale trade | 315.5 | 615.3 | 95.0 |
| Retail trade | 191.1 | 345.0 | 80.5 |
| Accommodation | 178.4 | 338.6 | 89.8 |
| Transport & storage | 374.4 | 770.3 | 105.7 |
| Communication services | 370.8 | 799.4 | 115.6 |
| Finance and insurance | 323.4 | 774.4 | 139.5 |
| Property, etc | 281.0 | 583.3 | 107.6 |
| Govt admin. and defence | 349.8 | 687.2 | 96.5 |
| Education | 367.0 | 599.6 | 63.4 |
| Health | 288.8 | 524.1 | 81.5 |
| Cultural services | 286.0 | 428.2 | 49.7 |
| Personal services | 317.9 | 550.6 | 73.2 |
| All industries | 311.3 | 582.2 | 87.0 |

*Source:* AUSSTATS, 6302.0, 6312.0

that employers require greater intertemporal flexibility with respect to labour deployment. On the supply side the growth in participation in post-secondary education and the growth in female labour force participation rates have meant that there are more workers with diverse and fragmented working time preferences (EPAC 1996, Ch.3).

We should add to this the effect of an emerging institutional framework that has facilitated working time deregulation. The push for labour market 'flexibility' by employers (Campbell 1993), the indifference of trade unions (Campbell 1996), the spread of enterprise bargaining and the de-collectivisation of the work force all facilitated a fundamental change in working time patterns. Manifestations of the deregulation of working time include: the extension of the spread of hours for the 'standard' working day or working week; the growth of evening and weekend employment; the growth in rotating and flexible working time patterns like split shifts and workers 'at call'; and the increase in unpaid hours, notably unpaid overtime, which has become averaged or an expected part of 'standard' working conditions.

## The level and distribution of wages

The structural shift in employment by industry has ramifications for the general level of wages, because the sectors which are declining in relative size are typically those which pay higher wages. In Table 10.6, average weekly earnings by ANZSIC Industry are shown for

**Table 10.7  Growth in award indexes, November 1983 to June 1997**

| Award index | Index growth |
| --- | --- |
| Male hourly earnings | 60.56 |
| Female hourly earnings | 69.60 |
| Persons hourly earnings | 63.28 |
| Male weekly earnings | 58.15 |
| Female weekly earnings | 64.57 |
| Persons weekly earnings | 60.09 |

*Notes:*  The Award Index (June 1976=100.0) for the period November 1983 to June 1985
was spliced to the corresponding award index (June 1985=100) to generate the
index growth rates. The weekly award index based on wages, rather than
salaries was employed in the weekly calculations.
*Source:*  AUSSTATS, 6302.0, 6312.0

the period November 1983 to August 1997. The table reveals that
the highest paying industries in November 1983 have experienced
the fastest rate of growth of AWE with a correlation of nearly
50 per cent. Earlier work pointed to the high rank correlation of
industry wages (Watts and Mitchell 1990b).

Table 10.7 shows the growth in Award Indexes for the period
November 1983 to June 1997 by gender. Female award wages have
risen significantly more quickly than male awards, albeit from a
lower base. This has not meant increased earnings equity, however.

The distribution of earnings in Australia has continued to widen
since the 1970s, despite frequent changes in the principles of wage
fixation and, in particular, a period of centralised wage fixation
between 1983 and 1987 (see King et al 1992; Watts and Mitchell
1990b; Gregory 1993; McGuire 1994; Watts 1997a). In the decade
to 1996, the adult, full-time distribution of wages was characterised
by increased polarisation, mainly through the downgrading of the
lower half of the wage distribution (Watts 1997a).[1] A major factor
appears to have been the differential rates of wages growth across
occupations. When changes in the structure of employment by
full-time and part-time status are also taken into account, the
distributional change is likely to be even greater. In the next section
we examine the changes in industrial relations and labour market
legislation enacted by the Federal Coalition government and their
potential impact on the level and distribution of wages.

## Changes to the wage determination system

### Workplace Relations Act

Under the previous government the Prices and Incomes Accord was
the central element in wage fixation. It evolved in the light of
changing economic circumstance through eight phases, from a

**Table 10.8  Key features of the Workplace Relations Act**

| Feature | Comment |
| --- | --- |
| Compulsory arbitration | Limited to minimum entitlements and emergency services disputes |
| Awards | Limited to 20 minimum entitlements Safety net adjustments for low paid |
| Certified agreements | Union and non-union agreements possible, vetted by IRC |
| Strikes | Limited to sanctioned bargaining periods |
| Trade unions | Closed shops illegal, non-union enterprise agreements possible, limited rights of workplace entry, more sanctions over behaviour |
| AWAs | Individual contracts, vetted by Employment Advocate |
| Role of IRC | Ratify certified agreements Award safety net adjustments Award simplification |
| Office of Employment Advocate | Facilitate and certify AWAs |

centralised indexation model to an increasingly decentralised model based on enterprise bargaining. The new government abandoned the Accord after it took office and introduced the Workplace Relations Act (WRA), which formalised the process of decentralisation and encouraged non-union enterprise bargaining at a time when employee trade union density was already low, with around 30 per cent of employees belonging to trade unions.[2] Table 10.8 shows the key features of the Workplace Relations Act.

The WRA imposed extensive regulatory sanctions against trade union activity and paved the way for employers to reduce award coverage and to move towards non-union bargaining. Some radical employers in the maritime industry (Melbourne's Webb Dock) and coal industry (Rio Tinto's, Hunter Valley No. 1 mine) have used the WRA in an attempt to diminish award and union presence at the workplace. In this anti-union context, Australian Workplace Agreements (AWAs) represent a key development of the WRA. These agreements attempt to formalise and facilitate individual employment contracts. They embody direct bargaining and do not require trade unions' presence or participation.[3]

The Department of Industrial Relations (DIR 1995, 1996) has suggested that the WRA will lead to a more direct and balanced relationship between employers and employees, with a reduced role for third party intervention. Further, it has claimed that there would be genuine freedom of association and a greater choice of union representation. The previous Accord system was considered by the

DIR to be too centralised, resulting in a lack of choice for employers and employees in the bargaining process, as well as giving too much power to the Industrial Relations Commission (IRC) and trade unions, thereby causing an unbalanced relationship between the employer and employee. Also, the system was considered to be too rigid, because there was insufficient scope for incorporating the different circumstances across enterprises. In particular, the award system was a barrier to flexible employment arrangements. In summary, the previous system was considered to be incompatible with microeconomic reform and responsible for Australia's major macro-economic problems, including unemployment and inflation.

There are now in effect three different processes in operation at the Federal level for determining wage increases. Under the award system minimum wage increases are established by the IRC to apply across enterprises for the particular award classification. Through enterprise bargaining wage increases are negotiated for the specific enterprise and/or workplace. Outside of these collective mechanisms are AWAs and other informal and direct arrangements between each employee and management. Only 35 per cent of employees are still covered by awards, while 35 per cent are covered by registered enterprise agreements and 30 per cent are covered by common law or individual contracts (Buchanan and Watson 1997, p.7). As a consequence, the award system which previously protected those employees with minimum bargaining power, and ensured that wage increases were distributed across the work force, is becoming less important in the Australian industrial relations system.

## The 1996 Living Wage Case

The Living Wage Case was conducted before the full bench of the IRC in 1996 and a decision announced in April 1997. The ACTU was initially seeking a $20 per week safety net wage increase, a minimum weekly wage of $380 per week and an award wage increase of 8.75 per cent, to be further supplemented by $20 per week wage increases in the following two years. The ACTU claimed that a large group of workers who were located within the Federal award system were missing out on enterprise based wage increases. Since real award wages have stagnated since 1993 the ACTU argued that these workers should receive 'safety net' wage increases. In addition it argued that there was a need to protect the lowest paid through increasing a Federal minimum award wage rate.

The Reserve Bank was particularly influential in its opposition to the claim, by suggesting that it would push up average wages growth to unacceptable levels, which would feed through into costs and threaten the inflation target and ultimately delay interest rate

cuts, thereby retarding economic growth and employment growth
(Reserve Bank of Australia Bulletin, December 1996). The Reserve
Bank also saw excessive wage increases as generating unemployment
through the over-pricing of labour. There was a tension in the
Reserve Bank's position. It could delay interest rate cuts as a result
of what it regarded as excessive wage increases. The delay in interest
rate cuts would prevent higher growth rates and employment
expansion, and the Reserve Bank would be vindicated because the
unemployment rate remained high or even increased.

The Federal government opposed the claim but did support an
$8 per week safety net increase. Apart from the ACTU a number
of welfare groups, including the Brotherhood of St Laurence, supported the claim on the basis of growing inequality and growing
numbers of working poor in the community.

In a split ruling the full bench of the IRC granted a $10 a week
safety net increase and increased the minimum wage to $359.40 per
week. Estimates suggest that around 2 million employees had not
received enterprise bargained wage increases, of whom around
200 000 were on minimum wage rates. The impact of the safety net
wage increase on average wages growth has been estimated to be
less than 0.5 per cent (Bellchamber 1997). In 1997 the ACTU
subsequently made a second round living wage claim of $58.60 over
two years together with a $20 per week safety net claim for those
unable to negotiate wage increases under enterprise bargaining.

Under the Accord, the macroeconomic wage outcome was considered to be of utmost importance in the quest for low inflation
and an internationally competitive economy. With the increased
decentralisation of the wages system, the timing and size of wage
increases have become less predictable. There are no longer wage
targets or coordinating mechanisms, characteristic of the Accord.
Thus there is a conflict between the push for enterprise bargains
and the Reserve Bank's insistence on using wage outcomes as its
guide to interest rate policy. There has been a de facto return to
centralised wage targets in Australia, which the Reserve Bank con-
cedes are based on misleading and partial aggregate wage data
(Reserve Bank 1996).[4]

Ironically, low wage workers are strongly represented in the
group whose wages continue to be largely controlled by the Commission through the setting of awards. The unfairness of imposing
the burden of wage moderation on the low paid was noted by one
of the Commissioners in a dissenting view at the Living Wage Case
(Buchanan et al 1998). In addition, as noted in the previous section,
the source of the polarisation of the adult full-time wage distribution
over the decade 1986–96 was the downgrading of the lower half of
the wage distribution, a trend which is likely to continue.

**Table 10.9 Average wages growth per different wage measures (%)**

| Year | Awards | AWE (ABS) | AWOTE (ABS) | AWE (National Accounts) |
|------|--------|-----------|-------------|-------------------------|
| 1993/94 | 0.99 | 2.89 | 3.06 | 2.59 |
| 1994/95 | 1.34 | 3.42 | 4.05 | 1.60 |
| 1995/96 | 2.03 | 2.48 | 4.52 | 4.23 |
| 1996/97 | 1.45 | 2.35 | 3.52 | 4.64 |

*Source:* Calculations from data in Reserve Bank *Bulletin*

The institutional intervention in the setting of awards is the only means by which any consistency between the structure of awards and bargained outcomes can be maintained, but, through its capacity to adjust interest rates the Reserve Bank can effectively veto any award adjustment which it views to be excessive. As the centralised role of the IRC in wage setting has diminished, the vacuum is being filled by the Reserve Bank (see also Buchanan et al 1998). Table 10.9 shows that the growth of the award index (both hourly and weekly) lagged appreciably behind the growth of average weekly earnings, even over the period of Labor government, when the award system covered nearly all workers and was central to wages policy. With the reduced coverage of awards and the increased burden on workers on awards to exercise wage moderation, it is inevitable that wage dispersion will continue to increase, particularly through the downgrading of the lower half of the wage distribution, unless there is intervention via a more generous social welfare system and/or a more progressive tax system. Given the budgetary stance of government, this would appear to be unlikely. Indeed, some commentators argue in favour of a reduction in benefits to restore the incentive to work (see, for example, Moore 1997). These changes will be exacerbated by the structural deterioration of the labour market, described in the first section of this chapter.

In Australia, the Labor and Liberal parties appear to believe that enterprise bargaining leads to increases in productivity and efficiency and hence international competitiveness, via improvements in work practices. This implies a link between less regulated workplace arrangements and the expansion of high wage, high productivity jobs, but this link has never been explained. The OECD Jobs Study (1994) and OECD (1996) point to the alleged benefits of the greater wage flexibility that characterises the American model, in the form of stronger growth and increased employment opportunities for *low skilled* workers which imply income gains for the economy as a whole. These are claimed to offset the social implications of wider wage differentials arising from the growth of low wage jobs. Workplace arrangements that sanction low wages are unlikely to promote high levels of investment, which, however, is the source of long-run increases in labour productivity. Finally, the failure of enterprise bargaining outcomes to reflect the growth in labour productivity raises the question of whether enterprise bargaining is an appropriate form of wage determination in this fragmented system.

The Australian industrial relations system has become more decentralised and less centrally coordinated through the demise of the Accord and the introduction of the WRA. Awards and safety net adjustments still provide for some degree of collectivisation and equity within the system. However, the Coalition has signalled further industrial relations legislation during its second term of office. Further award simplification, a diminished role for awards, inducements for AWAs, and further restraints on trade union activities are planned, signalling further decentralisation and de-collectivisation of the system. In this context important issues that will challenge policy include the position of the very low paid and the likely emergence of an underclass of working poor, as in the USA, growing earnings polarisation and the further deregulation of employment arrangements (especially working time). These changes will challenge the ability of the system to deliver both job and productivity growth.

## Labour market policy?

### The decline of labour market programs

Underpinning the Labor government's Working Nation policy was the explicit assumption that the constraint on reducing unemployment was structural, so that the first objective was to reduce the Non Accelerating Inflation Rate of Unemployment (NAIRU). Accordingly there were extensive targeted labour market programs which included wage subsidies for long-term unemployed and the preparation of the unemployed for employment through training schemes. However, in the absence of job creation, these policies merely shuffle the queue of unemployed workers (Thurow 1975). The provision of extra training is useless unless extra jobs are created via rising levels of aggregate demand. The Job Compact, which spelled out the mutual obligations of government and unemployed, was symptomatic of the shift in emphasis from passive income support to active programs.

In its first two budgets (1996/97, 1997/98), the Coalition government has radically reformed the program of employment assistance for the unemployed. It was claimed that both the efficiency and the effectiveness of assistance would improve through an employment services market that rewarded the service providers for placing clients into *real* jobs. The new arrangements were to be funded by scrapping most of the Labor government's labour market programs in 1998, with the exception of some entry-level training programs which support the objectives of the Modern Australian Apprenticeship and Traineeship System (see below) and regional assistance and employment strategies for Aboriginal and Torres Strait Islander peoples. These programs were designed to function alongside the employment services market. The New Enterprise Incentive Scheme (NEIS) was also retained to assist unemployed people to establish new businesses.[5]

Wage subsidies were to be available to employers who take on job-seekers being case managed or who have been unemployed for six months or more. Projected expenditures on labour market programs were to fall by $1.8 billion over four years in line with the government's strategy of deficit reduction. This budgetary strategy was claimed to increase the growth capacity of the Australian economy, and ultimately achieve sustained reductions in unemployment.

An integrated 'one-stop-shop' service delivery agency was developed which provided all the income support services including pensions and family payments currently provided by DSS; registration, assessment for, and referral to employment assistance services currently undertaken by the CES; enhanced self-help facilities to assist with job search for job-seekers; activity testing; provision of information, advice and guidance on government and community employment and welfare services; assistance for students; and special assistance for some groups, notably Aboriginal and Torres Strait Islander people, young people and migrants.

Labour market assistance to job-seekers was to be provided through competing 'employment placement enterprises' (EPEs) that are contracted by DEETYA, after a tendering process and an assessment of likely regional demand.[6] DEETYA is responsible for quality and the ongoing monitoring of contract performance by these agencies. Payment of a placement fee to an EPE will only be made if the EPE places an eligible job-seeker in a job listed on a national vacancy database. The fee would reflect the different needs of job-seekers and the levels of assistance required to place them into jobs. It was expected that approximately 60 per cent of available Intensive Employment Assistance (IEA) places and nearly 70 per cent of IEA funds were to be provided to long-term unemployed job-seekers, with the balance going to other job-seekers from special groups and those at high risk of long-term unemployment.

The early signs, following the implementation of this scheme in May 1998, were that the service to the unemployed had been reduced with more uncertainty over where to find assistance and jobs information.

Other changes to programs simplified administrative procedures and eliminated inconsistencies between different programs. The CESAC changes represented the first step in the transition from highly structured discrete programs with a complicated set of rules and regulations to a simple structure in which providers are claimed to have complete flexibility in the means they use to find their clients jobs.

## Apprenticeships

The Modern Australian Apprenticeship and Traineeship System (MAATS) was introduced to provide 'real' employment and train-ing opportunities for young people of Australia. It replaced the Australian Traineeship System (ATS), introduced in 1985. The new system was designed to be more flexible in response to industry and individual needs, by assisting employers to provide jobs that include a mix of work and training that suited both the employer and the trainee. Traineeships and apprenticeships were to be available in new industries to take advantage of growth and employment poten-tial, with a focus on opportunities in small and medium sized businesses in emerging technology, information and service indus-tries. Funding of $206 million, largely redirected from the labour market program budget, was to be provided over four years for MAATS (Biddle and Burgess 1998).

While the traditional apprenticeship system remains a significant source of entry level employment for young people, and the principal source of skilled manual workers in Australia, there has been a decline in the number of apprenticeships. The proposals to modern-ise and simplify the system and make it more flexible, with training driven by business interests, and expanding apprenticeships into new and emerging industries, should help to sell the system. It is unclear whether MAATS can overcome the problem of achieving widespread acceptance as an effective entry level training system in non-manufacturing industries, which eluded the Australian Traineeship System (Stromback 1996, p.9).

Active labour market programs still have an important role to play, and can improve the effective supply of labour and reduce skill and capacity bottlenecks, although the plethora of labour market programs established under Labor, with their differing requirements, must have been administratively inefficient. Even with the availabil-ity of jobs many unemployed people still require direct assistance and support in locating positions and in readying themselves to take up such positions. If anything, youth require more extensive and expensive labour market services, not fewer and cheaper labour market services (Fay 1996, p.32).

## Higher education

In the August 1996/97 Budget the Coalition government retained the income contingent character of the Higher Education Contributory Scheme (HECS) for university students, but replaced the flat rate HECS, which was introduced in 1989, with a three-tier HECS. The minimum level of taxable income at which repayment takes place was reduced to $20 701 and the schedule of repayment rates associated with different levels of income was steepened, with the initial rate of 3 per cent rising in increments of 0.5 per cent to 6 per cent for incomes of $37 263 and above.

There is a strong economic justification for students making a contribution to the cost of putting on their courses, because the acquisition of a university degree confers considerable (net) economic, cultural and social benefits to them. Since these benefits are not exclusively private, a subsidy should be paid by government to ensure that sufficient students have the incentive to complete university degrees (Chapman 1996, pp.44–5).

The Coalition's justification for the location of different fields of study across the three tiers is not merely to recover portion of the cost of the courses being mounted but, in addition, takes account of the prospective income stream of the graduate associated with the particular course. The linking of the current costs of educational services to the prospective income stream of their recipients has no justification in economic theory and has the capacity to distort preferences for different courses (see Watts 1997b).

From the beginning of 1998, universities could offer some places to local students for upfront fees, provided that the institution had filled its target number of places for HECS-only undergraduates. The minimum fee for these additional places will be set at the corresponding HECS charge for the particular course.

The increased emphasis on user pays has been accompanied by a decline in public funding of universities. Operating funds for universities in 1997 were projected to be 0.6 per cent over 1996 levels and 1.2 per cent below 1996 levels in 1998. In New South Wales enrolments of HECS undergraduates for 1998 fell significantly, which suggests that the change in the structure of HECS had a significant impact on students' decisions to enter university. More generous support policies may assist in reducing attrition rates for those in full-time education. The 20–24 years group face the prospect of tighter and less generous study allowances and increased fees for tertiary education.

The reduced outlays by the Coalition government on labour market programs and higher education, as announced in their first two budgets, would suggest that deficit reduction strategies take priority over improved training and job readiness of the unemployed. The House of Representatives Standing Committee on Employment, Education and Training 1997, p.121, concluded, 'Cuts to education, training and labour market programs are not justified and should be reversed. Active, and often expensive, case management is required to assist those disadvantaged youth, especially those seeking full-time employment without Year 12 qualifications.'

## Work for the Dole

To a large extent the Coalition government eschewed job creation and severely pruned the Federal public service in its first term.[7] One interesting development, which perhaps largely reflects the government's view of the obligations of the unemployed, rather than its desire to improve the functioning of the Australian labour market, was the introduction of the Work for the Dole legislation in 1997. It established a maximum number of hours of work for recipients of the dole per fortnight and allowed participants to receive an extra $10 a week to cover additional costs.

The Federal government piloted 178 Work for the Dole projects throughout Australia, involving over 10 000 participants. Many communities with the highest rates of youth unemployment received few or no projects, with the $21 million scheme skewed heavily in favour of Coalition regional electorates (McGeogh 1997). Young people aged 18 to 24 who had been unemployed for at least six months and had not been in a training or employment assistance program got priority. The programs run for a maximum of six months and participants will be required to work a maximum of two and a half six-hour days each week. It was anticipated that most participants will be volunteers, but some people had to work for their dole involuntarily. The projects are designed to formalise the principle of mutual obligation between taxpayers and the unemployed who receive financial support.

In January 1998 the Federal government toughened its dole policy by making it mandatory for all long-term jobless aged 18 to 24 to take part in training programs, to undertake voluntary or part-time work for at least six hours a week for a minimum of 14 weeks, or to relocate in exchange for benefits. Those refusing to fulfil their 'obligation' face loss of benefits, with a standard 18 per cent reduction in payments for 26 weeks applying for a first offence. As part of the policy, that applied from 1 July 1998, the pilot Work for the Dole scheme was expanded, with 20 000 new places out of 25 000 being associated with the requirement of 'mutual obligation'.

With the available places exceeding the supply of voluntary participants, many young unemployed workers were required to satisfy their obligation by participating in the other designated activities; it was announced that young people who live more than 90 minutes commuting time from any mutual obligation activity, and for whom literacy and numeracy distance education was not suitable, may be exempt from mutual obligation requirements and thus would not be forced to relocate. The government would also look at locating new Work for the Dole projects in areas where the different options were in short supply.

The government also planned to spend $383 million over four years on initiatives including a pilot program to provide mentors for job-seekers, a literacy and numeracy program, and measures to help young people forced back into the education system by the new dole requirements.

The Work for the Dole scheme is designed to break the cycle of unemployment. Most participants would be volunteers wishing to receive the benefits of employment experience, but members of the target group, who are characterised by the cycle of despair, low self-esteem and poor work ethic, are relatively less likely to volunteer and are more likely to need coercion into participating. Those who are forced to undertake this form of work and even volunteers are likely to be somewhat resentful, when their remuneration for two or two and a half days work a week is the same as unemployment benefits. The scheme has been described as purely a political gesture to appease commonly held prejudices about unemployed youth (Grattan 1997). It is not designed for older people, who make up a bigger proportion of the long-term unemployed.

A central theme of the strategies of employment assistance for the unemployed and Work for the Dole is to create real jobs. It is not clear what 'real' jobs are—if they are jobs that provide training, employment security and a career path, then virtually no youth jobs would qualify as real jobs. Work for the Dole schemes do not create real jobs, provide participants with marketable skills or reduce unemployment (Burgess and Biddle 1998). The unemployed require long-term jobs with pay and conditions and training and promotion opportunities similar to those already in employment. Only in these circumstances will they overcome the cycle of despair, low self-esteem and a poor work ethic. The House of Representatives Standing Committee on Employment, Education and Training agrees. They concluded (1997, p.120): 'The most significant factor influencing the employment of young people is the availability of jobs. The benefits of economic growth have not transferred into

jobs for young people. Many entry level positions have disappeared.'
Without sustained job creation relatively high unemployment rates
for all age groups will persist.

## Conclusions

In this chapter we have examined labour market trends and detailed
the Coalition's industrial relations and labour market policies during
their first two years in office which have ostensibly been designed
to facilitate the achievement of full employment with low inflation.
Two key points emerge from this analysis.

First, the central macroeconomic goals of the Coalition government are a reduction in the budget deficit and the maintenance of
a low rate of inflation. A small public sector is viewed as providing
the conditions for the expansion of the private sector. Labour market
and industrial relations policies are viewed as subordinate to the
achievement of these goals.

Second, unemployment is viewed as structural, which reflects an
industrial relations system which remains too rigid and a set of
labour market programs which have been overly complex to administer and inefficient in the provision of education and training and
employment assistance. The government's solution to structural
unemployment is further decollectivisation and decentralisation of
the wages system, the dilution of the award system and privatisation
of the public employment service. Combined with funding cuts for
labour market programs and the use of Work for the Dole programs
is a prevailing view that supply-side solutions will somehow generate
a large number of new jobs, especially for the unemployed.

It is our contention that these labour market and industrial
relations policies are fundamentally misguided. Unemployment per-
sists due to acute demand deficiency. Active labour market programs
have an important role to play in assisting disadvantaged job-seekers
to locate vacancies and to prepare them for work. Structural and
technological changes to the labour market mean that education and
training are becoming more important in the preparation of people
for work. Cuts in labour market programs and study allowances,
together with increased tertiary education fees, such as we have seen,
are unlikely to facilitate training and education.

# 11 Industry policy in Australia
## Robert Conlon

The term 'industry policy' in Australia has long been interpreted as *manufacturing industry* policy. For more than a century its dominant theme has been the protection of local manufacturing industries from import competition, and the story of protection in this country has largely been the story of the Australian tariff. However, over the last twenty years or so average tariff levels have steadily fallen and since the 1980s both major political parties have accepted (with some recent backsliding) the need for Australian industries to be more exposed to international competition. By the end of the century, the tariff will have been largely dismantled, but as tariffs have declined other, often less transparent, schemes have tended to take their place. For example, now, instead of taxing imports (or as a complement to import barriers), we subsidise exports implicitly or explicitly, or provide assistance for research and development. If tariffs were the 'old protection', these measures could be described as the 'new assistance'. Of course government help has not been restricted to manufacturing. Agriculture has also been assisted, mainly by taxation concessions, marketing schemes of various types (supported by taxpayers' funds), subsidies and adjustment payments of one form or another. These measures of assistance for industry—now known as business programs—have tended to proliferate. Indeed, over a long period programs to assist industry have grown more or less willy-nilly, often as a result of political expediency rather than from any underlying economic rationale.

In this examination of industry policy there are some important omissions. There is a legitimate case for including recent competition policy and the overall microeconomic reform agenda in the discussion. Policies designed to change (and improve) the competitive environment in both the public and private sectors of the economy will obviously affect the behaviour of firms, the structures of industries and the way they perform. Space, however, is limited. While industry policy in the broad sense encompasses activities in all sectors of the economy and all the policies aimed at modifying these activities, historically, governments both State and Federal have concentrated their attentions on manufacturing in the apparent belief that it is the only sector producing 'real' goods and 'real' jobs. This chapter will follow this lead. Its primary focus will be on the development of manufacturing industry policy in Australia—from the period when tariffs were dominant to the 'new' assistance measures which have been introduced by governments over the last two decades. It will also look at the future directions of industry policy following the recommendations of the recent Mortimer review of business programs, *Going for Growth*, and the response of the Federal Government to it, *Investing for Growth*.[1]

## Industry policy and institutions

### The early tariffs

Protective tariffs and other measures of trade control date from well before Federation. From the 1840s the colonies of New South Wales, South Australia and Van Diemen's Land pursued 'beggar-my-neighbour policies' (imposing protective measure and countermeasure) designed to foster their local industries at the expense of the other colonies. However, the beginning of overt protectionism in this country is usually considered to have had its origins in the Victorian gold rushes of the 1850s and the resulting immigration which produced an almost fourfold increase in the colony's population in the eight years to 1860.[2] When the gold rushes came to an end, tariffs were introduced to protect and expand the manufacturing base that had developed during the period.

Victoria's tariffs (which also provided a significant source of revenue for the colony's government) were an important and divisive issue in the long debate which eventually led to Federation. The free-trading colony of New South Wales was dominated by pastoral interests, and the proceeds of Crown land sales made it independent of tariff revenues. When Federation finally came about, there was a compromise on the issue, but one in which the balance of advantage was won by Victoria. Federation in 1901 brought the introduction of a common external tariff and, according to the Minister for Trade and Customs of the day, C.C. Kingston, 'at this time in our history neither free-trader nor protectionist can have his way entirely'. While the main objective of the first Australian tariff was raising revenue, 'protection, to existing industries at least, must accompany it'.[3] From that time, the protective element assumed increasing importance in various pre-World War I tariff revisions.

## The Tariff Board

During World War I manufacturing industries developed to replace the imports which were disrupted by lack of foreign supplies and available shipping space. Following the resumption of 'normality' at the end of the war came pressure on the Federal Government to provide protection for industries which had grown behind the prohibitive wartime barriers. As a response to these pressures (and to insulate the government from the political heat of the tariff-making process) the Tariff Board was set up in 1921. It was to inquire and report on:

(a) the necessity for new, increased or reduced duties, and the deferment of existing or proposed deferred duties;[4]
(b) the necessity for granting bounties for the encouragement of any primary or secondary industry in Australia; and
(c) the effect of the existing bounties or of subsidies subsequently granted.[5]

Despite its central role in influencing protection policy, by the end of the 1920s it had become a matter of concern to the Board that there was a 'danger of the tariff being used to bolster up the ever-increasing cost of production'. Moreover, there were instances of 'abuse' of protection 'where a highly protected industry returns to its shareholders, dividends considerably in excess of commercial rates'.[6] The Brigden Committee was formed to examine the role of protection and its report was broadly supportive of the way policy had operated to that time. Nevertheless the Committee suggested 'the tariff may be likened to a powerful drug with excellent tonic properties, but with reactions on the body politic which make it dangerous in the hands of the unskilled and the uninformed'. It concluded the tariff 'had reached its economic limits' and that 'no further increases in, or extensions of the tariff should be made without the closest scrutiny of the costs involved'.[7] Despite this, mainly as a result of measures introduced to deal with the Depression (especially the Scullin tariff of April 1930 which involved unprecedented increases in duties—though Scullin claimed this was not for the purpose of protection, but saving Australia's financial viability[8]), by World War II tariffs were about one-half as high again as they were in 1929.[9]

For much of the first fifteen or twenty years after World War II the tariff was essentially redundant as a means of protecting Australian industry. During the greater part of the 1950s, direct quantitative restrictions (quotas) operated through a system of import licensing, the result of foreign exchange shortages under a fixed (and overvalued) exchange rate regime. These quotas became the binding constraint on imports, though the government of the day stated explicitly to industry that it was not to take advantage of import controls as a protective barrier behind which it could expand. Needless to say the admonition was ignored.

The tariff once again became the dominant influence protecting manufacturing in the early 1960s when most direct import controls were scrapped. It was a tariff that was substantially unchanged since the 1930s; one in which the distorting influence of the Scullin tariff of more than 30 years before could still be discerned. Indeed, the Tariff Board had begun to lobby for an overall review of the tariff in the late 1950s, but the task of winning the government to the cause of tariff reform proved to be a long and difficult one. It took the Board more than a decade to convince the (McMahon) government of the need for a review, which finally began in 1971 and was to take seven years. The Whitlam government, which took office in 1972, continued the review process, and in 1974 formed the Industries Assistance Commission which subsumed the Tariff Board, broadening the scope of its activities from manufacturing to include industries in the rural, mining and services sectors. During this period the 25 per cent tariff cut of July 1973—made by the Whitlam government without reference to the Tariff Board—took place and remains the most significant single change in the tariff since World War II.[10]

How had the tariff shaped post-war Australian manufacturing? In 1965 the report of the Committee of Economic Inquiry (the Vernon Committee) commented that 'despite the difficulty of isolating [its influence], the tariff has been important in the expansion and increased diversity of industry, the development of labour skills, the advance of technology, the ability to absorb a rapid increase in population involving a high rate of immigration and the steady increase in capital investment essential to all these achievements'.[11] Ten years later the Committee to Advise on Policies for Manufacturing Industry (the Jackson Committee) examined the sector which for the preceding fifteen years had been sheltered by an industry policy centred almost solely on the tariff. It viewed the results with a far more jaundiced eye than Vernon. During that period, in the main, provided an industry could demonstrate technical efficiency, the Tariff Board had been willing to grant 'made-to-measure' protection.[12] The made-to-measure approach, together with the earlier period of direct import controls, 'had led to a very diverse and rather fragmented industrial structure. [One where] factories opened proudly in the early post-war years have become today's structural problems . . .'.[13] This then was the industrial environment in which the tariff review began. The Jackson Committee's evaluation of the problems which had accumulated behind the high protective barriers has been broadly accepted by both major political parties, as has (until recently) the appropriate response to it—lowering the protective barriers, while the Crawford Report in 1979 signalled the changing focus of future measures to assist industries and ease the pain of structural adjustment following tariff reform.[14]

## The Industries Assistance Commission and its successors

If there has been a watershed for post-war industry policy in Australia, it came with the formation of the Industries Assistance Commission. Until then its predecessor, the Tariff Board, had considered assistance to manufacturing almost exclusively, despite the reference in the *Tariff Board Act* to 'primary industry'. Advice to the government concerning policies towards industries in sectors other than manufacturing and mining, but especially agriculture, was provided elsewhere in the bureaucracy. There was no uniform set of criteria for this advice; no uniform set of objectives; and industry policy, in the broadest sense, was often a mish-mash of contradictory measures. The *Industries Assistance Act*, if nothing else, brought a prospect of coordination and the possibility of bringing some order to what had sometimes been a shambles of conflicting policies.[15]

Further rationalisation of sources of advice concerning assistance and regulation was brought about in 1990 with the merger of the IAC, the Inter-State Commission which had dealt with transport policies, and the Business Regulation Review Unit. The new body—the Industry Commission—among other things was to advise on ways to reduce unnecessary business regulation, facilitate structural adjustment and, most important, encourage the development of internationally competitive industries. Finally, the Howard government has merged the functions of the Industry Commission, the Bureau of Industry Economics (BIE) and the Economic Planning Advisory Commission (EPAC). From the merger the Productivity Commission has been formed, now virtually the government's only source of advice from the bureaucracy on matters of industry policy.

**Figure 11.1  Manufacturing: effective rates of protection**

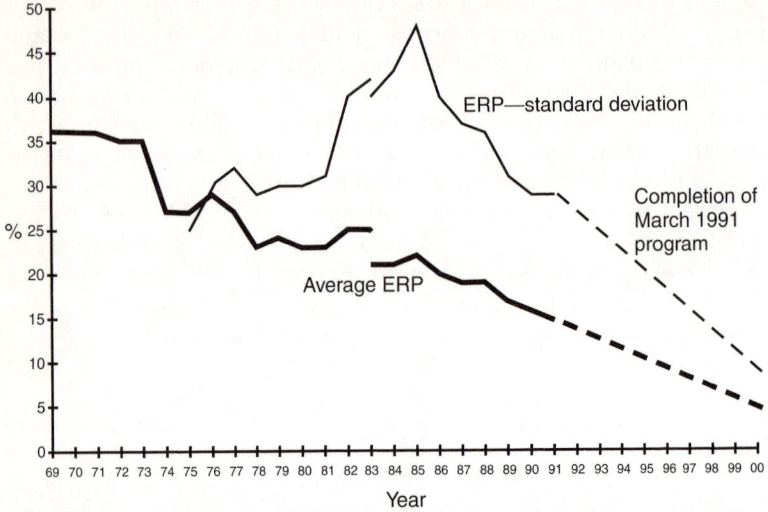

*Sources:* IAC/IC (1976, 1983, 1987, 1990, 1992)

## Assistance in the 1980s and 1990s

*Effective rates of protection (ERP)[16]*

Since the review of the tariff began in 1971, except for the 25 per cent tariff cut in 1973 average levels of assistance to manufacturing have only slowly declined. Table 11.1 shows the average effective rate of protection (ERP) of manufacturing fell from about 35 per cent in 1973 to about 27 per cent following the tariff cut.[17] By 1983 it had fallen only another 2 or 3 percentage points and by 1991 another 6 points to about 15 per cent. (The median was 8 per cent.) Under the program of tariff cuts announced by the Labor government in its March 1991 Economic Statement (and continued by the present Coalition government), the average ERP is currently 6 per cent and is scheduled to fall to 5 per cent by the end of the decade. However, there are two industries which stand out against the trend: automotive and textiles, clothing and footwear (TCF). Both shelter behind protective barriers substantially above those protecting any others, and will continue to do so well after the completion of the 1991–2000 program of tariff reform, following the Howard government's recent decisions to implement tariff pauses for both industries from 2000.

**Table 11.1  Average effective rates of protection: manufacturing industries and agriculture sector**

| ASIC (ANZSIC) industry | 1991/92 (%) | 1996/97 (%) | 2000/1 (%) |
|---|---|---|---|
| 21 (21) Food, beverages, tobacco | 4 | 3 | 2 |
| 24 (22) Textiles, clothing, footwear | 56 | 23 | 15 |
| *244 (223) Knitting mills* | *119* | *76* | *49* |
| *245 (224) Clothing* | *113* | *52* | *34* |
| *246 (225) Footwear* | *116* | *46* | *24* |
| 25 (23, 24; 292) Wood, wood products, furniture | 14 | 4 | 4 |
| 26 Paper products, publishing | 7 | 2 | 2 |
| 27 (25) Chemicals, petroleum & coal products | 8 | 3 | 3 |
| 28 (26) Non-metallic mineral products | 4 | 2 | 3 |
| 29 (27) Basic metal products | 8 | 4 | 4 |
| 31 Fabricated metal products | 18 | 4 | 4 |
| 32 (28) Transport equipment | 34 | 19 | 13 |
| *323 (281) Motor vehicles & parts* | *48* | *28* | *19* |
| 33 Other machinery & equipment | 16 | 5 | 5 |
| 34 (294) Miscellaneous manufacturing | 19 | 7 | 7 |
| **Total manufacturing** | 14 | 6 | 5 |
| Std dev. | 21 | 10 | 7 |

| | | 1994/95 | |
|---|---|---|---|
| **Total agriculture** | 15 | 11 | n.a. |
| Std dev. | 22 | 61[(b)] | n.a. |

*Notes:*
  (a)  ERP data was calculated by the Industry Commission for industries defined by the Australian Standard Industry Classification (ASIC). ASIC was replaced in 1992–93 by the Australian and New Zealand Industrial Classification (ANZSIC). To facilitate comparisons of data in this chapter this table provides an approximate concordance between the two classifications.
  (b)  Fresh milk and tobacco have ERPs > 200%.
*Source:* Industry Commission, *Annual Report 1992–93* (Canberra: AGPS, 1993)

## Protection and jobs in manufacturing

Tables 11.1 and 11.2 respectively show ERPs for manufacturing industries and their employment levels. More than 80 per cent of the 907 700 persons employed in manufacturing in 1995/96 were engaged in activities which sheltered behind ERPs of 7 per cent or less. Knitting mills, clothing and footwear,[18] and motor vehicles and parts employed a total of 100 000 people, about 11 per cent of the manufacturing work force, while sheltering behind ERPs far higher than any other industries in the manufacturing sector. Despite this, TCF (ANZSIC, 22) shed labour at a faster rate than any other group of industries over the five-year period 1990/91 to 1995/96. Employment at the end of the period was 18.8 per cent lower than at the

**Table 11.2 Employment in manufacturing**

| ANZSIC Industry | 1990/91 ('000) | 1995/96 ('000) | Percentage change |
|---|---|---|---|
| 21 Food, beverages, tobacco | 169.2 | 159.9 | –5.5 |
| 22 Textiles, clothing, footwear & leather | 91.0 | 73.9 | –18.8 |
| *223 Knitting mills* | *9.4* | *6.1* | *–35.1* |
| *224 Clothing* | *38.4* | *33.6* | *–12.5* |
| *225 Footwear* | *7.7* | *5.5* | *–28.6* |
| 23 Wood & paper products | 62.4 | 61.0 | –2.2 |
| 24 Printing, published & recorded media | 88.4 | 90.2 | +2.0 |
| 25 Petroleum, coal, chemical & assoc. products | 93.9 | 89.1 | –5.1 |
| 26 Non-metallic mineral products | 41.3 | 35.6 | –13.8 |
| 27 Metal products | 163.7 | 145.0 | –11.4 |
| 28 Machinery equipment | 216.7 | 202.2 | –6.7 |
| *281 Motor vehicles and parts* | *63.4* | *54.8* | *–13.6* |
| 282 Other transport equipment | 26.0 | 27.2 | |
| 29 Other | 54.7 | 50.9 | –6.9 |
| **Total** | **981.4** | **907.7** | **–7.5** |

*Sources:* ABS, Manufacturing Industry, 1990/91, 1995/96 (Cat. No. 8221.0)

beginning, while knitting mills (ANZSIC 223) and footwear (ANZSIC 225) together lost about one-third of their work forces over the period. Employment in motor vehicles and parts manufacture (ANZSIC 281) declined by 13.6 per cent, nearly twice the 7.5 per cent decline for the manufacturing sector as a whole. Clearly ERPs four times the sector average were insufficient to preserve the levels of employment in these activities, and these figures provide a good illustration of the poor insulating properties of even very high rates of protection. Moreover, the jobs in these industries were not without cost. To put these costs in perspective, the net subsidy equivalent (NSE)[19] of the protection per employee in 1992/93 (the latest year for which such data are available) was just over $19 000, while the average wage was then about $25 000. The corresponding figures for other transport equipment (the main component of which is motor vehicles and parts manufacture) were $20 600 (NSE per employee) and $32 300 (wages and salaries per employee). Wages and salaries per employee for motor vehicles and parts was $29 000. The NSE per employee for the manufacturing sector (omitting these industries) was about $6400 and the average wage $32 300.

The automotive and TCF industries, despite the phased reductions in their levels of protection under existing programs, have, and will continue to have, a disproportionate share of assistance well into the next century. Why have they been so successful in persuading governments of the merits of their cases for far higher levels of protection than any other industries? An important reason is the

**Table 11.3 Existing and proposed funding of business programs**

| | Existing programs current budget 1997/98 ($m) | No. of existing schemes | Mortimer programs five-year funding requirement ($m) | Mortimer average annual funding ($m) |
|---|---|---|---|---|
| Investment program | 24.00 | 16 | 1112.97 | 222.6 |
| Innovation program | 977.56 | 15 | 3639.33 | 727.9 |
| Export program | 398.21 | 12 | 1766.63 | 353.3 |
| Business competitiveness | 2675.66 | 23 | 13263.29 | 2652.7 |
| Sustainable resource management program | 172.59 | 10 | 967.98 | 193.6 |
| **Total** | **4248.02** | **66** | **20750.14** | **4150.0** |

Source: Mortimer, 1997, App.4

State and regional distribution of the activities. The TCF and auto-motive industries together contribute 20 to 25 per cent of the manufacturing industry work force in both Victoria and South Australia. In particular, the automotive industry is concentrated in these two States: 55 per cent of total employment in the industry is in Victoria, and 23 per cent in South Australia.[20] With this concentration, the potential electoral consequences of pressures imposed by alliances between State governments, unions and pro-ducers, all of whom see themselves as gaining from the protection of these industries, have proven too much for the Federal govern-ment to resist.

## The changing focus of assistance

As tariffs have fallen, at least partially replacing them have been other often less transparent means of assisting industries, broadly known as 'business programs'. Among them are various measures to assist exporters, to stimulate research, development and innova-tion, and various types of industry-specific arrangements, such as the Factor (F) scheme for the pharmaceuticals industry. These programs have recently been reviewed for the Commonwealth Gov-ernment by David Mortimer, Chief Executive of TNT Asia Pacific Region.

### An outline of existing business programs and the Mortimer Review

Irrespective of the fate of its policy recommendations, the Mortimer Review has performed a valuable function in merely identifying and providing costs of the many business programs currently operating.

**Table 11.4a  Summary: Commonwealth (State and Territory) budgetary outlays on industry**

|  | C'wealth 1991/92 ($m) | State/Terr. (1994/95) ($m) | C'wealth 1996/97 ($m) |
|---|---|---|---|
| Manufacturing[a] | 721.3 | 924.9 | 746.2 |
| Agriculture[b] | 893.2 | 682.2 | 555.6 |
| Mining[c] | 102.1 | 138.0 | 118.0 |
| Selected services[d] | 545.7 | 732.0 | 408.9 |
| **Total** | **2262.3** | **2477.1** | **1828.7** |

Mortimer lists 66 programs for industries in all sectors, which itself highlights one of the main weaknesses of the existing policies. The report sums up the fundamental problem well: 'The existing conglomeration of business programs has developed over many years on an *ad hoc* basis, often in response to short-term imperatives. The result is an array of programs which lacks direction, is duplicative and confuses business.'[21] Table 11.3 shows the broad allocation of budgeted funds for 1997/98 for existing programs, and an outline of the funding necessary for Mortimer's recommended programs over the five years ended 2002/03. For existing programs the total 1997/98 budget allocation is more than $4.2 billion, more than 60 per cent of which is devoted to business competitiveness programs (e.g. duty concessions or rebates of duties or taxes such as the diesel fuel rebate scheme).[22] Innovation programs (e.g. those encouraging research and development) take up almost 25 per cent of the budget, more than half of which is attributed to the 125 per cent tax concession for eligible R & D expenditure. Export programs (including assistance for the local tourism industry) are currently allocated just under 10 per cent, while sustainable resource management (e.g. the National Landcare Program) take up less than 5 per cent of funding.

The following section will provide an overview of non-tariff assistance to industries, and look selectively at some of the current programs.

*Industry assistance through the budget*

Table 11.4a shows Commonwealth budgetary outlays on industries in all sectors totalled more than $1.8 billion in 1996/97. Of this manufacturing received $746 million, agriculture $556 million, mining and (selected) services $409 million. This is only part of the story, however. Often overlooked is the assistance to industries provided by State and Territory governments. Their budgetary outlays totalled nearly $2.5 billion in 1994/95 (the latest available data) with manufacturing accounting for $925 million. At least some of

**Table 11.4b  Major components of Commonwealth budgetary outlays on manufacturing**

|  | 1991/92 ($m) | 1996/97 ($m) |
|---|---|---|
| **Manufacturing sector:** | | |
| Bounties | 244.7 | 86.6 |
| computers | (74.5) | (56.5) |
| Other industry specific | | |
| programs | 72.8 | 201.6 |
| Factor (F) | (23.6) | (189.1) |
| General industry programs | 178.3 | 325.6 |
| (excluding export outlays) | | |
| most technology programs | | |
| CSIRO manf. research | (-) | (98.2) |
| Export outlays | 225.5 | 132.4 |
| EMDGS | (50.0) | (81.8) |
| **Total manufacturing (a)** | **721.3** | **746.2** |

Sources: Industry Commission, *Annual Report, 1995–96* (Canberra: AGPS) (a) Table D5, (b) Table D4, (c) Table D6, (d) Table D7

these funds have been used in competitive bidding to attract the location of firms/industries to a particular State or Territory at the expense of others. This process, from the point of view of the Australian community, is essentially a zero-sum game.

For manufacturing the major forms of budgetary assistance (Table 11.4b) were the payment of bounties for local production, with the major budgeted expenditure ($56.5 million) for the production of computers. The major industry-specific program was the pharmaceuticals industry Factor (F) scheme (described later) with a budgeted expenditure of $189.1 million in 1996/97, while general industry programs (most technology programs, including the CSIRO, are included under this heading) had budgeted expenditure of $325.6 million.

## Measures assisting exports

In recent years Australian governments have strongly (and rightly) criticised the United States and the European Community for subsidising their exports of agricultural products. These subsidies have perverted world markets and are essentially self-defeating in much the same way as are the imposition of competitive 'beggar-my-neighbour' tariffs. Australia is hardly an innocent in this respect, of course, though some of Australia's export programs do attempt to correct market failures, or represent attempts to offset the unfavourable effects on industry exports of other government policies.

Commonwealth export measures affecting all sectors were estimated to be more than $1.1 billion. Of these measures, the Export

Market Development Grant (EMDG) scheme is the most expensive with a total of $204 million being paid in 1996/97.[23] Compensation for the adverse effects of tariffs on business costs, including refunds of duty paid (or duty which is payable, but forgone) under such schemes as duty drawback ($85 million in 1996/97) and Tariff Export Concession Orders (TEXCO) ($45 million), are also significant measures assisting exporters.

Other schemes are more complicated and even less transparent. For example, the Passenger Motor Vehicle (PMV) export facilitation scheme ($185 million) provides import credits to local producers equal to the value-added in their exports. The credits allow the holder to import PMVs and components duty free, and provide an implicit subsidy in that it is worthwhile for the firm to subsidise its exports as long as the subsidy paid is less than the duty it saves. However, as tariffs fall the implicit subsidy will decline. Another similar scheme is the TCF import credit scheme ($110 million) which provides firms with credits based on a proportion of the value-added in their eligible exports of TCF products.

## Assistance for research, development and innovation

The primary rationale for government support of R & D and innovation is that the benefits accruing to society from these activities exceed the (private) benefits to the firm undertaking them. If there are such 'spillovers', in market economies firms will not be fully compensated for all the social benefits they generate from their R & D, and as a consequence, from society's point of view the firm will tend to underinvest in these activities. This is an example of 'market failure': the failure of unregulated markets to optimally allocate society's resources to appropriate uses.

While Australia ranks highly on government expenditures on R & D as a percentage of GDP, its ranking on business R & D is poor. Moreover, the rate of technology diffusion in the business sector is low.[24] To deal with these shortcomings the Commonwealth Government is currently supporting twelve 'innovation programs'. Budgeted support for these is $810 million in 1997/98. The major component of this—$470 million—is the 125 per cent tax concession for eligible R & D.[25] Of the three remaining schemes, two provide venture capital ($20 million), while budgeted funding for cooperative research centres is $148 million.

Is this money well spent? The tax concession for eligible R & D (now 125 per cent, under the previous government 150 per cent) has had some history of being driven more by creative accounting than creative research. As well, recent theoretical developments have called into question at least some aspects of the usual arguments underpinning government support for R & D and related activities. In open economies such as Australia's, spillovers may be either local or international, either inter- or intra-industry, and appropriate policies may vary according to the circumstances. While very often subsidies for R & D *are* appropriate policies, there may be circumstances (e.g. where firms both cooperate and behave strategically) where firms may *overinvest* in R & D.[26]

## Industry-specific assistance

Especially over the last twenty years, particular industries have been singled out for special treatment. In manufacturing the need for special measures is an acknowledgment that for these industries the 'traditional' means of assistance—tariff protection—is unable to achieve the government's policy objectives. The automotive industry has long been such a case, with special arrangements going back well before World War II. (The history of assistance to the industry is described in some detail in an appendix to this chapter.) Indeed, it has been the subject of the best known of the recent industry plans—the Button Plan (the Motor Vehicle Policy 1984–1992).[27] Other significant industry-specific arrangements in manufacturing include the Steel Industry Plan (1984–1988), the still-current Factor (F) program for the pharmaceutical industry, and the TCF plan, both of which are briefly described below. In other sectors, specific arrangements have been made for adjustment assistance for dairying and wool, the waterfront and shipping.

The Factor (F) scheme was introduced to compensate manufacturers for the low prices they obtain for their products under the Pharmaceutical Benefits Scheme (PBS). Under the program, eligible companies receive compensatory payments (higher prices for selected products listed on the PBS) in return for commitments to increase domestic research and product development, local manufacture and exports. A review of the scheme by the Industry Commission found the scheme to have design flaws which limited its efficiency and effectiveness: 'Overall, the scheme was not found to be welfare enhancing, and its administration had been poor.'[28] Total support to the industry under the scheme was $130 million in 1995/96 and of this, export support was estimated to be $56 million.[29] The scheme will expire in 1999, but it will be replaced by a similar scheme, with reduced funding (capped at $300 million over five years).[30]

The TCF industry plan was announced in 1986, and as part of it, reductions in border assistance began in 1989. The plan has been modified on a number of occasions, but its objective remains the improvement of the industry's efficiency and international competitiveness, mainly by lowering tariffs, abolishing quantitative restrictions (from 1993), stimulating exports (via the import credit scheme), and providing adjustment assistance for firms and employees. Currently the industry is past the mid-point of a five-year program expiring in 2000, designed to assist firms to adjust to phased reductions in tariffs. There are four adjustment programs: a TCF Outreach Program to assist at least 100 firms in the industry to implement 'best practice' manufacture (with budgeted expenditure of $15 million over five years); a Quality Program to assist firms become more competitive by developing a 'quality culture' ($8 million); a TCF International Information Program to assist exporters ($1.3 million); and a TCF Infrastructure Program to fund projects such as training and investment promotion ($8 million). At the end of these programs, most tariffs applying to the products of the industry will be 15 per cent, but for clothing and finished textiles a rate of 25 per cent will apply—four times the rate scheduled for the remainder of manufacturing (excluding PMV). The government has now responded to the recent Industry Commission recommendations for the future of the TCF industry in much the same way as it responded to the Commission's recommendations for the PMV industry. It has rejected the majority recommendation for continued tariff phasing until 2008, by which time all TCF tariffs would have been 5 per cent.[31] Instead, the government has now decided on a tariff pause: tariff phasing will be suspended at the end of the current program in 2000, and the rates then applying will be maintained from 1 July 2000 until 1 January 2005, which has been termed a 'period of consolidation . . . [to] . . . enable TCF firms to strengthen their competitive position after a period of significant change'.[32]

## The Mortimer blueprint for future industry assistance

Mortimer's fundamental recommendation entailed the government adopting a target of doubling Australia's per capita income growth to 3.4 per cent. To assist in achieving the target, the Review proposed implementing 73 recommendations in programs devised to boost business investment, encourage innovation, expand exports, and enhance business competitiveness, while ensuring sustainable resource management. For any new program to be implemented Mortimer suggested it should pass eminently sensible threshold tests in which it must: (a) provide a net economic benefit; (b) address a market imperfection; and (c) not breach Australia's international obligations. The necessary funding for implementing all of the recommendations was estimated to be $20.75 billion over the five years 1998/99 to 2002/03 (an annual average of $4.15 billion). While these are very considerable sums indeed, in the main the proposals represent a reallocation of funding for existing programs, together with what may be considered to be, in the context of the overall government budget, a moderate net increase in expenditures of $843 million—less than $170 million per year—over the period. The major new expenditure recommended was an Investment Incentives sub-program which would have established a fund to allow expenditure of up to $1 billion over five years in approximately equal instalments. Partially offsetting this, the major saving was a recommended cut in funding for Cooperative Research Centres of $589 million over the period.

The government's response to the Review, *Investing for Growth*, commits it to a target 4 per cent annual growth rate on average during the decade to 2010.[33] It is a package which will see extra expenditure of nearly $1.3 billion on business programs over the next five years; however, some of the most important measures are more a partial restoration of funding cut from programs over the government's first 18 months of office than any 'new' spending.[34] The government has also significantly modified many of the Review's recommendations for future policy initiatives. For example, Mortimer's 'InvestAustralia' sub-program, with proposed funding of $113 million over five years for investment promotion, attraction and facilitation, has been cut to $28 million. More important, the government has rejected the centrepiece of the Review, the major new spending proposal, the $1 billion Investment Incentives sub-program. From the community's point of view (if not the potential recipients), the rejection is unlikely to be any great loss, however. This type of expenditure (which would have been at the discretion of the Industry Minister) to match incentive programs offered by other countries effectively involves competitive bidding among countries, encouraging firms to go to where the best incentive deal is offered. In the process the bidding may skim off much or all of any benefit accruing to the 'winning' country. However, at least partially negating the government's apparent rejection of competitive bidding is the appointment of a 'Strategic Investment Coordinator', Bob Mansfield, whose functions include advising the Cabinet 'on projects which may justify the provision of incentives or policy changes'.[35] While the government has stated that it is 'not disposed towards providing across the board investment incentives . . . [it] does acknowledge that in particular and special circumstances . . . there may be the need for some specific assistance . . . which could include grants, tax relief or the provision of infrastructure services'.[36] The provision of incentives will be subject to eligibility criteria, but in the end this may provide little comfort to Australian taxpayers: no costs have been provided and the scheme is apparently open-ended. In terms of providing access to senior members of the government and the types of assistance which may be provided, it smacks of the type of policies some of the Asian governments have used to attract foreign investment, with the disastrous results which have recently become apparent.

Other major measures in *Investing for Growth* include the extension of the EMDG scheme for a further two years at a total cost of $300 million. The scheme suffered a considerable cut in funding when it was capped at $150 million per annum in 1996/97, and was to be terminated in 2001/02. The existing duty drawback and export concessions schemes will be consolidated and simplified to become the TRADEX scheme, which is designed to give relief to businesses currently paying customs and excise duties and sales tax on products which are re-exported or which are inputs to exports. The total cost in terms of revenue forgone is estimated to be $105 million in the four years to 2001/02, though it is unclear if this will be extra 'expenditure' or the sum of expenditures under existing schemes. Complementing TRADEX is the apparent extension of existing provisions for manufacture in bond (MiB). MiB licence holders will be able to import goods, add value and then re-export without a duty/tax liability being incurred. The rather vague qualification for the scheme requires firms participating 'to demonstrate through their business plans that they are setting up new export activity dependent on the MiB arrangements'.[37] Funding for research and development, cut considerably in the government's first budget (mainly via the reduction of the rate of tax deductibility for eligible expenditure from 150 to 125 per cent) has now been partially restored by an expansion of the R & D Start program, to cost an extra $556 million over the next four years. However, no mention is made in the government's policy statement of the fate of Mortimer's recommendation that funding for the Co-operative Research Centre program be reduced by nearly $600 million over 5 years.

Measures in the government's program affecting other sectors include taxation changes designed to improve the competitiveness of the financial sector, which will cost the government a total of $81 million in revenue in the period to 2001/02, and under the broad heading 'The Information Age', a total of $47 million will be provided for such projects as establishing a network of software engineering centres to provide software development companies with access to the latest software.

*Evaluation*

Industry policy in Australia has lost none of its controversy, despite the passing (at the Federal level) of nearly 100 years. Initially the tariff (or more broadly, trade policy) was the major instrument of government policies promoting diversification of the substantially agricultural Australian economy (through the establishment of a manufacturing base), economic development and growth. In 1929 the Brigden Committee's view of the tariff as a means promoting these aims was on balance favourable, but it suggested 'the tariff had reached its economic limits' and advocated that any increases or extensions of tariff protection should be made only after the 'closest scrutiny of the costs involved'. The Depression which followed saw the introduction of the unprecedentedly high Scullin tariffs, but even these were not high enough for some. Despite their introduction it was said that 'the lobbies resound to the cries of the tariff touts', a quote which well describes the long history of rent-seeking behaviour which has been engendered by tariffs and other means of assistance provided by governments to business in this country.[38] The result was that tariff protection at the end of the 1930s was about 50 per cent higher than it was at the time of the Brigden Report, and its legacy was still felt into the 1970s. Like Brigden, the Vernon Committee of 1965 also looked favourably on the tariff's role in Austalia's economic diversification, development and growth. Its report came at the height of the power of Sir John MacEwan (leader of the Country Party, the predecessor of the National Party) with his policy of 'protection for all'. It was also probably the height of successful rent-seeking behaviour by local (and foreign-owned) business. As Freedman and Stonecash put it: the aim was to 'build a protective wall around Australian industry while simultaneously encouraging foreign investment . . . Companies in trouble, those facing competitive imports, could simply apply to the Tariff Board for more protection [and it] was ladled out to anyone who asked'.[39]

Once a manufacturing base was firmly established some of the costs of protectionism (and MacEwanism) began to be apparent. In 1975 the Jackson Committee, which was specifically asked to advise on policies for manufacturing industries, was highly critical of the tariff's role in fragmenting industries and creating structural problems for the Australian economy. Its views became widely accepted and, with the tariff review begun by the Tariff Board in 1971 under Chairman Alf Rattigan, was a major influence in beginning the process of tariff reform which in recent years has contributed to the creation of a more efficient and internationally competitive manufacturing sector.

The emphasis of government policy towards industry has now ostensibly shifted from providing assistance to particular activities (picking winners?) to the efficient allocation of resources across all sectors of the economy, including policies for the correction of market failure (real or apparent), and removing impediments to the efficient running of the economy. In many respects the title of the Mortimer review says it all: 'going for growth'. Continued support for research, development and innovation, some of the programs for encouraging exports (e.g. AUSTRADE's provision to firms of easily accessible information regarding export markets) and policies to overcome the limitation of capital markets (e.g. providing information on available investment opportunities) may be reasonably justified on grounds of market failure. Other programs are less easy to defend. The shift from import protection to export assistance, for example, substitutes for one measure another which in many ways is equivalent. Both tariffs and subsidies lead to distortions in production and consumption; depending on world supply and demand conditions, tariffs may improve the terms of trade while subsidies may worsen them.

The government's appointment of a 'Strategic Investment Adviser' shows the aim of encouraging foreign investment has not changed since MacEwan's day; only the means have changed. 'Picking winners' also has its equivalent in the government's 'action agendas', the first two of which are to foster the development of the information industries and the financial sector. The agendas are to be flexible strategies developed in concert with the industry concerned, and entail a process of analysis of current industry performance, identification of impediments to growth and development of priorities for reform. In the case of the agenda for the financial sector, for example, the projected cost is $81 million to 2001/02. Other industries which are likely to be the subjects of action agendas include tourism, chemicals and plastics, with the likelihood of more in the future. With tariff protection largely discredited, the emphasis for business as far as rent-seeking behaviour is concerned is now on business programs and action agendas. *Plus ça change . . .*

If Mortimer is correct, many of the existing business programs are poorly directed and designed. He recommended 'regular and rigorous program evaluation', noting that to date, 'evaluation has been *ad hoc* and findings have been inadequately implemented'.[40] The government has stated it will adopt design requirements based on Mortimer's recommendations, including establishing 'clear program objectives and performance indicators and undertaking regular independent evaluations of programs'.[41] The question arises: What happens if the program does not come up to the performance required? In these circumstances Mortimer advocated the withdrawal of assistance 'if firms cannot demonstrate clear increases in productivity within a reasonable time'.[42] While this is entirely reasonable, we have just had two reminders of the fact that firms and

**Table 11.5  Major Commonwealth export measures—industries in all sectors**

|                                      | 1991/92 ($m) | 19996/97 ($m) |
|--------------------------------------|:------------:|:-------------:|
| **Direct export measures**           | 802.8        | 821.5         |
| EMDG                                 | (134.0)      | (204.6)       |
|   Aust. Tourist Commission | (69.5)       | (76.8)        |
|   PMV export facilitation  | (161.1)      | (185.0)       |
|   TCF import credits       | (34.4)       | (1110.0)      |
|   Duty drawback & TEXCO    | (96.8)       | (130.0)       |
| **Other measures affecting exports** |              |               |
| Bounties (a)                         | 74.2         | 41.4          |
|   Computers                | (34.0)       | (25.8)        |
| Dairy products—market support        | 148.4        | 145.0         |
| Factor (F) pharmaceuticals (a)       | 17.4         | 99.8          |
| **Total manufacturing (a)**          | **1042.8**   | **1106.7**    |

*Note:*   (a) Export component of the programs only.
*Source:*  Industry Commission, *Annual Report, 1995–96*, Table C1

industries are unlikely to go quietly if assistance is withdrawn after a 'reasonable' time—however long that may be. The cases of the automotive industry and TCF have shown how loud and successful the cries can be and how (un)resisting to similar pressures governments are now and are likely to be in the future. The successful lobbying by these industries and their supporters in achieving the tariff pauses show that the days of special pleading and the 'tariff touts' are far from over. Here again the sense of having seen it all before is unmistakeable.

The government has now defined its fundamental goal: average growth of 4 per cent per annum for the decade to 2010. Policies removing obstacles to competition, providing adequate transport infrastructure, dealing with problems of market failure, and regularly evaluating the measures taken are all steps in the right direction to achieve the growth objective. It remains to be seen if some of the 'new assistance' measures lead in the same direction.

### Industry plans and the automotive industry: A cautionary tale

The automotive industry has long been at the centre of industry policy in Australia, and automotive industry 'plans' of one form or another have a very long history indeed in this country. Ford and General Motors have assembled passenger motor vehicles in Australia for more than 70 years and tariffs have at times played a crucial role in shaping the structure of the industry and its productive processes. However, at various times governments have recognised tariffs have either been insufficient or have been inappropriate instruments for achieving their policy goals. As a consequence the industry has been subject to an extraordinary number of sometimes quite extraordinary schemes. The following outline of government policies towards the industry is provided to illustrate how prescriptive some of these industry-specific policies have been and how, on occasion, their results have been far from satisfactory—or even perverse.

Until the mid-1930s the process of local manufacture essentially involved putting locally-built bodies, production of which was sheltered by high protective tariffs (moreover, fully-built imported bodies were fragile and bulky and therefore expensive to ship) onto locally assembled imported (CKD) chassis which were subject to low revenue duties.[43] In May 1936, without reference to the Tariff Board, the Lyons government introduced a set of policies designed to bring about the manufacture of 'complete' automobiles—including engines.[44] A fund was set up from revenue derived from a duty surcharge on imported chassis from which was to be paid a bounty for local engine manufacture (the measure eventually passed the Parliament as the *Motor Vehicle Engine Bounty Act 1939*). Later the Menzies government passed the extraordinary *Motor Vehicles Agreement Act* 1940, which would have given Australian Consolidated Industries an effective monopoly of domestic automobile manufacture. The measures (especially the latter) caused tremendous controversy, but ultimately nothing came of them. Eventually both Acts were repealed in 1945 as a condition for Chrysler, Ford, GM-H and International Harvester accepting the government's invitation to submit proposals for post-war manufacture of 'complete' passenger motor vehicles. After protracted negotiations, in 1945 GM-H agreed to begin local production, and in 1948 the first Holden rolled off the assembly line at Fisherman's Bend in Victoria.[45]

Since that time there have been a number of industry plans affecting automobile manufacturing in Australia. In 1964 two basic plans derived from a proposed Canadian local content scheme were implemented, which provided local producers with duty concessions (known as by-laws) on components, provided a specified level of local content was reached. Plan A involved participants raising local content to 95 per cent over five years, and B (subdivided into B1 and B2) was for low-volume producers who could obtain by-law concessions for more limited increases in local content. When the Tariff Board evaluated the plans in 1965 it had 'considerable doubts as to the possibility of some [models] obtaining economic volumes of production—at least in the foreseeable future'.[46] While the plans were made more flexible by 1971, the effects of more than half a decade of Plan-production were clear: rather than a small model range with high local content, it had resulted in model proliferation and, in particular, the fragmentation of the small car sector, that part of the market showing the highest rate of growth. The decision was therefore made to phase out the plans by 1974, but events were overtaking the decision. The industry's competitive position had been declining since the late 1960s and in 1974 Chrysler, Ford and GM-H threatened widescale retrenchments. The government responded by introducing as a 'short-term' stabilisation measure (it lasted ten years) an 80/20 market sharing arrangement—with quantitative restrictions used to limit imports to 20 per cent of the market. Shortly after the government extended to Nissan and Toyota what in these circumstances may be described as inexplicable invitations to become full manufacturers. Both companies accepted, so that by the second half of the 1970s there were five manufacturers in a market in which the competitive position of local producers was continuing to decline, despite (or perhaps because of) all of the government measures to assist them.

Following an inquiry by the Industries Assistance Commission in 1981, the government announced details of the assistance arrangements which would operate after 1984, but with the defeat of the Coalition government in March 1983 the proposed arrangements were superseded by what became known as the Button Plan, which was introduced in 1985. That year saw the peak in the level of assistance for the industry. It was supported by a 'complex package of assistance measures which automatically increased assistance when the industry's competitive position declined'.[47] The automotive sector of the industry was assisted by tariffs, quotas, duty concessions and export facilitation; the components sector by an 85 per cent local content requirement. Seemingly there was something for everyone—except the consumer. Among the Button Plan's objectives were to give the industry time to restructure and modernise and make it more efficient. The means included increasing import competition by the gradual reduction of tariffs and the removal of quantitative restrictions; and pursuing scale economies through industry rationalisation and export facilitation. The aim was that by 1992 there would be no more than three manufacturers, producing a total of no more than six models.

However, the significant devaluation of the Australian dollar in 1985 and 1986 considerably reduced the hoped-for gradual increases in competitive pressure caused by reductions in border assistance. As a consequence, a mid-term review of the plan was instituted, under which the government abolished import quotas, reduced tariffs from 57.5 to 45 per cent, and introduced phased tariff reductions to 35 per cent in 1992. The local content scheme was abolished from 1 January 1989. By that time the Button Plan was nearing its end and there was a need to consider arrangements for the post-Button era. The Industry Commission was asked to do the job. The Commission made its report in 1990 and recommended (and the government accepted), *inter alia*, that tariffs be reduced from 35 per cent at the end of 1992 to 15 per cent by 2000 through eight annual reductions of 2.5 per cent; export facilitation should continue and access to the scheme be broadened.

Though introduced by the previous (Labor) government, these measures will continue to operate until the end of the century, but controversy has now arisen over the post-2000 arrangements for the industry. It stems from the Howard government's rejection of the majority recommendations of the Industry Commission for continued annual tariff reductions of 2.5 percentage points to 2004, by which time, if adopted, the tariff would be 5 per cent. Instead, it accepted the substance of the minority recommendation for there to be a tariff pause at 15 per cent for five years from 1 January 2000. According to Deputy Prime Minister Tim Fischer, the rate will then be reduced to 10 per cent and '[t]his reduction will be the subject of legislation to ensure the industry has absolute certainty that it will receive tariff support at 15 per cent for 5 years from 2000, with tariff support [10 per cent] remaining at the end of the period'.[48]

For much of the last 70 years, in terms of the assistance they have been granted by governments of both major political persuasions, automobile producers in Australia have had privileged positions, and it is evident now that these privileges will remain for at least another decade. For the Australian community the support of the industry has been costly. By world standards, for most of the period cars produced in Australia have been expensive and often of poor quality. However, since World War II few if any industries in the manufacturing sector have been the subject of a greater variety of prescriptive measures than has the automotive industry. Many of these measures have even appeared to have been designed to make the industry less competitive than it would otherwise have been: the local content arrangements of the 1960s, and especially encouraging the entry of Nissan and Toyota in the late 1970s, for example, can at best be described as misguided. It is only in recent years with the Button Plan that policies have been explicitly directed towards improving market structure (e.g. encouraging fewer producers and models produced), but even here some of the measures encouraged (e.g. model sharing) have hardly been successful. Until the mid-term review of the Button Plan, and the increased competitive pressure from imports resulting from it, there was little evidence of improved performance in the industry. With greater competition since then, and particularly over the last three or four years, by virtually any measure local producers have improved the products they produce and their productivity rates in producing them. They are now comparable with all but the best of Japanese producers. The recent experience is an object lesson in how lowering trade barriers and greater competitive pressure from imports can play important roles in improving industry performance—but with the tariff pause to operate from 2000 to 2005 (and the similar policy adopted for TCF), it is a lesson the Howard government seems determined to ignore.

# 12 Australia and the Kyoto Protocol[1]

## *Anthony D. Owen*

Increased atmospheric concentrations of greenhouse gases (GHGs) have led to global concern that human activities could cause accelerated changes in climate patterns. The ultimate objective of the 1992 United Nations Framework Convention on Climate Change (UNFCCC) is to stabilise greenhouse gas concentrations in the atmosphere at a level that would prevent dangerous human interference with the climate system. However, it soon became evident that in order to meet this objective, it would be necessary to establish a legal instrument that would provide a sound basis for long-term co-operative global action. Negotiations concluded in Kyoto in December 1997 with the release of the Kyoto Protocol. Subsequently, at Buenos Aires in November 1998, a two-year plan of action to finalise outstanding details of the Protocol was adopted.

The Kyoto Protocol establishes a legally binding obligation on Annex I Parties[2] (subject to entry into force) to reduce emissions of greenhouse gases (GHGs) by an average of 5.2 per cent below 1990 levels[3] by the years 2008–2012.[4] The Protocol will become legally binding when at least 55 countries, including developed countries accounting for at least 55 per cent of these countries' 1990 carbon dioxide emissions, have signed and then ratified. As of November 1998, developed country signatories accounted for 78.7 per cent of the group's emissions. However, only two countries had ratified, and both of these were developing nations (Fiji and Antigua and Barbuda). There are no obligations on developing countries under the Protocol. The Protocol makes reference to a second commitment period to succeed the first, and stipulates that negotiations to define corresponding commitments shall start no later than 2005. Emission reductions obtained over and above commitments in the first period may be 'banked' to set against commitments in the subsequent period.

The key elements are:

- A global target of a reduction in GHG emissions by Annex I countries amounting to 5.2 per cent in the first five-year accounting period, 2008–2012;
- Differential targets for Annex I Parties;
- Six GHGs to be covered:[5] $CO_2$, $CH_4$, $N_2O$, HFCs, PFCs, $SF_6$ which, together, account for virtually all anthropogenic[6] greenhouse gas emissions in the industrialised world;
- Comprehensive coverage of sources and sinks;[7]
- Emission trading adopted in principle for Annex I countries;
- Clean Development Mechanism (CDM) allows Annex I countries to receive emissions reduction credits for project activities in non-Annex I countries;
- No commitment sought from developing countries; no evolution article for future commitments, and no voluntary undertakings;
- The Protocol will enter into force 90 days after ratification by at least 55 countries accounting for at least 55 per cent of total Annex I $CO_2$ emissions.

The Kyoto Protocol provides significant flexibility for Parties to achieve the targets. Individual countries, to achieve their particular emissions target, can adopt a complex array of alternative approaches. There are no mandatory policies and measures to be undertaken—individual Annex I countries will be able to select those policies and measures best suited to economic circumstances, community concerns and other national criteria. Policy decisions could require differing contributions by individual gases and by individual industry sectors as well as individual sources.

The inclusion of legally binding targets on Annex I Parties will affect economic (trade) competitiveness and contribute to the transfer ('leakage') of emissions, investment and jobs to countries outside the target group. International negotiators accepted a Kyoto Protocol with significant, but unquantified, economic implications for both developed and developing countries. Annex I countries will now need to assess their potential obligations under the Kyoto Protocol. They will need to consider the policies and measures best suited to achieve the emission targets and timetables required and the overall cost to their country.

With much of the detail surrounding key elements of the Kyoto Protocol still subject to determination it is impossible to predict the overall impact of either universal or partial adoption by Annex I Parties. Future meetings will be held on many of the areas of detail that must still be developed, including the rules and guidelines for emissions trading and the procedures for the certified emissions reduction certificates to be established under the CDM.

In general, the qualifying sources include industrial and agricultural activities. In most industrialised countries emissions from land clearance in 1990 were negligible. For Australia, however, land clearance accounted for over 20 per cent of its 1990 $CO_2$ emissions; in the closing hours of the Kyoto negotiations, Australia successfully inserted a sentence enabling it to include these emissions in its 1990 base inventory.

Limited provision was also made to offset national emissions through absorption of greenhouse gases through 'sinks' resulting from direct human-induced land use changes and forestry activities, limited to afforestation, reforestation and deforestation since 1990, measured as verifiable changes in stocks in each commitment period.

Although developing countries were not committed to any action, current or future, by the Kyoto Protocol, cooperation between developing countries and Annex I countries will be essential to achieve global stabilisation of emission concentrations in the long term. The electricity generating capacity of Brazil, China, India, Indonesia and Russia, in aggregate, is expected to more than quadruple between now and 2020. In this same period, 80 per cent of the existing electricity capacity in these five countries would be replaced through normal turnover. Installation of cleaner, more efficient technology throughout this transition could lead to dramatic reductions in the growth of greenhouse gas emissions in this group, particularly as older, dirtier plants are retired.

## Mechanisms for international flexibility among Annex I parties

### Bubbling

A 'bubble' provision enables any group of countries, at the time they ratify the Protocol, to redistribute their emission commitments in ways that preserve the collective total, and it establishes legal responsibilities in the event that the collective commitment is not achieved. The provision is the direct result of the European Union agreement in March 1997 on sharing out a collective 10 per cent emission reduction between its member states, in a way that spanned a 30 per cent reduction for Luxembourg, 25 per cent reductions for Germany, Denmark and Austria, through to increases ranging up to 40 per cent in the case of Portugal.

While the bubble provision was established mainly for the EU, it does raise the possibility of some non-EU OECD nations (specifically Japan and the USA) forming a bubble with Russia and the Ukraine in order to use the latter's 'hot air'.[8]

## Emissions trading[9]

In an emission trading system that is part of an international environmental agreement, there are two main goals:

- economic efficiency through a trading system with low transaction costs that provides access to lower cost mitigation; and
- environmental security through an assurance that the agreed environmental goal will be achieved through compliance with national emission limits.

Emission trading is an intrinsic and irreversible part of the Kyoto Protocol, which is independent of the commitment to negotiate specific rules and procedures under which such trading operates.

In an emission trading system, each emitter has an obligation to limit its emissions to a specified quantity. If an emitter (a country or firm) remains below its allowed limit, it can sell permits to emit to another country or firm whose emissions exceed its limit. Through trading, a market price for the permits emerges which reflects the marginal cost of emission reduction. Each emitter can decide whether it is cheaper to reduce its own emissions or to purchase permits from others. Total emissions from all emitters in the trading system do not exceed the agreed environmental objective (i.e. the sum of all emission limits).

Under an international emission trading system, a country with low greenhouse gas mitigation costs could reduce emissions below its national emission target. That country could then sell permits to emit to a country with high mitigation costs. This would allow the purchasing country to increase emissions above its target. Emissions from all Annex I Parties would remain at the agreed environmental objective which is represented by the sum of Annex I Party emission targets, but the cost of achieving the objective would be lower.

In an emission trading system, greenhouse gas emission targets would be an asset to be managed as cost-effectively as possible. Any emission reductions below an emission target could be sold. Participants in the emission trading market with low mitigation costs would therefore have an incentive to reduce the greenhouse gas intensity of their activities as much as they can. This should encourage innovation, boost the rate of diffusion of low or no greenhouse gas technology, and encourage development of new technology. Thus emission trading could make it more likely that the agreed emission targets will be met. The price of permits would provide information on the cost of greenhouse gas mitigation. This information, and the lower mitigation costs that may be possible through trading, may facilitate decisions to revise emission targets in the future.

## Joint implementation

The Protocol enables emission savings arising from cross-border investments between Annex I Parties to be transferred between them. This is 'joint implementation' at the project level, occurring between entities of countries that are both subject to legally binding constraints. An estimate must be made of the emissions 'saved' by the project, as compared with what otherwise would have been emitted. The emission savings agreed between the Parties then becomes equivalent to an international emissions trade, being deducted from the allowed emissions of the host country and added to the allowed emissions of the investing country (on a pro rata basis, where appropriate). Since the combined emissions from the countries involved remains unchanged, it is of secondary importance from the standpoint of both the Protocol and the environment, and is simply a matter for negotiation between the governments and industries concerned. An example of a potential joint implementation project would be the rehabilitation of leaking Russian gas pipelines, the methane saved by such a project yielding emission allowances for the investing country.

## Clean Development Mechanism

The Protocol also establishes a Clean Development Mechanism (CDM) which, in principle, enables activities similar to joint implementation to proceed with non-Annex I countries. The Annex I investing country could then utilise certified emission reductions to contribute towards compliance. Commencing in the year 2000, these reductions can be banked for eventual use over the 2008 to 2012 accounting period. However, such investments must be 'new' money invested in projects that would not have proceeded in the absence of the CDM. Essentially, this condition has been imposed to prevent redirection of existing aid flows specifically into projects that will return emission credits.

### How will emissions trading operate?

Under the Kyoto Protocol, the combined quantity of emissions from Annex I countries is effectively capped. Thus emissions trading could occur on a government-to-government basis when one country which wished to exceed its emissions limit would purchase emission permits from a country which could adapt to a lower limit. If governments also implemented domestic emission trading systems, domestic trading would involve individual industries and large firms where these were either a significant source of emissions or a significant source of emission credits. Such firms or industries may also be authorised to trade internationally.

However, it would be neither economically nor practically feasible to include small emission sources in a domestic trading system because of the complexity of setting emission limits for small emitters and controlling greenhouse gas emissions at the point of emission. Emissions from households, vehicles and small businesses could be capped by the regulation of energy suppliers. Governments might also choose to implement other policies and measures for road transport, small businesses and households, such as carbon or energy taxes, energy efficiency standards or voluntary agreements, as part of the national obligation to reduce national emissions.

To permit emissions trading it is essential that good quality emission data be recorded across all trading countries. Clearly it is conceivable that emissions could actually rise as the result of a trade between a purchasing country with precise emissions data and a seller with poor data (if the emission reduction were over-estimated). A further problem stems from the degree of uncertainty attached to the measurement of $CO_2$ emissions from some sources (e.g. forestry), other GHGs and sinks. This may have to be resolved by establishing separate markets for each major greenhouse gas source and sink. The effect of this would be to fragment the greenhouse gas emission trade market and thus reduce its economic efficiency.

The design features of a trading system must include details of:

- the greenhouse gases included in national emission limits;
- the stringency of emission limits (together with the cost of greenhouse gas mitigation);
- the length of budget periods; and
- the nature of non-compliance provisions.

Neither these nor other key design parameters for a trading system have yet been decided.

To enhance environmental security it would be necessary to impose a high degree of emission data quality assurance, with strict domestic monitoring and reporting requirements. The introduction of such a system could be one of the criteria on eligibility to trade. In the short run, this may limit trading to $CO_2$ emissions arising from the combustion of fossil fuels alone, since this is relatively easy to estimate and verify and is also the single largest contributor.

## The evolution of a trading system

### Market mechanisms

As long as there is profit to be made, a variety of market mechanisms will emerge to facilitate trading. A number of existing mechanisms such as stock exchanges, information services and payments mechanisms could be used for emission trading. Other mechanisms may need to be set up, or could develop in response to market needs. As in other commodity markets, a variety of market variations would emerge with real-time markets for immediate delivery of greenhouse gas units, perhaps with a settlement period, futures trades, and contracts or options to buy or sell at a future date. However, if not all greenhouse gas units were identical, specialised knowledge of the countries or industries from which the units came might be needed, in which case trading would be more likely to take place through brokers than exchanges.

Trades could occur through forward transactions before the beginning of the first budget period. However, incentives to trade based on future budget allocations will be weak until the budget periods are binding.

It would be difficult to implement a system that covered, from the outset, all greenhouse gases, all sources and sinks, and all Parties. Such difficulties would cause delays, during which time opportunities to trade would be lost. An international emission trading market would be likely to develop gradually over time towards more fully comprehensive trading of different greenhouse gases, evolving into a system with many trades, many participants, and hence greater cost savings and flexibility.

The number of participants might start small to avoid the uncertainties of trading with participants in countries that could not fully verify their emissions. The number of participating countries could increase as more countries opt to take on appropriate monitoring and other requirements. Domestic trading systems are also likely to develop over time, which would facilitate private trades among individual emission sources. The number of greenhouse gases covered by an international emission trading system could also gradually expand from fossil fuel derived carbon dioxide to all greenhouse gases.

### Banking

Participants may be allowed to 'bank' greenhouse gas units, i.e. save them for future use or to sell to other participants in the future. If banking is allowed, greenhouse gas units could be used either to offset emissions in the year the units were issued or, if they were not used, the units could remain valid to offset emissions in future years.

Banking could be a feature of any emission limitation commitment, regardless of whether an emission trading system were established.

Banking would not adversely affect the environment. Increased emissions in future that are above the agreed emission limits will have been offset by earlier reductions. Cumulative emissions and greenhouse gas concentrations will not therefore be affected. Banking would provide certainty that unused greenhouse gas units could be used to offset future emissions or to sell to others. Participants may therefore be willing to go further than their required emission limit in early years if it were cost-effective for them to do so. Banking could add to the liquidity of the market for greenhouse gas units by creating a larger pool of units that could be traded, which would reassure participants that units would be available in the future. Thus banking could improve market confidence, increase liquidity and smooth price fluctuations.

## Borrowing

'Borrowing' is another way to increase flexibility and lower the economic cost of greenhouse gas reductions. Borrowing allows future allocations of greenhouse gas units to be used to offset emissions in excess of the emission limit in the current period. As with banking, borrowing could be a feature of any emission limitation commitment, regardless of whether an emission trading system were established. Borrowing could allow participants to mitigate greenhouse gas emissions at lower cost if mitigation costs were expected to be lower in future periods (probably as the result of developments in less carbon-intensive technologies).

However, borrowing raises a number of problematic issues. If participants were to use or sell large amounts of future greenhouse gas units and could not cover these through future mitigation or by purchasing from others, they could face the equivalent of bankruptcy in not being able to meet their commitments. Borrowing would also make it more difficult to check that participants were in compliance or moving towards their agreed emission limit unless borrowing were only permitted over a short period and a limitation on the extent of reliance on borrowing imposed. Further, if the majority of participants were to borrow from their future emissions allocations rather than trade, market liquidity could suffer, making it more difficult to achieve a fully operating international market for greenhouse gas units.

## Economic implications of Annex I commitments and flexibility mechanisms

Grubb and Vrolijk[10] have developed an International Trade in Emission Allowances (ITEA) model to permit exploration of key issues

relating to defining and trading commitments in the Kyoto negotiations. They use official projections of Annex 1 countries of $CO_2$
emissions to the year 2010 to reflect a 'business as usual' scenario,
together with the adoption of some degree of 'no regret' (i.e. free)
reductions. Prominent among the latter are the removal of fossil fuel
subsidies (which currently amount to around US$100 billion a year
in Annex I countries) and improved efficiency in the transport sector
(via higher energy efficiency standards and the imposition of full
polluter pays charges). The EU is treated as one unified group,
assuming that it will use the bubbling provisions and trading to
distribute emission reductions at minimum cost. Under these
assumptions, Australia was expected to increase $CO_2$ emissions by
40.8 per cent over its 1990 level (Table 12.1), far ahead of the
second largest emitter (the USA with 23.2 per cent). The low growth
expected in the EU is largely due to low population growth and the
shift from coal to gas for power generation. Australia was also
among the highest nations for potential for 'free' reductions. Other
GHGs were included in terms of their Global Warming Potential
(GWP), and again Australia was significantly above all other emitters (largely due to land clearance emissions).

The model mimics behaviour that minimises total abatement
costs among the Annex I countries. In principle, that could be
achieved by using any combination of the three Annex I flexibility
mechanisms (bubbling, emissions trading and joint implementation), together with each country taking optimal choices about the
mix of different gases and sources to be limited. Thus, for example,
Japan could contribute to meeting its formal commitment by trading or investing in Russian methane reductions, if that were cheaper
than limiting its domestic $CO_2$ emissions. The model assumes
competitive behaviour, which means, for example, that Russia will
'sell' its methane reductions to the highest bidder (which also
defines the average price of emission quotas). In an addition to
the scenario, Russian and Ukrainian 'hot air' was removed from
the analysis, with these two countries assumed only to trade emission reductions below their projected 'business as usual' emissions
levels.

The implication of trading for different regions is summarised
in Table 12.1. The most conspicuous result to emerge from the
analysis is the size of the gap between domestic emissions and the
overall Kyoto commitment in some OECD countries. Emissions in
the EU end up close to the Kyoto commitment in aggregate (a little
lower if hot air is excluded), which reflects the low 'business as
usual' projection. Within the EU, however, emission levels could be
widely distributed with the more developed countries such as Germany and the UK, in the range 10–20 per cent below 1990 levels,

**Table 12.1  Estimated increase in $CO_2$ emissions**

| | Basic assumptions | | Implications of trading | | Cost implications | | |
| Regions | BAU $CO_2$ growth (% 1990) | Free reduction (% BAU) | Commitment (%1990) | No restriction | No hot Air | $/capita no trade | $/capita no hot air |
| --- | --- | --- | --- | --- | --- | --- | --- |
| EU | 4.1 | 6 | −8 | −7 | −10 | − | −0.02 |
| USA | 23.2 | 10 | −7 | +11 | +6 | 5.44 | 0.55 |
| Japan | 14.9 | 5 | −6 | +7 | +5 | 2.09 | 0.17 |
| Australia | 40.8 | 12 | +8 | +6 | +1 | − | −0.26 |
| Canada | 18.5 | 10 | −8 | +7 | +2 | 2.12 | 0.32 |
| O-OECD | 22.8 | 4 | −1.8 | +1 | −2 | 0.26 | 0.02 |
| Russia | −19.5 | 14 | 0 | −28 | −32 | − | −0.34 |
| Ukraine | − | − | 0 | −28 | −32 | − | −0.34 |
| N-EU | −9.9 | 10 | −6.6 | −19 | −23 | 0.14 | −0.34 |
| O-CEEC | −27.5 | 12 | −8 | −36 | −39 | − | −0.47 |

*Source:*  Adapted from Grubb, M. and Vrolijk, C. (1998)

being offset by the growth in some of the less developed member states. Countries faced with high costs to limit domestic $CO_2$ emissions will take the cheaper options of action on other gases and emissions trading, leaving domestic $CO_2$ emissions at higher levels. By 2010, under either set of assumptions, comprehensive gas coverage and emissions trading leaves domestic $CO_2$ emissions in Japan and the USA at 12 to 16 percentage points higher than their Kyoto commitment. Australia appears likely to comfortably meet its commitment.

Grubb and Vrolijk contend that the large gaps between the commitment and actual $CO_2$ reductions for countries like the USA and Japan starkly illustrate both the dangers and the opportunities offered by emissions trading. Taken at face value, the Kyoto agreement could still leave $CO_2$ emissions in the USA and Japan around 10 per cent above 1990 levels without breaching the formal agreement (and that is before considering additional flexibility from sinks and the CDM). Grubb and Vrolijk maintain that this is not the intended outcome of the US or Japanese positions. Particularly if some of this represents hot air trading, such an outcome would risk bringing mechanisms for flexibility and efficiency into serious disrepute and delay still further the time when developing countries accept the need to act themselves.

These latter results are not very sensitive to differing assumptions within plausible ranges, given the official 'business as usual' projections as a basis. This is because certain fundamental characteristics are almost universally accepted: across Annex I countries it is cheaper to achieve a given reduction relative to 1990 levels in eastern Europe than in the major OECD countries, and it is easier to do so on multiple gases than on $CO_2$ emissions alone. It is therefore inevitable that flexibility results in OECD $CO_2$ emissions being above the level of the Kyoto commitment. More pessimistic assumptions about the costs of limiting $CO_2$ emissions would only widen the gap between domestic $CO_2$ and the Kyoto commitment further.

The two final columns of Table 12.1 contain an illustration of the approximate cost implications of the commitments and the impact of emissions trading on different regions. These are expressed in terms of token dollars per capita (in other words, they are unit free and are only useful for comparison across countries and not as absolute measures of true dollar values). Commitments in Australia, the EU and most of eastern Europe can be met through 'no regret' measures alone, given the scope assumed for such reductions, particularly concerning non-$CO_2$ gases, combined with the modest baseline projections for the EU and the very large contribution of non-fossil fuel sources in Australia. Most other OECD countries incur costs which emissions trading reduces typically by a factor of around 10, because of the access they have to the large pools of low cost reductions in eastern Europe and the smaller OECD countries. Australia and eastern Europe benefit significantly from quota exports.

Grubb and Vrolijk emphasised that these results were preliminary and, like all such analysis, dependent upon input assumptions. Nevertheless, they believed that the general pattern of results was robust, with the caveat that costs to the EU and Japan would be higher if their official 'business as usual' emissions projections were overly optimistic.

The above analysis suggests that the mechanisms for flexibility would be very heavily used, including large-scale trading of surplus emission quotas likely to be available from Russia and the Ukraine, to the extent that $CO_2$ emissions in the USA and Japan would probably remain well above 1990 levels in the commitment period. Grubb and Vrolijk were uncertain how acceptable this would be in practice, and what implications it could hold for the subsequent evolution of the regime and the ultimate objective of stabilising levels of GHGs in the atmosphere. They felt that the perverse Russian and Ukrainian allocations negotiated in Kyoto may cause problems for many years to come, although excluding trading of genuinely surplus hot air quotas could avoid some of these problems and result overall in stronger reductions. The inclusion of sinks and the CDM add further dimensions of flexibility that, at present, cannot be quantified.

## Conclusions

Greenhouse gases are well suited to international trading because the location of greenhouse gas emission reduction does not affect the climate. International greenhouse gas emission trading among countries with emission limits would enable them to achieve compliance with national emission limits at minimum cost, while allowing countries full flexibility to reduce domestic emissions in ways that best suit their national circumstances. Certain features of emission trading, such as banking, could also provide flexibility over when greenhouse gas mitigation can take place and provide an incentive for early action to reduce greenhouse gas emissions where this is cost-effective.

# Notes

## Chapter 1

1  The source for all data is DX data base.

## Chapter 2

1  We should be wary of concluding from these figures that these countries
   have actually surpassed Australian living standards. Dowrick and
   Quiggin (1993) demonstrate that, when account is taken of the com-
   paratively large amount of leisure enjoyed in Australia, there is a strong
   presumption that Australian living standards are in fact higher—a
   proposition which is endorsed by much of the commentary emanating
   from Japan itself on the very long working hours and lack of leisure.
2  On the other hand, general taxation reduces the private returns to
   investment and hence inhibits investment. In general there will be a
   level of tax-funded public investment in education, research and infrastructure that will be economically optimal.

## Chapter 3

No Notes

## Chapter 4

1  Analysis of the links between unemployment and crime is presented in
   Crow et al (1989).
2  See Whitfield (1987) for a survey of such research.
3  For analysis of the unemployment–vacancies relationship in Australia
   see Harper (1980) and King (1986).

4   See the Green Paper, Chapter 8, for analysis of the way the existing benefits policy might be improved.

5   See the Green Paper, Chapters 4–6, for details on Labour Market Program recommendations.

## Chapter 5

No Notes

## Chapter 6

1   In particular two arguments are *not* discussed. One is that deficit financing of public expenditure does not stimulate the economy, since the public will save to pay expected increases in taxes that will be imposed to reduce public debt in the future. The second is that economic policy can have effects on the economy only if policy makers trick the public by making unexpected policy changes after the public have made their decisions. Australian policy makers and advisors have (rightly) never given much credence to either of these arguments.

2   This is discussed in more detail in Chapter 7.

3   If one looks at the thirteen years ending in 1996/97 (when Australia had a floating exchange rate) the adjusted square of the correlation coefficient is 0.07, which is nowhere near being statistically significant.

4   This is not surprising. As we have seen, when the economy grows rapidly this in itself will tend to reduce the deficit. It will also lead to increases in the current account deficit which in turn will lead to rises in interest rates.

5   If there is an increase in imports, in the short run the savings gap also increases through an extension of trade credit, and the current deficit increases. If the Reserve Bank fears a substantial devaluation, it may raise interest rates to encourage foreign lending to Australia. This will also reduce Australian investment and the planned savings gap.

## Chapter 7

1   The authors would like to thank Ian McDonald, Nilss Olekalns and Graham Voss for comments on this chapter.

2   At the time of writing the nature of prudential regulation is undergoing some changes. A newly created body, the Australian Prudential Regulatory Authority, will be taking over some of the functions previously fulfilled by the RBA.

3   Detailed discussion of Australia's recent unemployment experience can be found in Chapter 3.

4   The expected inflation rate is used because, at the time of decision, it is the expected inflation rate which influences borrowing and lending decisions.

5   A similar argument is that discretionary policy will lead governments to try to reduce unemployment before an election in order to help them get re-elected. Implicit in this view is that the probably higher inflation

that results from this policy will not be as apparent to the electorate as any reduced unemployment.

6　See Milbourne (1990, section 4b) and the references contained within.

7　Six quarters seems to be the average lag of monetary policy. Milbourne (1990) surveys the empirical evidence.

8　A more complete description is contained in Milbourne (1990). There seemed to be a considerable difference between the Treasury and the RBA for the reasons for monetary contraction: the former argued that high interest rates were necessary to contain the current account deficit; the latter argued for the importance of price stability. See the quotes in Bewley and White (1990).

9　RBA *Bulletin*, April 1993, p. 2.

10　RBA *Bulletin*, April 1993, p. 2.

11　See Chapter 2.

12　Though as noted above, this role is currently undergoing some changes as a result of the recommendations of the Wallis Committee report (see note 2).

13　For further details see the RBA website, at www.rba.gov.au

## Chapter 8

1　Valuation of such goods and services by market prices is generally not available.

2　An offset to this implied overstatement, from the treatment of transfer payments in public sector measurement inherent in estimating its effective control over resource use, arises from the government's general regulatory powers. The actual impact from government use of these powers is often well in excess of the input costs of implementing such regulatory measures. Hence an input measurement strategy tends to understate the actual extent of public sector control over the private sector, the coercive features of which are seen as the essential characteristic of government, which measurement of its size needs to capture.

## Chapter 9

1　A good survey of the optimal tax literature is provided in Heady, C. (1993) 'Optimal taxation as a guide to tax policy: A survey', *Fiscal Studies* 14(1):15–41; Cullis, J. and Jones, P. (1992) *Public Finance and Public Choice*, Chapters 16–17.

2　Meade (1978).

3　An excise duty is often called a specific tax. This is because it is on specific units of *output* of a good such as litres of petrol or alcohol or kilograms of tobacco. These taxes should be contrasted with a GST or a WST which are ad valorem taxes—that is, taxes on the *value* of goods and services.

4　See Pender and Ross (1995), pp.14–16. A recent study by Chennells and Griffith (1997) has examined further the OECD statistics but not the case of Asian countries.

5　See Warren (1997, 1990) and Harding, Lambert and Warren (1998) for a discussion of the issues and intertemporal estimates.

6 A progressive tax is typically defined as one where the ratio of the marginal tax rate to the average tax rate is greater than unity. Another way to put this is that a progressive tax is one where the average tax rate increases with increasing income.

7 The Federal Treasury web site (www.treasury.gov.au) contains a wealth of information on taxation and tax reform, Federal Budget papers and tax expenditures. Also visit the Australian Tax Office (www.ato.gov.au) and Customs Department (www.customs.gov.au) web sites for other important tax information.

8 Fringe benefits are taxed at a flat effective tax rate of 48.5 per cent. Therefore, if an employee receives a fringe benefit of $100, the fringe benefit tax liability for the employer is $(0.485/(1-0.485)) \times \$100$ or $94. Put differently, if a person confronting a marginal tax rate of 48.5 per cent received a gross amount of $194, after tax they would receive $100.

9 If the company tax rate is 36 per cent and a person receives a full franked dividend of $74, then dividends are included in their personal income tax return as having a gross value of $100 ($74/(1-.36)) but with a tax credit claim of $36. A franking credit can be used to reduce your tax liability but it cannot be used to obtain a refund. See further discussion of this issue on pages 163–65.

10 In June 1998, the threshold for the assets test for singles and couples was $90 000 higher for non-home owners than home owners. See information at www.centrelink.gov.au

11 In 1884, South Australia was the first Australian State to levy a general income tax (Smith 1993, p.145).

12 The Medicare levy has its own threshold of $13 127 for a single person and $22 151 + $2 100 × K where K is the number of children. However, these thresholds are clawed back so that for singles above $14 347 and couples above $24 209 + $2 295 × K, a flat rate of 1.5 per cent applies. It should also be noted that those in receipt of government pensions and benefits and self-funded retirees are entitled to special tax rebates which significantly increase the effective tax threshold for these groups.

13 A flat tax should be contrasted with a linear tax, the latter being distinguished by having a tax-free threshold.

14 See Head and Krever (1990).

15 *Taxation Review Committee Preliminary Report*, 1 June 1974, AGPS, Canberra.

16 *Commonwealth Taxation of Goods and Services*, Treasury Taxation Paper No 5, October 1974, AGPS, Canberra, p.6. This view was also echoed in *Taxation Review Committee Full Report*, 31 January 1975, AGPS, Canberra, pp.511–16.

17 A VAT (Value Added Tax) is a multiple stage retail sales tax and is levied in all European Community countries. Canada and New Zealand also impose a VAT but call it a Goods and Service Tax.

18 The DWP BBCT was a single stage tax at the retail level, that is, a retail sales tax. This is in contrast to a VAT which is a multiple stage retail sales tax.

19 See *Draft White Paper*, (1985).

20 A Bit Tax is a tax on bits of information. For example, there are 8

bits in one byte, 1024 bytes in one kilobyte and 1024 kilobytes in one megabyte. A Bit Tax is therefore a tax on electronic data flows and pays no regard to what is actually transmitted.

## Chapter 10

1 The latest available data is May 1996, so an analysis of changes in the distribution of earnings since the election is not possible.
2 Coalition State governments (including Victoria and Western Australia) had already implemented similar or more far-reaching reforms.
3 Details about AWAs are kept secret. The Employment Advocate registers AWAs and has a duty to ensure that they were not enforced under duress and that the agreements do not seriously disadvantage employees.
4 With the advent of enterprise bargaining it is now very difficult to interpret aggregate wage data. The problem is that not everyone is covered by enterprise bargains, wage increases may be granted in exchange for trade-offs in other conditions and there are major compositional changes occurring in the work force (Burgess, 1995).
5 The programs to be scrapped were determined by a cost-benefit analysis undertaken by the CESAC.
6 The tendering process appears to have disadvantaged companies which had a good record of achievement but were not competitive in terms of the price they offered (*Sydney Morning Herald*, 1998).
7 In the 1996/97 Budget the Commonwealth provided $41.6 million over the following three years to establish the Green Corps (Young Australians for the Environment), which would give Australians aged 17–20 the opportunity to work on environmental projects. It was anticipated that the Green Corps would be built up so that by the end of a three-year period 3500 young Australians would have participated.

## Chapter 11

1 D. Mortimer, *Going for Growth*, Canberra AGPS, June, 1997 (hereafter 'Mortimer'); *Investing for Growth*, Canberra, AGPS, December, 1997.
2 Between 1852 and 1860 Victoria's population increased from 150 000 to 540 000.
3 C.C. Kingston, Minister for Trade and Customs, quoted in Brigden, 1929, p.148.
4 Deferred duties were a form of anticipatory protection.
5 *Tariff Board Act* 1921, Section 15(1)(d) (e) and (f).
6 Tariff Board, *Annual Report, 1927*, Canberra: Commonwealth Government Printer, p.18.
7 Brigden (1929), pp.6–7.
8 A. Capling and B. Galligan, *Beyond the Protective State*, Cambridge University Press, 1992, p.97.
9 R.J. Jackson et al, *Policies for the Development of Manufacturing Industry* (Report), Canberra: AGPS, 1975, p.27.
10 The tariff cut was implemented not as an industry or tariff policy, but

as a macroeconomic measure to increase the flow of imports and so reduce inflationary pressures.

11  Vernon 1965, p.368.

12  Often this entailed setting tariffs to equalise ex-factory prices of locally made goods and the landed cost of competing imports—setting a so-called 'scientific tariff'. The broad principle of the made-to-measure approach was to provide sufficient protection to maintain employment and profitability in the protected industry without consideration of its effects on possible user industries. It resulted in a 'cascading' of the tariff structure with different (and higher) levels of protection at different (and higher) stages of the production process.

13  Jackson 1975, p.34.

14  The adjustment measures suggested by Crawford included assistance for exports, R & D and modernising capital equipment. *Report of the Study Group on Structural Adjustment* (Crawford Report), Canberra, AGPS, 1979, p.78.

15  Under the Act, among the requirements of the Commission's recommendations were the need to ensure that any measures of assistance to, and development of industries were integrated with national economic policies as a whole; that they would achieve balanced growth and improve efficiency in the use of the community's productive resources, would facilitate structural adjustment; and recognise the interests of consumers. However, amendments to the Act by the Fraser government in the late 1970s—a time of rising unemployment—imposed on the Commission the requirement, when making its recommendations, to report *inter alia* on the level of assistance necessary to maintain employment at the level which existed at the beginning of the inquiry. If adopted, here was the made-to-measure approach reborn: protection tailored to fit the least efficient firm in an industry.

16  The ERP is a measure of the net assistance to an activity provided by the protective structure. Essentially it is a measure which is the net of the advantage to local producers provided by protection against competing imports and the disadvantage (the tax effect) they may suffer from any prtotection applying to their importable inputs.

17  The reason the average ERP did not fall by the full 25 per cent is that many imported goods were already free of duty.

18  The Commonwealth Statistician's industry classification was changed in 1992/93 (see note to Table 11.1). The concordance of industry classifications in Tables 11.1 and 11.2 should be viewed as approximate.

19  This is the subsidy that would have had to be paid to provide the same level of net assistance to the industry as the current assistance arrangements (e.g. tariff protection).

20  See Industry Commission, (Draft Report) *The Automotive Industry*, Canberra, 1996, Table 17; ABS, *Labour Force, Australia* (Cat. 6203.0); ABS, *Manufacturing Industry Australia* (Cat. 8221.0).

21  Mortimer, p.47.

22  The diesel fuel rebate is the most expensive of these schemes and is budgeted to cost almost $1.5 billion in 1997/98 (Mortimer, p.221).

23  From 1997/98 the program expenditure will be capped at $150 million per year.

24  Mortimer, pp.55, 106.

25  The sum allocated refers to the 25 per cent component of the 125 per cent tax concession.

26  See, for example, D. Leahy and J. P. Neary, 'R & D spillovers and the case for industrial policy in an open economy', *Centre of Economic Performance, Discussion Paper No. 65*, April, 1997 (London School of Economics).

27  Named after Senator John Button, who was Industry Minister from 1983 to 1993.

28  Industry Commission, *Annual Report 1995/96* (Canberra, AGPS) p.281. See also Industry Commission, *Annual Report, 1991/92* (Canberra AGPS) and Industry Commission, *The Pharmaceutical Industry*, Report No.51 (September, 1996).

29  Productivity Commission, *Stocktake of Progress in Microeconomic Reform* (Canberra: AGPS, June 1996), p.125; Industry Commission, *Annual Report 1995/96*, (Canberra: AGPS), p.102.

30  Mortimer, p.170.

31  Industry Commission, *The Textiles, Clothing and Footwear Industries*, Report No. 59 (Canberra: AGPS, 1997).

32  J. Howard and J. Moore, Joint Press Release, 10 September 1997.

33  Following publication of the review, in July the Treasurer had rejected Mortimer's proposal for a growth target, but the government's final response to Mortimer, *Investing for Growth*, included an overall growth target (rather than a per capita target) of 4 per cent.

34  For example, an extra $670 million is budgeted for encouraging innovation (the main component of which is $556 million to expand the R & D Start program) which is about one-third of the R & D funding cut from the government's 1996/97 Budget. (*Investing for Growth*, p.87; *Australian Financial Revue*, 9 December 1997, p.10.)

35  J. Howard, Address to the National Press Club, 8 December 1997.

36  *Investing for Growth*, p.47.

37  *Investing for Growth*, p.56.

38  G.H. Winder and C. MacPherson, *The Delusion of Protection* (Sydney, 1931), p.129.

39  C. Freedman and R. Stonecash, 'A survey of manufacturing industry policy: From the Tariff Board to the Productivity Commission', *Economic Record*, June 1997, p.176.

40  Mortimer, pp.78–9.

41  *Investing for Growth*, p.94.

42  Mortimer, p.60.

43  CKD—completely knocked down (i.e. disassembled). In those days, for customs' purposes the 'chassis' included the engine.

44  The industry became an important part of the Lyons government's short-lived policy of 'trade diversion'. Measures were implemented to divert trade from 'unfavourable' trading partners (including the United States and Japan) to 'favourable' partners (essentially countries of the Sterling bloc including, of course, the United Kingdom). Following the

controversy surrounding the measures concerning the automotive industry, the government reluctantly referred the matter of 'complete' manufacture to the Tariff Board, a majority of which rejected the government's strategy of 'development [of the industry] in one step', preferring a more gradual approach.

45  During the 1950s vehicles with varying degrees of local content were also produced by Ford, British Motor Corporation and Chrysler.

46  Tariff Board, 1965, p.16.

47  Industry Commission, Draft Report, *The Automotive Industry*, p.K5.

48  Speech to the Federation of Automotive Products Manufacturers Annual Convention, Canberra, 16 June 1997.

## Chapter 12

1  This chapter is largely based upon presentations given at the 'Climate After Kyoto: Implications for Energy' Conference convened by the Royal Institute of International Affairs, Chatham House, London, 5–6 February 1998.

2  Annex I Parties comprise all OECD nations (with the exceptions of Turkey, Mexico and Korea) and the 'transition' market economies of Eastern Europe: a total of 38 countries.

3  A different base year is allowed for some of the transition economies of central Europe and for industrial trace gases.

4  Most countries were allocated an 8 per cent reduction commitment. Major exceptions to this figure were those permitted increases: Iceland (+10 per cent), Australia (+8 per cent), and Norway (1 per cent), no change: New Zealand, Russia, and Ukraine (0 per cent); and smaller decreases than the norm: Japan (–6 per cent) and USA (–7 per cent).

5  $CO_2$ = carbon dioxide; $CH_4$ = methane; $N_2O$ = nitrous oxide; HFCs = hydrofluorocarbons; PFCs = perfluorocarbons; $SF_6$ = sulphur hexafluoride.

6  Man-made.

7  'Sources' are the principal physical origins of GHGs, while 'sinks' are means by which GHGs can be absorbed, principally reforestation.

8  As a result of the country's economic transition $CO_2$ emissions in the former Soviet Union have fallen by 25–30 per cent since 1990. Although the Russian and Ukraine economies are recovering, emissions are unlikely to return to their 1990 levels for many years. Consequently, surplus emission quotas are available to these countries following allocation to them of a zero growth target in the Kyoto Protocol. This surplus is referred to as 'hot air'.

9  See Owen (1995) for a more detailed discussion of emissions trading in the context of the broader topic of economic instruments for use in environmental regulation.

10  Grubb, M. and Vrolijk, C. (1998).

# Bibliography

Abramovitz, Moses (1986), 'Catching up, forging ahead and falling behind', *Journal of Economic History* 46, 385–406.

ACAC (1987) *National Wage Decision*, Print G6800, Commonwealth Government Printer, Melbourne.

ACTU-Trade Development Council (1987) *Australia Reconstructed*, AGPS, Canberra.

Affirmative Action Agency 1992, *Integration of Permanent Part-time Worker*, Workshift Information Series No. 3, Department of Industrial Relations, AGPS, Canberra.

Agreements Data Base and Monitor (ADAM), Australian Centre for Industrial Relations Research and Teaching, Sydney.

AIRC (1991a) *National Wage Decision*, Print J7400, Commonwealth Government Printer, Melbourne.

——(1991b) *National Wage Decision*, Print K0300, Commonwealth Government Printer, Melbourne.

——(1993) *National Wage Decision*, Print K9700, Commonwealth Government Printer, Melbourne.

——*Safety Net Review—Wages*, AGPS, Canberra, 1997.

Akerlof, G., Dickens, W. and Perry, G. (1996) 'Low inflation or no inflation: should the Federal Reserve pursue complete price stability?' *Challenge* Sept–Oct: pp.11–7.

Alexander, M. and Green, R. (1992) 'Workplace productivity and joint consultation', *Australian Bulletin of Labour*, 18/2.

ALP-ACTU (1983) Statement of Accord by the Australian Labor Party and the Australian Council of Trade Unions Regarding Economic Policy, ALP-ACTU.

Anderson, P., Dwyer, J. and Gruen, D. (1995) *Productivity and Growth*, Proceedings of a Conference, Reserve Bank, Sydney.

Argy, V. (1992) *Australian Macroeconomic Policy Part II*, Allen & Unwin, Sydney.

Aschauer, D.A. (1989) 'Is public expenditure productive?' *Journal of Monetary Economics*, 23, pp.177–200.

Asprey Report (1974) *Taxation Review Committee Preliminary Report*, 1 June, AGPS, Canberra.

Asprey, K.W. (Chairman) (1975) *Taxation Review Committee Full Report*, 31 January, AGPS, Canberra.

Atkinson, J. (1987) 'Flexibility or fragmentation?—the United Kingdom labour market in the eighties', *Labour and Society*, Vol. 12, pp.87–105.

Australian Bureau of Statistics (1989) 'Development of multifactor productivity estimates for Australia 1974–75 to 1987–88', Catalogue No. 5229.0, April, ABS, Canberra.

——(1993) 'Australian National Accounts multifactor productivity, 1991–92', Catalogue No. 5234.0, April, ABS, Canberra.

——(1992) *The Australian Consumer Price Index: 12th Series Review*, Catalogue no. 6450.0, ABS, Canberra.

Australian Centre for Industrial Relations Research and Teaching (1996) 'A Profile of Low Wage Employees', Living Wage Case Submission, Sydney.

Australian Government–ACTU (1990) Agreement between the Federal Government and ACTU, AGPS, Canberra.

——(1993) *Putting Jobs First*, AGPS, Canberra.

——(1995) Sustaining Growth, Low Inflation and Fairness, AGPS, Canberra.

Baekgaard, H. (1997), *The Distribution of Household Wealth in Australia for 1986 and 1993*, paper presented to the 1997 National Social Policy Conference, University of NSW, Sydney, 16–18 July.

Ball, L. (1993) 'How costly is disinflation? The historical evidence', *Federal Reserve Bank of Philadelphia Business Review* Nov–Dec: pp.17–28.

Barro, Robert J. and Lee, Jong-wha (1993) *Losers and Winners in Economic Growth*, NBER Working Paper No. 4341.

Barro, Robert J. and Sala-i-Martin, Xavier (1995) *Economic Growth*, McGraw-Hill, New York.

BCA (Business Council of Australia) (1989) *Enterprise Based Bargaining Units: A Better Way of Working*, BCA, Melbourne.

Bellchamber, G. (1997) 'Bank confused on numbers', *Australian Financial Review*, June 13.

Bennett, L. (1994) 'Women and enterprise bargaining: The legal and institutional framework', *Journal of Industrial Relations,* Vol. 36(2), pp.191–216.

Bewley, R. and White, G. (1990), 'Do high interest rates improve the current account?', *Economic Papers*, pp.19–33.

Biddle, D. and Burgess, J. (1998) *Youth Unemployment and Contemporary Labour Market Policy in Australia*, paper presented at AIRAANZ Conference, Victoria University of Wellington, February 1998.

Borland, J. (1997) 'Unemployment in Australia—prospects and policies', *Australian Economic Review*, 30,4.

Boskin, M.J. et al (1998) 'Consumer prices, the Consumer Price Index, and the cost of living', *Journal of Economic Perspectives*, Winter: pp.3–26.

Brigden, J.B. (1929) *The Australian Tariff*, Melbourne University Press, Melbourne.

Brown, W., Hayles, J., Hughes, B. and Rowe, L. (1980) 'Occupational pay structures under different wage fixing arrangements: A comparison of intra-occupational pay dispersion in Australia, Great Britain and the United States', *British Journal of Industrial Relations*, Vol. 18, pp.217–30.

Buchanan, J. and Callus, R. (1993) 'Efficiency and equity at work: The need for labour market regulation', *Journal of Industrial Relations*, Vol. 35(4), pp.515–27.

Buchanan, J. and Watson, I. (1997) *The Living Wage and the Working Poor*, The National Social Policy Conference. Brisbane.

Buchanan, J., van Barneveld, K., O'Loughlin, T. and Pragnell, B. (1997) 'Wages policy and wage determination in 1996', *Journal of Industrial Relations*, 39, 1, pp.96–119.

Buchanan, J., Woodman, M., O'Keefe, S. and Arsovska, B. (1998) 'Wages policy and wage determination in 1997', *Journal of Industrial Relations*, 40, 1 (forthcoming).

Budget 96—Questions and Answers, http//www.deet.gov.au/budget96/qanda/q&a2.htm#6

Burgess, J. (1995) 'Aggregate wage indicators, enterprise bargaining and recent wage increases', *Economic and Labour Relations Review*, 6, 2, pp.216–33.

Burgess, J. (1996) *Labour Economics*, Heinemann, Melbourne.

——(1997) 'Labour economics', *Economics*, 33, 2, pp.9–16.

Burgess, J. and Campbell, I. (1993) *Moving Towards a Deregulated Labour Market, Part-Time Work and the Recession in Australia*, ESC Working Paper No. 11, University of Newcastle.

Callus, R. et al (1991) *Industrial Relations at Work: The Australian Workplace Industrial Relations Survey*, AGPS, Canberra.

Campbell, I. (1993) 'Labour market flexibility in Australia', *Labour and Industry*. 5, 3, pp.1–31.

——(1996) *The End of Standard Working Time? Working Time Arrangements and Trade Unions in a Time of Transition*, National Key Centre in Industrial Relations Working Paper No. 39, Monash University, Melbourne.

Campbell, I. and Webber, M. (1996) 'Retrenchment and labour market flows in Australia', *Economic and Labour Relations Review* (forthcoming).

Carlin, W. and Soskice, D. (1990) *Macroeconomics and the Wage Bargain*, Oxford University Press, Oxford.

Carmichael, J. (1990) 'Inflation: performance and policy' in S. Grenville (ed.), *The Australian Macro-Economy in the 1980s*, Reserve Bank of Australia, Sydney.

Chapman, B.J. (1990) 'The labour market' in S. Grenville (ed.), *The Australian Macro-Economy in the 1980s*, Reserve Bank of Australia, Sydney.

Chapman, D.R. and Junor, C.W. (1981) 'Profits, variability of profits, and the Prices Justification Tribunal' *Economic Record* 57, June, pp. 128–39.

Chisholm, A. (1993) 'Indirect taxation, effective tax rates and consumption efficiency' in J.G. Head (ed.) *Fightback! An Economic Assessment*, Conference Series 12, Australian Tax Research Foundation, pp.309–50.

Clark, T.E. (1998) 'Progress toward price stability: a 1997 inflation report', *Federal Reserve Bank of Kansas City Economic Review 83*, First Quarter, pp.5–21.

Clark, K. and Summers, L. (1982) 'The dynamics of youth unemployment' in R. Freeman and D. Wise (eds) *The Youth Labour Market*, University of Chicago Press, Chicago, pp.199–230.

Collins, D. J. and Warren, N.A. (1998) *Understanding Consumption Taxes: Everyone's Guide*, Research Study 30, Australian Tax Research Foundation, Sydney.

Committee on Employment Opportunities (1993) *Restoring Full Employment*, Commonwealth of Australia (The Green Paper).

Commonwealth of Australia (1996) *Budget Statements 1996/97*, Canberra.

——(1997) *Budget Strategy and Outlook, 1997/98*.

Corden, W. M. (1979) 'Wages and unemployment in Australia', *Economic Record*, Vol. 55, pp.1–19.

Costello, P. (1998) 'Tax Reform: not a New Tax, a New Tax System, AGPS, Canberra.

Covick, O. (1984) 'Productivity-geared wages policy, labour's share of Gross Product, and the "real wage overhang"', in B.J. Chapman, et al (eds), *Australian Labour Economics: Readings*, 3rd Edition, Macmillan, Melbourne.

Crow, I., Richardson, P., Riddington, C. and Simon, F. (1989) *Unemployment, Crime and Offenders*, Routledge, London.

Davis, K. (1991) 'The development of Australian monetary policy during the last decade' in *Developments in Australian Economics*, C. Kearney & R. MacDonald (eds), Longman Cheshire, Melbourne.

Davis, M. (1996) 'We're not extravagant people, battlers tell wage bench', *Australian Financial Review*, December 9.

Dawkins, P. and Norris, K. (1990) 'Casual employment in Australia', *Australian Bulletin of Labour*, Vol. 16, pp.156–73.

De Long, J. Bradford and Summers, Lawrence H. (1992) 'Equipment investment and economic growth: how strong is the nexus?', *Brookings Papers on Economic Activity* 2:1992, pp.157–99.

Debelle, G. and Stevens, G. (1995) *Monetary policy goals for inflation in Australia*, Research Discussion Paper RDP 9503, Reserve Bank of Australia, Sydney.

DEETYA (1996), Green Corps: Young Australians Working for the Environment, http://www.deet.gov.au/minwn/vanstone/v70_20_8.htm

——(1997a) Green Corps Project Begins in Sydney. http://www.deet.gov.au/minwn/abbott/am100697.htm

——(1997b), Work for the Dole Legislation, http://www.deet.gov.au/minwn/kemp/k10_19397.htm

DEIR (Department of Employment and Industrial Relations) (1986), *Industrial Democracy and Worker Participation*, AGPS, Canberra.

Department of Industrial Relations, *Equal Pay Unit Newsletter* (various issues).

——(1992) *Equal pay: policy statement*, AGPS, Canberra.

——(1993) *The Spread and Impact of Workplace Bargaining: Evidence from the Workplace*, research project prepared by M. Short, A. Preston and D. Peetz, AGPS, Canberra.

——(1995) *Enterprise bargaining in Australia: Developments under the Industrial Relations Reform Act, Annual Report 1994*, AGPS, Canberra.

——(1996) *The Reform of Workplace Relations*, Implementation Discussion Paper, Canberra.

——(1996a), *Changes in Federal Workplace Relations Law: Legislative Guide*, AGPS, Canberra.

——(1996b), *Enterprise Bargaining in Australia*, AGPS, Canberra.

Dowrick, Steve (1990) 'Explaining the productivity slow-down of the 1980s', *Australian Bulletin of Labour* 16(3), September, pp.174–97.

——(1992) 'Technological catch up and diverging incomes: patterns of economic growth 1960–88', *Economic Journal* 102, pp.600–10.

——(1995) 'The determinants of long-run economic development', in *Reserve Bank Conference Proceedings*, Reserve Bank of Australia, Sydney.

Dwyer, T.M., and Larkin, J.T., (1995) *The Taxation of Company and Business Income*, Research Study 35, Australian Tax Research Foundation, Sydney.

Economic Planning and Advisory Council (EPAC) (1991) *Australia's Inflation Problem: Office of EPAC Seminar*, EPAC Background Paper No. 11, AGPS, Canberra.

EPAC (1996) *Future Labour Market Issues for Australia*, AGPS, Canberra.

Evatt Foundation (1995) *Unions 2001: A Blueprint for Trade Union Activism*, Evatt Foundation, Sydney.

Fay, R. (1996), Enhancing the Effectiveness of Active Labour Market Policies: Labour Market and Social Policy Occasional Paper No. 18, OECD Paris.

Feldstein, M. (1997) *Capital income taxes and the benefit of price stability*, Working Paper 6200, National Bureau of Economic Research, September.

*Fightback! Fairness and Jobs* (1992) Liberal Party of Australia, Canberra, 18 December.

FitzGerald, V.W. (1993) *National Savings*, AGPS, Canberra.

Foster, W. and Gregory, R. (1983) A flow analysis of the labour market in Australia' in R. Blandy and O. Covick (eds), *Understanding Labour Markets*, Allen and Unwin, Sydney.

Friedman, M. (1968) 'The role of monetary policy', *American Economic Review*, Vol. 58.

Gittins, R. (1996) 'What happens when we don't have a wages policy any more?' *Sydney Morning Herald*, March 16.

Goodhart, C. (1994) 'What should central banks do? What should be their macroeconomic objectives and operations?' *Economic Journal*, November, pp. 1424–36.

Grattan, M. (1997) 'Work with no job,' *Australian Financial Review*, February 11.

Green, R. (1991) 'Change and involvement at the workplace: Evidence from the Australian Workplace Industrial Relations Survey', *Economic & Labour Relations Review*, 2/1.

——(1992) 'Productivity and comparability in Public Service pay', *Labour Economics and Productivity*, 4/2.

——(1994) 'Wages policy and wage determination in 1993', *Journal of Industrial Relations*, 36/1.

——(1996) 'Productivity: Current trends and prospects', in *Industrial Relations Under the Microscope*, ACIRRT Working Paper No. 40, University of Sydney.

Green, R. & Macdonald, D. (1992) 'The Australian flexibility paradox', *Journal of Industrial Relations*, 33/4.

Green, R.H., Mitchell, W.F. and Watts, M.J. (1997) 'The Accord, trade unions and the Australian labour market' in *The Australian Economy: The Essential Guide 2*, (ed.) P. Kriesler, Allen and Unwin, Sydney.

Gregory, R.G. (1993) 'Aspects of Australian and US living standards: The disappointing decades 1970–1990', *Economic Record*, Vol. 69, pp.61–76.

Groenewegen, P. (1990) *Public Finance in Australia. Theory and Practice*, Third Edition, Prentice Hall, Sydney.

Grubb, M. and Vrolijk, C. (1998) *The Kyoto Protocol: Specific Commitments and Flexibility Mechanisms*, paper presented at the 'Climate After Kyoto: Implications for Energy' Conference convened by The Royal Institute of International Affairs, Chatham House, London, 5–6 February.

Gruen, F.H. (1978) *Some Thoughts on Real Wages and Unemployment*, Centre for Applied Economics Research Paper No. 4, University of New South Wales, Sydney.

Hall, P. and Fruin, D. (1994) 'Gender aspects of enterprise bargaining: The good, the bad and the ugly', in D.E. Morgan (ed.) *Dimensions of Enterprise Bargaining and Organisational Relations*, UNSW Studies in Australian Industrial Relations, No. 35, Industrial Relations Research Centre, UNSW, Sydney, pp.77–129.

Hancock, K. (1985) *Australian Industrial Relations Law and Systems*, Report of Committee of Review, AGPS, Canberra.

——(1987) 'Regulation and deregulation in the Australian labour market', *Australian Bulletin of Labour*, vol. 13(2), pp.94–107.

Hanusch, Horst (ed.) (1988) *Evolutionary Economics: Applications of Schumpeter's Ideas*, Cambridge University Press, Cambridge.

Harding, A. 1995, *The Impact of Health, Education and Housing Outlays on Income Distribution in Australia in the 1990s*, Discussion Paper 7, National Centre for Social and Economic Modelling, University of Canberra.

Harding, A. and Polette, J. (1995) 'The price of means-tested transfers: Effective marginal tax rates in Australia in 1994', *Australian Economic Review*, 3rd Quarter, pp.100–6.

Harding, A., Lambert, S. and Warren, N.A. (1998) *Income Distribution Report No. 8*, National Centre for Social and Economic Modelling, University of Canberra, Canberra.

Harper, I. (1980) 'The relationship between unemployment and unfilled vacancies in Australia', *Economic Record*, Vol. 56, No. 154, pp. 231–43.

Harrison, B. and Bluestone, B. (1990) 'Wage polarisation in the US and the "flexibility" debate', *Cambridge Journal of Economics*, Vol. 14(3), pp.351–73.

Head, J.G. and Krever, R. (eds) 1990, *Flattening the Tax Rate Scale: Alternative Scenarios and Methodologies*, Longman-Cheshire, Melbourne.

Heiler, K. (1998), 'The petty pilfering of minutes, or what has happened to the length of the working day in Australia' in R. Harbridge, C. Gadd and A. Crawford (eds) *Current Research in Industrial Relations*, Victoria University of Wellington, pp.167–76.

Hughes, B. (1973) 'The wages of the weak and the strong', *Journal of Industrial Relations*, vol. 15, pp. 1–24.

——(1994) *Wage questions*, ESC Working Paper No. 19, University of Newcastle, December.

*IMF Survey 1994*, May, International Monetary Fund, Washington D.C.

Ingles, D. (1997) *Low Income Traps for Working Families*, Discussion Paper No. 363, Centre for Economic Policy Research, Australian National University, Canberra.

Isaac, J. et al (1993) *Small Business and Industrial Relations: Some Policy Issues*, Industrial Relations Research Series No. 8 (DIR), AGPS, Canberra.

Junankar, P.N. and Kapuscinski, C.A. (1992) *The Costs of Unemployment in Australia*, EPAC Background Paper No. 24, AGPS, Canberra.

Keating, P. (1993) Speech to the Institute of Directors, April 21.

Kelley, A. and Schmidt, R. (1979) 'Modelling the role of government policy in post-War Australian immigration', *Economic Record*, Vol. 55, No. 149, pp.127–35.

King, J. (1986) 'How large is the structural element in the current unemployment?', *Australian Bulletin of Labour*, Vol. 12, No. 2, pp. 102–18.

King, J.E. (1990) *Labour Economics, An Australian Perspective*, Macmillan, Melbourne.

King, J.E., Rimmer, R.J. and Rimmer, S.M. (1992) 'The law of the shrinking middle: Inequality of earnings in Australia 1975–89', *Scottish Journal of Political Economy*, Vol. 39(4), pp.391–412.

*Labour Market and Social Policy*, Occasional Papers No. 18, OECD, Paris.

Lansbury, R. (1975) 'The return to arbitration: Recent trends in dispute settlement and wages policy in Australia', *International Labour Review*, 117.

Leeves, G. (1997) 'Cyclical properties of labour market gross flows in Australia', *Economic and Labour Relations Review*, Vol. 8, pp.116–27.

Lewis, H. 1990, *Part-time work: trends and issues*, Department of Employment, Education and Training, AGPS, Canberra.

Lipsey, R.G. (1960) 'The relation between unemployment and the rate of change of money wage rates in the United Kingdom, 1862–1957: A further analysis', *Economica*, Vol. 27.

Lowe, P. (1995) 'Labour productivity growth and relative wages: 1978–1994', in P. Anderson, J. Dwyer and D. Gruen (eds) (1995) *Productivity and Growth*, Proceedings of a conference, Reserve Bank, Sydney.

Lucas, R. (1972) 'Expectations and the neutrality of money,' *Journal of Economic Theory*, 4, April, pp.103–24.

Macfarlane, I.J. (1995) 'Inflation and changing public attitudes', *RBA Bulletin*, December, pp.9–15.

——(1996) 'The economy and wages', *RBA Bulletin*, May, pp.17–22.

——(1998) 'Statement to Parliamentary Committee', *RBA Bulletin*, May, pp.1–6.

McDonald, T. and Rimmer, M. (1989) 'Award restructuring and wages policy', in J. Nevile (ed.), *Wage Determination in Australia*, CEDA, Melbourne.

McGeogh, P. (1997) 'Dole projects timed to perfection', *Sydney Morning Herald*, November 10.

McGuire, P. (1994) 'Changes in earnings dispersion in Australia, 1975–92', *Labour Economics and Productivity*, Vol. 6, pp.27–53.

McTaggart, D. (1992) 'The cost of inflation in Australia' in A. Blundell-Wignall (ed.) *Inflation, Disinflation and Monetary Policy*, Reserve Bank of Australia, Sydney.

Melzer, T.C. (1997) 'To conclude: Keep inflation low and, in principle, eliminate it', *Federal Reserve Bank of St. Louis Review* 79, November/December: pp.3–7.

Menon, J. (1993) 'Exchange rates, import prices, and the macroeconomy', *Economic Papers*, 12 March, pp.37–48.

Milbourne, R.D. (1990) 'Money and finance,' in S. Grenville (ed.) *The Australian Macro-Economy in the 1980s*, Reserve Bank of Australia, Sydney.

Mishell, L. and Schmitt, J. (1995) *Beware the US Model: Jobs and Wages in a Deregulated Economy*, Economic Policy Institute, Washington.

Mitchell, D. (1984) 'The Australian labour market' in R.E. Caves and L.B. Kruse (eds) *The Australian Economy: A View from the North*, Allen and Unwin, Sydney, pp.127–93.

Mitchell, R. & MacIntyre, S. (eds) (1989) *Foundations of Arbitration: The Origins and Effects of State Compulsory Arbitration 1890–1914*, Oxford University Press, Melbourne.

Mitchell, W. and Watts, M. (1997) 'The path to full employment', *Australian Economic Review* 30,4.

Mitchell, William F. (1987a) 'The NAIRU, structural imbalance and the macroequilibrium unemployment rate', *Australian Economic Papers*, Vol. 26, pp.101–18.

Mitchell, William F. (1987b) 'What is the full employment unemployment rate?' *Australian Bulletin of Labour*, vol. 11(1), pp.321–36.

Moore, D. (1997) 'The effect of the social welfare system on unemployment', *Australian Bulletin of Labour*, 23/4, pp.275–94.

Mulvey, C. (1986) 'Wage levels: Do unions make a difference?' in J. Niland (ed.) *Wage Fixation in Australia*, G Allen and Unwin, Sydney, pp.202–16.

Munnell, A.H. (1992) 'Policy watch: Infrastructure investment and economic growth', *Journal of Economic Perspectives* 6(4), pp.189–98.

Musgrave, R. A. (1969), *Fiscal Systems*, Yale University Press, New Haven.

National Pay Equity Coalition 1989, *Submission to House of Representatives Standing Committee on Legal and Constitutional Affairs Inquiry into*

*Equal Opportunity and Equal Status for Australian Women*, Volume 2, s326–s374.

——(1990) *Enterprise Based Bargaining Units: Company Unions: No Equity, No Unions*, Discussion Paper, The Coalition, Sydney.

National Women's Consultative Council (1990), *Pay Equity for Women in Australia Labour Research Centre*, AGPS, Canberra.

Nevile, J.W. (1979) 'Inflation in Australia' in J.W. Nevile (ed.), in *Policies Against Stagflation*, Longman Cheshire, Melbourne.

Nguyen, T. (1991) 'Inflation and economic growth' in *Australia's Inflation Problem: Office of EPAC Seminar*, EPAC Background Paper No.11, AGPS, Canberra.

Norris, K. (1980) 'Compulsory arbitration and the wage structure in Australia', *Journal of Industrial Relations*, Vol. 22, pp.249–63, November 10.

O'Connor, D. (1994), 'Equity in the workplace: The implications of the *Industrial Relations Reform Act* 1993', *The Journal of Industrial Relations*, Vol. 37(1), pp.63–71.

OECD (1990) *OECD Economic Surveys: Australia, 1989/1990*, OECD, Paris.

——(1993) *Employment Outlook*, OECD, Paris.

——(1994) *The Jobs Study—Facts, Analysis Strategies*, OECD Paris.

——(1996) *The OECD Jobs Strategy: Pushing Ahead with the Strategy*, OECD, Paris.

——(1997) *International Greenhouse Gas Emission Trading*, OECD, Paris.

——(1997) *Questions and Answers on Emission Trading Among Annex I Parties*, OECD, Paris.

Otto, G. and Voss, G.M. (1994) 'Public capital and private sector productivity', *Economic Record*, Vol. 70, pp.121–32.

Owen, A. D. (1995) 'The environment: The role of economic instruments' in P.R. Kriesler (ed.) *The Australian Economy, The Essential Guide*, Allen & Unwin, Sydney.

Peetz, D. (1990) 'Declining union density', *Journal of Industrial Relations*, 32/2.

Pender, H. and Ross, S. (1993) *Income Tax and Asset Choice in Australia*, Research Paper No. 3, AGPS, Canberra.

——(1995) *Business Taxation in Australia and Asia*, Commission Paper No. 4, AGPS, Canberra.

Phelps, E.S. (1967) 'Phillips curves, expectations of inflation and optimal unemployment over time', *Economica*, Vol. 34.

Phillips, A.W. (1958) 'The relation between unemployment and the rate of change of money wage rates in the United Kingdom, 1861–1957', *Economica*, Vol. 25.

Plowman, D. (1992a) 'Industrial relations and the legacy of new protection', *Journal of Industrial Relations* 34/1.

——(1992b) 'An uneasy conjunction: Opting out and the arbitration system', *Journal of Industrial Relations*, 34/2.

Preston, A. (1994) 'Taxation policy and Australia's competitiveness' *Economic Roundup*, Spring edition, AGPS, Canberra.

*Reform of the Australian Tax System* (1985), September 19, AGPS, Canberra.

Reserve Bank of Australia (1994) 'Measuring "underlying" inflation', *RBA Bulletin*, August, pp.1–6.

——(1996), 'Measuring wages', *RBA Bulletin*, June, pp.7–11.

——(1997a), Semi-annual Statement on Monetary Statement, *RBA Bulletin*, May, pp.1–33.

——(1997b), Semi-annual Statement on Monetary Statement, *RBA Bulletin*, November, pp.7–46.

——(1998) 'Semi-annual statement on monetary policy', *RBA Bulletin* May, pp.7–53.

Rodgers, G. and Rodgers, J. 1989 (eds) *Precarious Jobs in Labour Market Regulation*, International Institute for Labour Studies, International Labour Office, Geneva.

Romer, Paul M. (1986), 'Increasing returns and long-run growth', *Journal of Political Economy*, 94, pp.1002–37.

——(1990), 'Endogenous technological change', *Journal of Political Economy* 98 (2), S71–S102.

Rowthorn, B. (1977) 'Conflict, inflation and money', *Cambridge Journal of Economics*, 1/1.

Samuelson, P.A. (1954) 'The pure theory of public expenditure' in R.W. Houghton (ed.) (1973) *Public Finance*, Penguin Books, Harmondsworth, pp.181–5.

Saunders, P. (1992) *Poverty, Inequality and Recession*, Centre for Applied Economic Research, Working Paper No. 5, University of New South Wales, Sydney.

Saunders, P. (1993) 'Deregulation and inequality', *Economic Papers*, Vol. 12(3), pp.28–43.

Schelde-Andersen, P. (1992) 'OECD country experiences with disinflation' in *Inflation, Disinflation and Monetary Policy*, A. Blundell-Wignall, (ed.) Reserve Bank of Australia, Sydney.

Sheehan, Peter J. (1992) *Economic Theory and Economic Strategy: The New Growth Models*, paper delivered at the 21st Conference of Economists, University of Melbourne, July.

Singleton, G. (1990) *The Accord and the Australian Labour Movement*, Melbourne University Press, Melbourne.

Sloan, J. and Wooden, M. (1987) 'The Australian labour market, December 1987', *Australian Bulletin of Labour*, Vol. 11(1), pp.295–320.

Solow, R. (1997) 'Labour market flexibility', *Keynes Lecture*, British Academy, London.

Stegman, T. (1982) 'The estimation of an accelerator type investment function with a profitability constraint by the technique of switching regressions', *Australian Economic Papers*, pp.379–91.

——(1990) 'The sectoral composition of capital expenditure in Australia', *Economic Papers*, Vol. 9, No.1, pp.41–54.

——(1993) 'Unemployment' in G. Bell and B. Hession (eds), *The Economy in Reform: Readings in Australian Economic Policy*, VCTA, Melbourne.

——(1997) 'Implications for wages policy in Australia of the Living Wage Case', *Economic and Labour Relations Review*, Vol. 8:1, pp.143–55.

Stevens, G. (1992) 'Inflation and disinflation in Australia: 1950–91' in *Inflation, Disinflation and Monetary Policy*, A. Blundell-Wignall (ed.) Reserve Bank of Australia, Sydney.

Steward, A. (1994) 'The Industrial Relations Reform Act 1993: Counting the cost', *Australian Bulletin of Labour*, Vol. 20(2), pp.140–61.

Stilwell, F. (1986) *The Accord and Beyond: The Political Economy of the Labor Government*, Pluto Press, Sydney.

Stromback, T. (1996) *The Modern Australian Apprenticeship and Traineeship System (MAATS)*, Centre for Labour Market Research, Curtin University of Technology, Perth.

Summers, R. and Heston, A. (1993) 'The Penn World Table (Mark 5): An expanded set of international comparisons, 1950–88', *Quarterly Journal of Economics* 106(2), 327–68 (1991), subsequently updated to Mark 5.5, available from National Bureau of Economic Research, Boston, Mass.

*Tax Expenditure Statement* (1996), AGPS, Canberra.

Temple, J. (1999) 'The new growth evidence', *Journal of Economic Literature*, 37(1), pp.112–56.

Tobin, J. (1972) 'Inflation and unemployment', *American Economic Review*, Vol. 52.

Wailes, N. and Lansbury, R. (1997) *Flexibility versus Collective Bargaining. Patterns of Australian Industrial Relations Reforms During the 1980s and 1990s*, Australian Centre for Industrial Relations Research and Teaching, Working Paper No. 49.

Warren, N.A. (1990) *A Goods and Services Tax for Australia*, Research Study No.11, Australian Tax Research Foundation, Sydney.

——(1991) *The Changing Incidence of Federal Indirect Taxes: 1975/76 to 1988/89*, EPAC Background Paper No.13, EPAC, AGPS, Canberra.

——(1993) *The Looming Fiscal Crisis and Australia's Indirect Tax Options*, Research Study No.21, Australian Tax Research Foundation, Sydney.

——(1995) 'Erosion of the indirect tax base: possible solutions' in R. Krever and J. Disney, (eds) *Restoring Revenue: Issues and Options*, Centre for International Law, ANU and Law and Policy Research Institute, Deakin University, Canberra.

——(1996) *GST: The Long, Winding Road*, Institute of Chartered Accountants, Sydney.

——(ed.) (1997) *Reshaping Fiscal Federalism in Australia*, ATRF Conference Series, Australian Tax Research Foundation, Sydney, pp.168.

——(1998) *Tax Facts and Tax Reform*, Research Study No. 31, Australian Tax Research Foundation, Sydney.

Watts, M.J. (1993) *The Impact of Occupational Sex Segregation on Female Employment Opportunities in Australia, 1978–92*, report prepared for the Department of Employment, Education and Training under the Women's Research and Employment Initiatives Program, 1991–92.

——(1996) 'The dispersion of gender wage distributions in Australia: Some further evidence and tentative explanations', mimeo, Department of Economics, University of Newcastle.

——(1997) 'Gender segregation in higher educational attainment in Australia 1978–94', *Higher Education*, 33, pp.1–17.

Watts, M.J. and Mitchell, W.F. (1990a) 'Australian wage inflation, real wage resistance, hysteresis and incomes policy 1968(3)–1988(3)', *The Manchester School*, June, pp.142–64.

——(1990b) 'The impact of incomes policy in Australia on the male inter-industry wage structure', *Journal of Industrial Relations*, Vol. 33(3), pp.353–69.

Watts, M.J. and Rich, J. (1991), 'Equal opportunity in Australia? The role of part-time employment in occupational sex segregation', *Australian Bulletin of Labour*, vol. 17, pp.155–74.

Whiteford, P. (1995), *Is Australia Particularly Unequal*, paper presented to the workshop, Contract State, Social Charter or Social Compromise: Towards a New Australian Settlement, University of Sydney.

Whitfield, K. (1987) *The Australian Labour Market*, Harper & Row, Sydney.

Whitfield, K. and Ross, R. (1995), *The Australian Labour Market* 2nd edition, Harper Educational, Sydney.

Withers, G. et al (1986), 'Wages and labour market adjustment: A cross country causality approach', *Economic Record*, Vol. 62, pp.415–26.

Wooden, M. (1996) 'The youth labour market: Characteristics and trends', *Australian Bulletin of Labour*, 22, 2, pp.137–60.

# Index

1996 Living Wage Case, 191–4
  'safety net' wage increases, 191
Abramovitz, M., 21, 244
ABS, *see* Australian Bureau of
  Statistics
Accord, xiv
  and inflation, 41, 125
  defined, xiv
  government, 190, 192, 194, 205
  labour productivity, 18–19
  unit labour cost, 41
ACTU, *see* Australian Council
  of Trade Unions
Agriculture, 131, 144
  assistance, 201
  budgetary outlays on, 210
  Diesel Fuel Rebate, 160
  employment in, 185–8
  outlay, 142–3
Akerlof, G., 40, 244
Alexander, M., 244
Anderson, P., 244
Anti-inflation policy
  monetary policy, 50, 126
Appreciation/Revaluation
  Australian dollar, 4
  defined, xiv

fixed exchange rate, xiv
floating exchange rate, xiv, 237
reserve bank, xiv
Apprenticeships, 196–7
Apps, P., 168
Argy, V., 245
Arrow's impossibility theorem, 138
Arsovska, B., 246
Aschauer, D., 15, 245
ASEAN Countries, 4
Asia
  domestic investments tax
    rates, 157
  income tax trends, 157–8
  nominal company tax rates,
    158, 178
Asian crisis
  Asian Currency Unit, 90
  Asian Monetary System, 90
  Australia's recession, 90
  bank failure, 87
  Bank of Japan, 86
  Bretton Woods Committee, 91
  Camdessus, Mr, 91
  contagion, 84, 91
  crisis capital account, 3
  currency crisis, 87

Dow Jones, the, 84
East Asian financial crisis, 20
Euro, 90
Group of Seven, 84
Habibie, 86
Hang Seng index, 84
hyperinflation, 84
IMF assistance, 82
implications of, 76
Indonesian rupiah, 82
International Monetary Fund, 92
Japan, 84–6
Mahathir, 86
Malaysia, 82, 83
Nikkei index, 84, 86
Philippines, 82
predatory speculation, 86
reform of financial markets, 90
Reuters, 92
Singapore, 82
Soros, 86
South Korea, 84–6
speculative property developments, 87
stock market crash, 1987, 91
Suharto, 84, 86
Thai baht, 82
Thailand, 87
unemployment, 2
Asprey, K.W., 245
Asset sales, structural deficit, 108
Atkinson, J., 245
Australian Bureau of Statistics
base weight, 28
consumption: details of Australia, 6–8
contribution of technical progress, 17
current weight, 28
defined, xiv
employment, 187
income compensation, 32
Laspeyres index, 28
Paasche index, 28
price indexes, 28
social accounting, 8

unemployment, 52, 54, 55, 56, 65, 70
Australian Council of Trade Unions
1996 Living Wage Case, 191–4
'safety net' wage increase, 191
Australian economy
after Asian crisis, 1–5
Australian dollar, 2, 120
Australian Tax Office, 163, 170, 239
balance of trade, 2
capital account, 3
capital flows, 1
European currencies, 4
exchange rates, 2
exports, 1, 201
external financing requirements, 76
floating exchange rate, 100
foreign debt, 2, 3
foreign exchange markets, 120
implications of Asian financial crisis, 76
import substitution, 3
imports, 1, 201
industrial relations, 1
industry policy, 1
inflation, 1, 126
inflation experience, 38–64, 121, 126
inflation, 1, 126
international competitiveness, 1, 193, 201
international debt, 2
international trade, 1
investment in value added, 3
Japan, 2
local taxes, 160
nominal company tax rates, 158
public expenditures, 5
real effective tax rate, 157
recession 1990s, 3, 185
recovery, 185
tax debate, 1

tax revenue to level of
  government, 159
taxation, 5, 146–80
unemployment, 2, 3
USA, 2
world interest rates, 2
Australian Industry, international
  competitiveness, 5, 193, 201
Australian Petroleum Resources
  Rent Tax, 146
Australian Prudential Regulatory
  Authority, 127, 237
Austria
  local taxes, 160
  tax revenue to level of
    government, 159
Automotive industry
  Button Plan, 213, 221–2
  Chrysler, 220
  Ford, 219–20
  General Motors, 219–20
  industry plans, 219–23
  Lyons government, 220
  Menzies government, 220

Baekgaard, H., 245
Balance Budget Multiplier
  defined, 95
  theorem, 95
Balance of payments
  Asian financial crisis, 82–92
  Asian trading partners, 80
  Australian securities, 75
  Australian's foreign
    indebtedness, 79, 80
  constraint to economic
    growth, 64, 72
  corporate bonds, 75
  current account balance, 75
  current account deficit, 76
  debt position, 80
  defined, xiv, 76
  exchange rate, 79, 93
  financial assets, 75
  fiscal policy, tight, 76
  fiscal surplus, 76
  GDP ratio, debt to, 81

interest rates, 75, 79
monetary policy, 75, 76
net external debt, 80
net incomes, 76
open economy, 75
portfolio managers, 75
recession, 76
servicing burden, 80
transfer payments, 76
Balance of trade, 2
Ball, L., 46, 47, 245
Barro, R.J., 245
Belgium
  tax revenue to level of
    government, 159
  tax unit, 168
Bellchamber, G., 192, 245
Bennett, L., 245
Beveridge Curve, 66–7
  Solow, 66
  USA, 66
  Europe, 66
Bewley, R., 238, 245
Biddle, D. 182, 196, 199, 245
Bit tax, European Union, 179
Bluestone, B., 249
Borland, J., 52, 245
Boskin, M.J., 245
Boskin, Commission, The, 29
Bracket creep, defined, 167
Bradford, 247
Brigden, J.B. 246
Brigden Committee, 203, 217, 240
Brooks, 149
Brotherhood of St Laurence
  1996 Living Wage Case, 192
  poverty line, 181
Brown, W., 246
Buchanan, J., 191, 193, 246
  Living Wage Case, 192
Budget
  1996/97 Budget cuts, 145
  efficiency auditing, 141
Budget deficit, fiscal policy
  stance indicator, 95
Bureau of Industry Economics, 205
Burgess, J., 245, 246

Business Council of Australia, Great Depression, 108
Business cycle
  business cycle, 6
  monetarist, 120
  short-term fluctuations, 10–11
  unemployment, 70
Button, J., 242

Cable television, 134
Calculus of consent, defined, 138
Callus, R., 246
Campbell, I., 71, 188, 246
Canada
  local taxes, 160
  public debt, 99
  tax revenue to level of government, 159
Capling, 240
Capital, trend growth, 11
Capital Account, defined, xiv
Capital adequacy ratios
  Australia, 127
  OECD, 127
Capital gains, income tax, 148
Capital-intensive industries, average labour productivity, 63
Carlin, W., 246
Carmichael, J., 31, 125, 246
Cash rate
  Australian experience, 123
  relation to other rates, 117
Chand, Sheetal K., 112
Chapman, B., 40, 41–2, 197, 246
Chapman, D.R., 246
Chennells, 238
Child care services, 136, 139
Chisholm, 163, 246
Clark, K., 247
Clark, T., 48, 247
Clean Development Mechanism
  aims, 228–9
  carbon or energy taxes, 229
Coal industry, Rio Tinto, 190
Collins, D.J., 247
Committee to Advise on Policies

for Manufacturing Industry, 204–05, 217
Committee of Economic Inquiry, 204, 217
Commodity Prices, 39
Commonwealth Treasury
  Tax Expenditure Statement, 160
  Taxation, 239
Communications, outlay, 142–3
Consumer Price Index
  Boskin Commission, 29
  budgetary policies, 33
  defined, xiv
  housing, 33
  inflation, xiv, 126
  monetary policy, 33
Consumption
  details of Australia, 7
  rise, 9
Consumption taxation, 5, 96, 238
  and the internet, 180
  defined, 170–5
  New Zealand, 174
  Preliminary Report by the Asprey Committee, 170–1
Corden, W.M., 247
Cost–benefit analysis
  and resource allocation, 141
  shortcomings, 139
Costello, P., 170, 174, 247
Covick, O., 247
CPI, see Consumer Price Index
Crawford, 241
Crawford Report, 205, 241
Crow, 236, 247
Crowding out
  defined, xiv
  fiscal policy, 108
  government expenditure, xiv
  Keynesian fiscal policy, 97
  private investment, 103
  statistics, 108
CSIRO, industry program, 211
Cullis, 238
Current account

balance of trade in goods and
    services, 77
defined, xv, 76
exports, 77
imports, 77
merchandise trade balance, 77
net income, xv, 4, 77
services balance, 77
Current Account Deficit
defined, 100
fiscal policy, 110
size of, 98–102
Customs Department, 239

Davis, K., 247
Davis, M., 247
Dawkins, P., 247
Dead weight loss, taxation,
    163
Debelle, 51, 247
DEETYA, 247
Defence, 131, 135, 136, 144
employment in, 185–8
outlay, 142–3
DEIR, 247
    see Department of
        Employment and Industrial
        Relations
De Long, J., 16, 247
Department of Employment and
    Industrial Relations, 191
Depreciation/devaluation
Australian dollar, 99
currency, 4
defined, xv
exchange rate, xv
fixed exchange rate, xv
inflation rate, 26
Deregulation
defined, xv
exchange rate, xv, 42
financial markets, xv, 125
labour market, 5, 191–4
OECD, 23
product markets, 187
trade unions, 188
Dickens, 50, 244

Discouraged workers, 54–5
effect of, 60
Dowrick, S., 248
Dwyer, T., 169, 170, 244, 248

East Asia, crisis of 1997, 10
Econometric modelling, 121
Economic growth
business cycle, 6
depletion of natural
    resources, 8
environmental degradation, 8
growth and inflation, 6
growth of consumption, 6
Reserve Bank of Australia, 115
social accounting, 8
unemployment, 52
Economic Planning and
    Advisory Committee
and working hours, 187
Productivity Commission,
    205, 242
Education, 12, 131, 132, 133, 144
employment in, 185
HECS, 134
objectives of, 140
outlay, 142–3
protests about, 145
Effectiveness, defined, 140
Efficiency
defined, 140
taxation, 147
Eisner, R., 112
Elasticity, defined, xv
Emissions trading, 227–35
Employment
by industry, 185–6
changing nature, 183–8
motor vehicles, 209
Enterprise bargaining, 193
Environment
degradation, 8
Global Warming Potential, 232
greenhouse gases, 224–35
International Trade in
    Emission Allowances,
    232–4

EPAC, 248
  see Economic Planning and
    Advisory Committee
Equi-marginal rules, maximum
  welfare approach, 137
Equity
  intergenerational, 149
  taxation, 147
Europe
  capital income, 178
  European currencies, 4
European Union
  Bit Tax, 179
  emission gases, 226
  export subsidising, 211
Exchange rates, 2
  'pass-through' of, 42
  Australian economy, 2
  fixed, 120
  inflation, 42
  monetary policy, 119
Expenditure taxes, 149
  and market failure, 150
Exports
  balance of payments, 108
  Export Market Development
    Grant, 211–12
  Factor (F) scheme, 209, 211,
    213
  growth rate, 72
  Passenger Motor Vehicle, 212
  Tariff Export Concession
    Orders, 212
  TRADEX scheme, 216
Externalities, 134
  pollution, 134

Fay, R., 197, 248
Federal Constitution, 130, 150
Feldstein, M., 44, 45, 48, 49, 248
Fightback, 171–2
Financial commentaries, 4
Financial account
  official component, 78
  non-official component, 77
Fiscal policy
  after Keynes, 93

Australian economy, 2
  balance of payments, 93
  balanced budget multiplier, 94
  crowding out, 97
  current account deficit, 110
  defined, xv
  employment, 93
  'equilibrium', 102
  exchange rate, 93
  floating exchange rate, 100
  inflation, 110
  involuntary unemployment, 102
  Keynes, 93, 103
  lump sum taxation, 94
  monetary policy, 97, 98
  national savings, 110
  neo-classical, 102
  poll tax, 94
  private investment, 98
  Second World War, 93
  setting of, 72
  short-run interest rates, 98
  stance of, 96, 104–09
  structural policy, 97
  tight, 3
  traditional tools, 4
  transfer payments, 129, 130
  unemployment, 93
  United States of America, 104
  vertical fiscal imbalance, 153
  volume of money, 98
Fischer, Tim, 222
Fitzgerald, V.W., 248
Fixed Capital Equipment,
  government expenditure, 103
Floating Exchange Rates, 38
  Australia, 101
Foreign debt
  import substitution, 3
  investment in value added, 3
  domestic capacity, 3
Foreign investment, expected
  exchange rate changes, 3
Foster, W., 58, 248
France
  domestic investments tax
    rates, 157

nominal company tax rates, 158
tax unit, 168
Freedman, C., 217, 242
Frictional unemployment,
    defined, 65–7
Friedman, M., 45, 120, 248
Fruin, D., 249

Galbraith, J.K., 113, 128
Galligan, 240
GDP, see Gross Domestic Product
Germany
    domestic investments tax
        rates, 157
    local taxes, 160
    nominal company tax rates, 158
    tax revenue to level of
        government, 159
    tax unit, 168
    unemployment, 110
Gittins, R., 248
Going for Growth, 202
    outline, 215–16, 240
    TRADEX scheme, 216
Goodhart, C., 248
Government
    bonds, 106
    business, 5
    constitution, 131
    expenditure on economic
        infrastructure, 103
    federal, 131, 138, 141, 144,
        150, 180, 202, 204, 210
    financial markets, 3
    government failure, 135–6
    local, 131, 175
    media, 3
    rhetoric, 3
    state, 131, 144, 202
    tax revenue to level of
        government, 159
    Uniform Income Tax Act, 150
Grattan, M., 199, 248
Great Depression
    Australia, 108
    Business Council of Australia,
        108

fiscal policy, 108
Green R., 244, 248, 249
Greenhouse gases, 224–35
Global Warming Potential, 232
    International Trade in Emis-
        sion Allowances, 231–4
Green Paper
    Labor Government paper, 71,
        237
    Labor market programs, 73,
        194–5
Gregory, R., 58, 248, 249
Griffith, 238
Groenewegen, P., 249
Gross Domestic Product
    Australian economy, 6–9
    CPI, 29
    defined, xv
    domestic final demand, 29
    implicit price deflators, 29
    inflation, 29
    unemployment, 64
Growth
    contribution of physical
        investment, 15–17
    contribution of technical
        progress, 17–20
    'multi-factor productivity
        growth', 17
Grubb, M., 231–4, 243, 249
Gruen, D., 244
Gruen, F.H., 249
GST, see Consumption taxation

Habibie, 86
Haig-Simmons accretions
    principle, taxation, 148–9
Hall, P., 249
Hancock, K., 249
Hanusch, 23, 249
Harding, A., 162, 166, 238, 249
Harper, I., 236, 249
Harrison, B., 249
Hayles, J., 246
Head, J., 239, 247, 250
Heady, 238
Health, 131, 132, 133, 144

as government failure, 136
consumer price index, 33
employment in, 185–8
maximum welfare approach,
  138
Medicare levy, 156, 239
outlay, 142–3
HECS, *see* Higher Education
  Contribution Scheme
Heiler, K., 250
Heston, A., 254
Higher education, 197–8
  HECS, 197
Hilmer Report, 134–5
Hong Kong
  Asian financial crisis, 83
  economic growth, 20
  Hang Seng index, 84
Household savings
  current account deficit, 111
  savings gap, 111
Housing
  Consumer Price Index, 33
  outlay, 142–3
  owner-occupied, 149, 160,
    165, 176–7
  public, 130, 131, 144
  Reserve Bank of Australia, 115
Howard, J., 242
Howard government, 132, 144,
  181
  and Senate, 138
  consumption tax, 174
  enterprise bargaining, 193
  expenditure cutting, 141
  higher education, 197–8
  Higher Education Contribu-
    tion Scheme, 197
  House of Representatives
    Standing Committee on
    Employment, Education
    and Training, 198–9
  industrial relations, 181–200
  industry commission, 222,
    241, 242, 243
  labour market programs,
    194–6

Productivity Commission,
  205, 242
tariffs, 206, 223
unemployment, 181
Work for the Dole, 181,
  198–200
Workplace Relations Act,
  190–1
Hughes, B., 246, 250

IMF, *see* International Monetary
  Fund
Immigration
  labour force, 11–15
  population growth, 11–15
Imports
  balance of payments, 108
  growth rate, 72
  tariffs, 201
Income taxes, 148
  and the internet, 180
  capital gains, 148
Indexation, taxation, 167
Indirect taxes
  defined, xv
Indonesia,
  domestic investments tax
    rates, 157
  nominal company tax rates, 158
Industrial relations, 181
  Australian Workplace
    Agreements, 190
  Workplace Relations Act, 190
Industrial Relations Commission
  1996 Living Wage Case,
    191–4
  Workplace Relations Act, 191
Industries Assistance
  Commission, 205
  automotive industry, 221
Industry Commission, 205, 242
  automotive industry, 221–2,
    241, 243
  Business Regulation Review
    Unit, 205
  defined, xv
  Howard government, 222

Inter-State Commission, 205
productivity growth, 19–23
TCF industry, 214
Inequality, 181
Inflation
Australian experience, 38–64, 121, 124, 126
bracket creep, 167
causes of, 34-44
'conflict theory', 37
consumer price index, 126
cost increase, 35
cost-push, 36
costs of, 27, 44–50
defined, xv
depreciation, 26, 37
devaluation, 37
dividends, 165
excess demand, 35
fiscal policy, 40
government policy changes, 31
Hawke government, 41
import, 26
income, 165
indexation, 167
indirect taxes, 37
'inertial' inflation, 37
interest, 165
measurement, 27
monetary policy, 40, 125, 126
New Zealand, 51
rate of, 4, 110
target, 121
taxation, 167
and terms of trade, 125
and wages growth, 125
Inflation Tax, 106
Ingles, D., 166, 250
Interest rates
Reserve Bank of Australia, 117
overnight loans, 117
Intermediate Good, defined, xv
International capital mobility, and taxation, 178–80
International Debt, Australian economy, 2

International Monetary Fund, Asian Financial Crisis, 90
International Technology Transfer, consequence 20–3
International trade
and taxes, 146, 150, 172
Industries Assistance Commission, 204
international competitiveness, 201
quotas, 204
Scullin Tariff, 203–04, 217
tariffs, 201
The Tariff Board, 203–05, 217, 220, 243
International Trade in Emission Allowances defined, 231–4
Internet
and taxation systems, 179
international capital mobility, 178
labour mobility, 179
Investing for Growth!, 202
Investment, spillover benefits, 16
Isaac, J., 250

J-Curve
defined, xv
balance of trade, xv
Jackson, 240, 241
Jackson Committee, see Committee to Advise on Policies for Manufacturing Industry
Japan
Asian financial crisis, 84–6
Australian economy, 2
Bank of Japan, 86
domestic investments tax rates, 157
economic growth, 20
government expenditure, 103
Kyoto, 5
Kyoto protocols, 5
Nikkei index, 84, 86
nominal company tax rates, 158
Sony, 86
Yen, 4

Jones, 238
Junankar, 46, 47, 250
Junor, W., 40, 246

Kaldor, N., 23
Kapuscinski, 46, 47, 250
Kearney, C., 247
Keating, P., 250
Kelley, P., 60, 250
Keynesian
  balance of payments, 93
  demand-pull inflation, 35
  employment, 93
  exchange rate, 93
  fiscal policy, 103
  inflationary process, 36
  monetary policy, 120, 125
  rate of inflation, 93
  unemployment, 45, 93
King, J., 236, 250
Kingston, C.C., 202, 240
Korea
  domestic investments tax
    rates, 157
  nominal company tax rates, 158
Krever, R., 239, 250

Labor Government
  1993/94 Budget, 138
  and Senate, 138
  Button Plan, 213, 221–2
  draft white paper, 171
  enterprise bargaining, 193
  National Tax Summit, 171
  tariffs, 206
  unemployment strategy, 72
  Working Nation, 58, 194–5
Labour force
  contribution, 11–15
  defined, xv, 54
  economic growth, 11
  output-employment elasticity, 11
  participation,15, 54–6
  population, 11
  size, 60
  trend growth, 11

unemployment, 59
  women, 15, 284
Labour-intensive industries, 63
Labour market
  average weekly earnings, 38
  changes in, 170
  flows of, 69
  schemes, 72
  tightening, 43
  unemployment programs, 59,
    181
Labour market programs
  Job Compact, 194
  Modern Australian Appren-
    ticeship and Traineeship
    System, 195–7
  NAIRU, 194
  New Enterprise Incentive
    Scheme, 195
  Working Nation, 58, 194–5
Labour productivity
  average, 63
  defined, 18
  enterprise bargaining, 193
  Europe, 19
  USA, 19
Lambert, P., 162, 238, 249
Lansbury, R., 250, 254
Larkin, J., 169, 170, 248
Laspeyres, 28
Lawrence, H., 247
Leahy, D., 242
Lee, J., 245
Leeves, G., 71, 250
Lewis, H., 250
Lipsey, R.G., 250
Lobby groups
  arts community, 145
  business lobby groups, 145
  social welfare lobby groups, 145
Long-term unemployment, 182
Lowe, P., 250
Lucas, R., 121, 250

MacDonald, R., 237, 249, 247
McDonald, T., 251
MacEwan, J., 217, 218

Macfarlane, I., 26, 50, 251
MacIntyre, S., 251
MacPherson C., 242
McGeogh, P., 198, 251
McGuire, P., 251
McTaggart, D., 44, 45, 47, 251
Mahathir, 86, 92
Malaysia
    domestic investments tax
        rates, 157
    nominal company tax rates, 158
Manufacturing
    budgetary outlays, 210
    employment, 208
Maritime industry, Webb Dock,
    190
Market failure, 135
    and taxes, 146, 150
Maximum welfare approach
    defined, 137–138
    equi-marginal rules, 137
Maxwell, P., 112
Meade, J., 238
Melzer, T., 48, 251
Menon, 42, 251
Merit goods, 135
    examples of, 135
Microeconomic reform
    agenda, 5
    policy settings, 72
Milbourne, R., 238, 251
Mining, budgetary outlays on, 210
Mishell, L., 251
Mitchell, D., 251
Mitchell, R., 251
Mitchell, W.F., 249, 251, 255
Monetarist
    monetary policy, 120
    NAIRU, 36
    theories of, 120
    unemployment, 45
Monetary policy
    activist policy, 120
    Australian economy, 2, 120
    business investment, 115
    classical economists, 120
    defined, xv

deregulation, 125
fine-tuning, 115, 120
fiscal policy, 43
goals of, 114–15
housing, 115
indicators, 115–18, 126
inflation, 119, 125, 126
Keynesian, 97, 120
operation of, 118–21
Reserve Bank of Australia, 113
settings of, 72
stance of, 115
theories of, 120–1
tight, 2
traditional tools, 4
transmission mechanism of,
    119–20
Unites States of America, 120
yield curve, 118
Money
    broad, 116
    Monetary Aggregates, 116–17
    narrow, 116
    stock, 116
    targeting, 121
Money Stock, defined, 116
Money Wages, defined, 67
Moore, D., 193, 251
Mortimer Review, 202
    Co-operative Research
        Centre, 215–16
    'Invest Australia', 215
    outline, 209–10
    recommendations, 214–16,
        218, 240, 242
Mulvey, C., 251
Mundell, 16
Munnell, A.H., 251
Musgrave, R., 135, 251

NAIRU, 35
    monetarists, 36
    natural rate output, 36
    see Non-accelerating inflation
        rate of unemployment
National Savings
    current account deficit, 110

savings gap, 110
size of, 98–102
Natural Rate Hypothesis
defined, xvi
formulated, 45
Friedman, Milton, 45
Phelps, Edmund, 45
monetary policy, 120
NBFIs, see Non-Bank Financial
Intermediaries
Neary, J.P., 242
Net Foreign Debt, 2
Net income, 2, 4
Netherlands
domestic investments tax
rates, 157
tax unit, 168
Nevile, J., 39, 112, 252
New Classical
inflation, 45
sacrifice ratios, 47
New Classical Macroeconomics
and monetary policy, 125
defined, xvi
New Zealand
consumption tax, 154
income tax, 166
inflation, 51
tax unit, 168
Nominal values, defined, xvi
Non-accelerating inflation rate
of unemployment
defined, xv, 65
labour market programs, 194
Non-Bank Financial
Intermediaries, 116
and money definition, 122
financial deregulation, 125
Norris, K., 247, 252
NRH, see Natural Rate
Hypothesis
Nyuyen, T., 27, 252

O'Connor, D., 252
OECD, see Organisation for
Economic Co-operation and
Development

O'Keefe, S., 246
'Okun's Law', 62–5
O'Loughlin, T., 246
Olekalns, N., 237
Olympic Games, 135
OPEC, see Organisation of
Petroleum Exporting Countries
Open Economy, defined, 75
Organisation for Economic
Co-operation and
Development Australia,
taxation low rate, 102
average ratio, 99
capital adequacy ratio, 128
defined, xvi
domestic investments tax
rates, 157
income tax trends, 157–8
Jobs Study, 193
local taxes, 160
nominal company tax rates, 158
property taxation, 175
public sector size, 132, 186
Sweden, 156, 166, 178
tax revenue to level of
government, 159
trends in taxation, 153–9, 178
United Kingdom, 156
Organisation of Petroleum
Exporting Countries
defined, xvi
oil price increase, 40
Otto, G., 16, 252
Owen, A., 243, 252

Paasche, 28
Pareto efficient
public goods, 139
voluntary exchange models, 137
Participation rate, defined, xvi
Part-time work, 183–8
Peetz, D., 252
Pender, H., 238, 252
Perkins, J.O.N., 112
Perry, G., 50, 244
Pharmaceuticals industry, Factor
(F) scheme, 209, 211, 213

Phelps, E., 45, 252
Phillips, A., 252
Phillips Curve, defined, xvi
Plowman, D., 252
Polette, 166, 249
Population
  baby boom, 11
  economic growth, 11
  immigration, 11
Population growth
  immigration, 60
  natural increase, 60
Poverty, unemployment, 181
Pragnell, B., 146
Pressman, S., 112
Preston, A., 252
Prices Justification Tribunal, 40
Private goods
  defined, 133
  exclusion principle, 133, 134
  rivals in consumption, 133
Private investment, 15
  crowding out, 16
Private sector, net wealth, 176–8
Privatisation
  efficiency gains, 135
  Hilmer Report, 134
  OECD, 23
  utilities in Australia, 134
Productivity
  defined, xvi
  growth, 19
Program budgeting, short-
  coming, 139
Prudential Regulation, banks,
  114, 127–8
Public Debt
  Canada, 99
  government expenditure, 105
  media commentators, 99
  size of, 98–102
Public expenditure
  cost–benefit analysis, 139,
    141
  efficiency auditing, 141
  maximum welfare approach,
    137–8

program budgeting, 139
  sources of, 131
  state vs commonwealth, 144
  theories of 133–6
  voluntary exchange models,
    136–7
Public good, 133–6
  defined, 133–4
  Pareto efficient, 139
  voluntary exchange models,
    137
Public Investment, 15
Public savings
  defined, 101
  to increase, 112
Public sector
  contracting out, 135
  employment, 132, 186
  measurement of 132–3
  OECD, 132
  size of, 133–6
Public services, corrective
  services, 135, 136, 138
Public Trading Enterprises
  defined, xvi
  outlays from, 130

Quiggin, J., 236

Rational expectations
  defined, xvi
  hypothesis, 121
Rattigan, Alf, 217
Real interest rate, defined, 118
Real values
  current prices, xvi
  defined, xvi
  nominal values, xvi
Recreational services, 131
  employment in, 185–8
Relative Wages, defined, 67
Research and Development
  Factor (F) scheme, 213
  government support, 212–13
Reserve Bank of Australia

1996 Living Wage Case, 191–3
Asian Financial Crisis, 92
balance of payments, 75
and business cycles, 122
business investment, 115
capital adequacy ratios, 128
credit, 116
economic growth, 115
evolution of policy, 125–8
exchange rates, 118, 237
financial account, 78
housing, 115
housing starts, 118
inflation, 26, 36, 50, 118, 121, 126, 127
interest rates, 113
Keynesian, 125
Macfarlane, 26
monetary policy, 115, 118
money supply, 113, 125
New Classical theory, 125
prudential regulation of banks, 127–8, 238
target cash rate, 118, 121
unemployment, 74, 118
Rich, J., 255
Richardson, P., 247
Riddington, C., 247
Rodgers, G., 253
Rodgers, J., 253
Romer, P., 23, 253
Ross, R., 255
Ross, S., 238, 252
Rowe, L., 246
Rowthorn, B., 253

Samuelson, P., 137, 253
Saunders, P., 54, 253
Savings
    defined, xvi
    tax treatment of, 176
    see also national savings
Savings By Section, GDP, 111
Savings Gap, current account deficit, 110
Schelde-Anderson, P., 46, 47, 253

Schmidt, 60, 250, 251
Schumpeter, J., 23
Scullin tariff, 203–04
    depression, 217
Seasonally Adjusted Data, defined, xvi
Second World War, 93
Senate
    Democrats, 138
    Independents, 138
SGC, see Superannuation Guarantee Levy
Sheehan, P., 253
Simon, F., 247
Simplicity, taxation, 147
Singapore
    domestic investments tax rates, 157
    nominal company tax rates, 158
Singleton, G., 253
Sloan, J., 253
Smith, Adam, 147, 239
Social security, see Transfer payments
Solow, R., 55, 253
Sommerhalder, 168
Soros, George, 83, 86
Soskice, D., 246
Stagflation, defined, xvi
State government, 131, 202
    ACT, 144
    budgetary outlay on industry, 210
    Financial Institutions Duty (FID), 180
    franchise taxes, 150
    New South Wales, 202
    Queensland, 144, 180
    South Australia, 144, 202
    Tasmania, 144
    taxation revenue, 151–3, 159, 175
    Victoria, 202
'Strategic Investment Coordinator', 215–16
    Bob Mansfield, 215
Stegman, T., 253

Stevens, G., 30, 38, 46, 47, 51, 247, 254
Steward, A., 254
Stilwell, F., 254
Stock Market Crash, 43
Stock of Money, 97
Stonecash, R., 217, 242
Stormback, T., 2, 254 196
Structural deficit
    as measure of stance of fiscal policy, 96, 104–09
    inflation, 105
    oil shock, 105
Structural unemployment, defined, 65–7
Subsidies, 37, 132
Suharto, 85, 86
Summers, L., 16, 247
Superannuation, private sector wealth, 176–7
Superannuation Guarantee Levy, defined, 156–7
Supply of Money, defined, 116
Sweden
    capital income, 166, 178
    income tax, 156
    tax unit, 168
Switzerland
    local taxes, 160
    tax revenue to level of government, 159

Taiwan
    domestic investments tax rates, 157
    nominal company tax rates, 158
Tariffs
    Australia, 201
    Industries Assistance Commission, 204
    Scullin Tariff, 203–04
    textiles, clothing and footwear, 206–09
    The Tariff Board, 203–05, 217, 220, 243
    World War I, 203
    World War II, 204

Tax, see taxation
Tax incidence, defined, 161–4
Taxation
    Australian Petroleum Resources Rent Tax, 146
    Australian Tax Office, 163, 170, 239
    bracket creep, 167
    company taxation, 168–70
    on consumption, 170–5
    correct market failure, 146, 150
    criteria for good taxation system, 147
    deadweight loss, 163
    economic efficiency, 147
    equity, 147
    expenditure taxes, 149
    guns levy, 156
    Haig-Simmons accretions principle, 148–9
    income taxes, 148, 180
    indexation, 167
    inflation, 167
    internet, 179–80
    jobs levy, 156
    local taxes, 160
    Medicare levy, 156, 239
    property taxation, 175
    real effective tax rates, 157
    revenue sources, 151–3
    revenue to levels of government, 159
    simplicity, 147
    Sweden 156, 178
    tax haven, 179
    tax incidence, 161–4
    tax unit, 168
    training levy, 156
    trends in OECD, 154–9, 178
    trusts, 170
    types, 148–50
    United Kingdom, 156
    voluntary exchange models, 137
    wealth taxes, 148
    wholesale sales tax, 150
    work–leisure choice, 149

TCF, *see* Textiles, clothing and footwear
Technical progress, trend growth, 11
Telstra, 134
Temple, J., 24, 254
Terms of Trade
  and inflation, 125
  defined, xvi
Textiles, clothing and footwear, tariffs, 206–09
Thailand
  domestic investments tax rates, 157
  nominal company tax rates, 158
Thurow, L., 194
Tobin, J., 254
Transfer payments, 131
  outlay, 142–3
  pensions, 129, 132, 156
  unemployment benefits, 129, 132, 156
Transport, 136
  outlay, 142–3
Twin Deficit, 100

'Underlying' or 'Core' Inflation, defined, xvi
Unemployment, 182–3
  anti-inflation wages policy, 74
  Australian economy, 2
  Australian Industrial Commission, 74
  capital-intensive industries, 63
  causes of, 64–9
  Commonwealth Employment Service, 74
  current account deficit, 76
  defined, xvi, 54
  demand management policy, 68
  GDP growth, 59, 62
  inflation, 68
  inflationary pressure, 59, 64
  international competitiveness, 68, 193, 201
  involuntary, 102
  Keynesian, 45

labour force, 59
Labour Government paper, 71
labour market deregulation, 5
labour market flows, 69–71
labour market programs, 59, 181, 194–5
labour market schemes, 72
labour productivity, 63
labour-intensive industries, 63
long term, 58, 105, 182
male–female relatives, 68
measurement, 54–5
monetarist, 45
natural rate, 45, 65, 120
'non-accelerating inflation rate of, 5
participation rate, 60–5
poverty, 181
profit margins, 68
social costs, 54
social service benefits systems, 72
unit labour costs, 68
United States of America, 110
wages as cause, 69
working nation, 58
youth, 68, 182
Uniform Income Tax Act, 150
United Kingdom
  company taxation, 169
  domestic investments tax rates, 157
  interest withholding tax, 156
  nominal company tax rates, 158
  tax unit, 168
United Nations Framework Convention on Climate Change, 224
United States of America
  Aschauer, 16
  Australian economy, 2
  banking system, 128
  company taxation, 169
  dollar, 4
  domestic investments tax rates, 157
  economic growth, 20

empirical work, 104
export subsidising, 211
fiscal policy, 110
labour market, 193–4
local taxes, 160
nominal company tax rates, 158
public capital, 103
tax revenue to level of
    government, 159
tax unit, 168
unemployment rate, 110
US Treasury, 179
wage flexibility, 193

Value added tax
    OECD, 154, 239
    see also Consumption tax
van Barneveld, K., 246
VAT, see Value added tax
Vernon, 240
Vernon Committee, see
    Committee of Economic Inquiry
Vertical fiscal imbalance, 153
Voluntary exchange models
    defined, 136–7
    pareto efficiency, 137
Voss, G., 16, 237, 252
Vrolijk, 231–4, 243, 249

Wages, 125, 190, 192, 194
    and inflation, 125
    as cause of unemployment,
        67–9
    policy settings, 72
Wailes, N., 254

Wallis Committee, 238
Walsh, M., 97
Warren, N., 238, 247, 249, 254
Watson, 191, 246
Watts, M.J., 249, 251, 254–5
Wealth taxes, 148
    intergenerational equity, 149
Webber, 71, 246
Welfare, maximum welfare
    approach, 138
White, 238, 245
Whiteford, P., 255
White Paper
    jobs compact, 73
    national training wage, 73
    unemployment, 73
Whitfield, K., 236, 255
Withers, G., 255
Wooden, M., 182, 253, 255
Woodman, M., 246
Women
    in workplace, 14, 15
    part-time work, 184
Work for the Dole Scheme, 181,
    198–200
Working Nation, 58, 194
Workplace Relations Act
    Australian Workplace Agree-
        ments, 190
    decentralisation, 194
    defined, 190–1
World Recession, 109

Youth unemployment, 182